WHITE LIKE HER

WHITE LIKE HER

My Family's Story of
Race and Racial Passing

By Gail Lukasik, PhD

AS SEEN ON *GENEALOGY ROADSHOW*
Foreword by Kenyatta D. Berry

Skyhorse Publishing

Skyhorse Publishing books may be purchased in bulk at special discounts for sales promotion, corporate gifts, fund-raising, or educational purposes. Special editions can also be created to specifications. For details, contact the Special Sales Department, Skyhorse Publishing, 307 West 36th Street, 11th Floor, New York, NY 10018 or info@skyhorsepublishing.com.

Skyhorse® and Skyhorse Publishing® are registered trademarks of Skyhorse Publishing, Inc.®, a Delaware corporation.

Visit our website at www.skyhorsepublishing.com.

10 9 8 7 6 5 4 3 2 1

Library of Congress Cataloging-in-Publication Data is available on file.

Cover and interior photographs courtesy of the author

ISBN: 978-1-5107-2412-9
eISBN: 978-1-5107-2415-0

Printed in the United States of America

For my mother, Alvera Frederic Kalina, whose courage lit the way. Thank you, mom, for your bravery and sacrifice.

The Central Figures in *White Like Her*

Gail Lukasik
B: Sept. 9, 1946

Alvera Frederic Kalina————Harold J. Kalina
B: Oct. 21, 1921, NO   B: Aug. 26, 1918, Ohio
D: Apr. 5, 2014, Ohio   D: Dec. 20, 1996, Ohio

Maternal First Cousin
Ula Duffant B: 1931, NO

Grandparents
Azemar Frederic————————Camille Kilbourne
B: Jan. 1897, NO   B: Jan. 1905, NO
D: July 1946, NO   D: Oct. 1982, NO

Stephen Kalina———————Mary Thiery
B: 1895, Ohio   B: 1893, Ohio
D: 1949, Ohio   D: 1967, Ohio

1st Great Uncle and Aunt
Edward Nicholls——————Laura Baker
B: 1883, NO   B: 1884, NO
D: 1948, Ohio   D: 1968, Ohio

2nd Great-Grandfather and Grandmother

Leon Frederic Jr.————————Celeste Girard
B: Aug. 1868   B: 1872
D: Sept. 30, 1913   D: July 2, 1930

3rd Great-Grandfather and Grandmother

Leon Frederic, Sr.————————Philomene Lanabere
B: 1838, NO   B: 1840, NO
D: 1905, NO   D: 1891, NO

4th Great-Grandfathers and Grandmothers

Ursin Frederic————————Roxelane Arnoux
B: Aug. 1, 1792   B: 1808, Cuba
D: 1856   D: 1882

Bernard Lanabere————————Felicite Dauphin
B: 1811   B: 1808
D: 1883   D: 1878

5th Great-Grandfathers and Grandmothers

Joseph Frederick Lestinet————Luison Santilly
B: abt. 1743   B: 1765
D: 1813   D: ?

Catiche Dauphin————————Manuel Mayronne
B: 1782   B: 1790
D: 1849   D: 1850

6th Great-Grandfathers and Grandmothers

Pierre Santilly—Native American Woman   Marta   Pierre Dauphin
B: 1735   B: 1759   B: 1754
D: 1783   D: 1805   D: 1804

7th Great-Grandmother
Maria: B: abt. 1744 D: ?

Foreword

By Kenyatta D. Berry, JD
Host, *Genealogy Roadshow* (PBS)

WHEN THE producers of *Genealogy Roadshow* approached me prior to the second season and said, "We have a story for you," I was hesitant at first. It was a story about racial passing. Gail Lukasik, a mystery author, had come to the *Roadshow* asking if her mother had passed for white. She wasn't sure of her mother's racial heritage. I hesitated because I didn't know how much Gail truly knew about her mother.

In the African American community, it is an unwritten rule that you do not "out" a person who is passing for white. And I was going to "out" her mother on a national television show. I felt as if I was betraying Gail's mother, because I understood that she made a great sacrifice and a painful choice. As an African American woman who had family members who passed, I knew Gail's mother had turned her back on her family, her friends, and her heritage. And in doing so, she'd assumed an identity that she barely knew but worked so hard to achieve. Her mother must have always lived in fear that someone might find her out. What if her children were born with darker skin? How could she explain that to her white husband?

The producers assured me that Gail knew about her mother's secret. But I still had trepidations. How would Gail react to me telling her story? How would our viewers react to this subject? But I knew it was a story that needed to be told.

Gail showed up at *Genealogy Roadshow* with her family and lots of anticipation. She had no idea what I would reveal about her mother's ancestry or how it would change her life. We were both nervous, but once we started talking our nerves subsided.

After learning more about her mother's racial ancestry, I knew Gail would be compelled to write a book. I also knew that we would share a special bond because she took this journey with me.

White Like Her: My Family's Story of Race and Racial Passing is the culmination of that journey. This book adds to the ongoing conversation about race and racial identity in America because it looks at the ramifications of institutionalized racialism and racial passing through one family's story—the Frederic family—a multiracial family with deep roots in Louisiana.

Passing is something we don't talk about in our society, but in the African American community we know it exists. It's part of our collective history as Americans. I would guess that most Americans, especially those of the younger generation, have never heard these terms. The "one-drop" rule is one of the many reasons that Gail's mother and many African Americans choose to pass for white. Passing meant better opportunities for jobs, education, and quality of life. According to statistics, between 1880 and 1925 approximately twelve thousand blacks "crossed the color line" each year in hope for a better life.[1] Considering those statistics, I would also guess that many Americans, like Gail, have benefitted from an ancestor who "crossed the color line" to hide their racial identity and have no idea of their mixed racial heritage.

In *A Chosen Exile* by Allyson Hobbs, the first chapter is titled "White Is the Color of Freedom." If you think about it, that idea has been true since slavery began in America and is still true. Racism and the continued oppression of African Americans exist today. So, imagine yourself born in Louisiana with white skin and multiracial ancestry but classified as black because of the one-drop rule. You would face discrimination, low or no education, and dim job opportunities. What would you do? Would you choose to leave your family behind? These are the questions that *White Like Her* raises that will help us as a nation continue the discussion about racial identity. In her exploration of racial identity, Gail points out that not all African Americans who could pass for white did, adding another dimension to the racial discourse.

The book also tells the Frederic family's story, which is important in helping us understand America's complex racial history. This family's genealogy exposes the various sexual relationships between white men, free people of color, female slaves, and white women. By giving the historical background connected to each generation, the book shows that while the roles were firmly defined, the races were less defined because of blurred racial lines when it came to their offspring. White men had children with free women of color and slaves. The status of the child was dependent upon the status of the mother. In Louisiana, this created a social system where free people of color were a step above slaves but below the poorest white farmer.

But *White Like Her* is not just about genealogy. It also explores the social and cultural history of Louisiana, rich with African, French, and Spanish heritage. Racial classifications such as quadroon (one-quarter) and octoroon (one-eighth) were often used to describe the offspring of white planters and women of African and European descent. This created the multi-racial ancestry that most African Americans have today. The Frederic family is an example of those blurred lines of black, white, free people of color, master, and slave.

As a professional genealogist and host on *Genealogy Roadshow*, I celebrate the uniqueness of Gail's personal journey of discovery and her willingness to share it. In learning to forgive and understand her mother and her choices, Gail lets go of the judgment and tries to imagine how hard it must have been for her mother to pass for white. Along the way she is able to embrace her heritage and discover what it truly means to be a family. Most people want a connection to their ancestor or are trying to solve a family mystery. Sometimes when you start this journey it leads you down an unexpected road.

One incident in *White Like Her* that really stood out for me was the moment when Gail discovered her maternal grandfather, Azemar Frederic, listed as "B" on a census record. Uncertain and shocked, she approached a volunteer to get clarification on this designation. The woman stated that "B" meant black. She also made racially insensitive jokes to Gail, and this was in the 1990s. The woman had no idea that this was Gail's grandfather.

I realized that this is what her mother went through every day of her life when she made the decision to pass, enduring the jokes and having to smile as if she agreed or brushing them aside. Her mother must have been hurt because they were talking about her parents, grandparents, and her. I cannot even imagine the sadness she endured. I am sure Gail's mother would have never thought her curious daughter would be enduring this pain and sadness in her quest to discover her mother's ancestors.

It was fascinating to me to get the backstory and to understand Gail's personal struggles before she came on the show. With each document or explanation, it left her more confused and conflicted about the one-drop rule. What did that mean to her and her family's identity? Yet, she still chose to come on *Genealogy Roadshow* and reveal her family's secret to America.

I am very fond of Gail, and I think she is extremely brave to go on *Genealogy Roadshow* and reveal her family story—a story that was shared by many but often kept to themselves. Gail and I hit it off instantly and as her story unfolded, I could tell that she was thinking of her mother and her childhood. I could see it in her eyes. It was as if her mother's peculiar behaviors, such as meticulously applying face makeup to cover her olive complexion and avoiding the sun, were being examined.

After Gail's story aired, I remember being at the RootsTech conference in Salt Lake City. A white man came up to me and he almost started crying. He couldn't understand why Gail's mother had to pass for white. He knew why, but the story touched him so much, he just said, "It wasn't right. It wasn't right."

That was the goal of sharing Gail's story and her mother's journey—to open up a dialogue, to get whites and blacks talking about slavery and Jim Crow.

White Like Her adds to that dialogue by exploring the trials and tribulations of a mixed-race family and, more importantly, the impact of racial identity. This book will be the impetus to conversations about periods in history that have been forgotten but still resonate in people's lives today whether they know it or not. Some too painful to remember, but we know "it wasn't right."

1

PBS's *Genealogy Roadshow* Season Two Taping

August 2014, St. Louis, Missouri

WILD WITH ANTICIPATION, I hurry up the granite steps of the St. Louis Central Public Library, oblivious to the blistering heat and humidity. A family secret I've kept for seventeen years is about to be exposed in the most public way possible—on a national television show, *Genealogy Roadshow*. Although I'm a published mystery author, I've never been able to solve this mystery with any certainty. Today it will be solved.

Already there's a queue of people on the left waiting to enter the imposing library for the show's taping. La Monte Westmoreland, one of the producers, instructed me to bypass the line. "If you have any problems, call me on my cellphone."

Tucked in my purse are his cellphone number and my notes from the Skype interview with Rachel from casting in California. Last night, unable to sleep, I rehearsed my questions for the genealogist, reciting them over and over as if they were an incantation that could conjure my mysterious, elusive grandfather, Azemar Frederic of New Orleans.

He and his ancestors hold the key to my racial identity that was deeply buried by my mother, Alvera Frederic Kalina.

As I reach the top step I spot the film crew on the right, lugging their equipment inside the library. Before I can follow them, Sarah Hochhauser, the Assistant Producer, appears. In her lovely Welsh accent, she tells me that she'll be doing a short interview prior to the taping and then another interview after the taping to get my reaction to the revelations.

"Do you know what the genealogist found out about my grandfather?" I ask Sarah, adrenaline spiking through me at the thought of multiple interviews.

"No, I don't," she answers. "You'll have to tell me your reaction to the revelations in the post interview. That makes all the interviews more spontaneous for both of us."

Does she really not know? I study her face, which is impossible to read.

As we walk inside, a million thoughts and emotions spark through me, from curiosity about what they discovered to anxiety about whether I should have ever agreed to do this. From the moment I completed the online application to learning my story was chosen for the show, I've struggled with doubt. Am I honoring the vow I made to my mother so long ago to keep her secret, or am I dishonoring it? Though I know it's too late for second thoughts, still they won't leave me, nagging at me with a daughter's worry. Even now, four months after my mother's death, I want to protect her. From what, I'm not sure.

"You'll be fine," Sarah says, patting my shoulder. And then she's gone, hurrying toward the Great Hall, where the filming will take place.

My family joins me. They've been waiting patiently for me to finish my conversation with Sarah. Today's revelations affect them as well. My husband, Jerry; our son, Chris; daughter, Lauren; daughter-in-law, Charlyne; and our two granddaughters, Ainsley and Quincy, and I walk toward the Great Hall. We stand on the threshold silently watching.

Everything is unreal from the crew setting up cameras and lights to the large screen that will show our family's history to the table where Jerry and I will sit and listen to Kenyatta Berry, one of *Roadshow*'s genealogists. The air is palpable with excitement and energy.

I let it all wash over me, thinking back to that chilly winter day nearly twenty years ago when I uncovered a family secret in a Family History Center in Buffalo Grove, Illinois. The day that I found out I wasn't who I thought I was. That everything I knew about myself wasn't everything. That a crucial part of my mother's family history had been hidden from me.

The producer tells us it's time. My husband and I follow him into the room and take our places. Across from us sits Kenyatta, who's dressed in a crisp white suit that contrasts with her warm brown skin. Behind us stands our family who surrounds us like an embrace.

My breath catches as I glance at the script that rests beside the laptop computer Kenyatta will use to display the key documents of my mother's story. It's thick with secrets.

The director calls for silence. The Great Hall goes quiet and the three cameras start to roll. Kenyatta smiles knowingly at me and says, "Your mother had a secret she was determined to take to the grave."

I nod, realizing the trueness of her words, and how my mother's death freed me from my vow, and how if it weren't for my persistent curiosity, she would have taken her secret to her grave.

"I'd like to show you the 1940 Louisiana census," Kenyatta says, opening the document on the computer with her long, slender fingers. We all turn toward the large screen to see what she has revealed.

It takes me a moment to find my mother on the census. As I stare at her name, I feel myself slip out of time. It is the first of many surprises.

That morning I couldn't have imagined that my appearance on *Genealogy Roadshow* would mark the start of an adventure involving a movie and TV producer/documentarian, historians, genealogists, archivists, librarians, women with stories similar to mine, and the discovery of a lost family. My journey would uncover ancestors spanning continents and centuries tied to important historical events—some known, some unknown—as well as stories at the heart of this country's beginnings.

After the taping, Stuart Krasnow, the show's executive producer, said to us, "This story is going to be an example of what America is now. Most of us are not aware of our true ancestry."

I nodded my head in agreement thinking not only about my mother's true ancestry but the countless other family stories that have been buried for generations, out of fear or shame or time. We all think we know who we are. We all believe what our parents tell us about our families. Sometimes what they don't tell us is the real story.

2

Secrets and Lies

Parma, Ohio

WHEN I WAS a young girl, my mother would tell me about her life in New Orleans before she came north to Ohio to marry my father. Each story so carefully fashioned, so artfully told I never questioned their validity. It was one of the rare times I'd be allowed to sit on my parents' double bed in the cramped downstairs bedroom that faced the street, its north window inches from the neighbor's driveway where a dog barked sometimes into the night.

The room was pristine with its satiny floral bedspread, crisscrossed white lacy curtains, and fringed shades. Area rugs surrounded the bed like islands of color over the amber shag carpet. A large dresser held my mother's perfumes neatly arranged on a mirrored tray. An assortment of tiny prayer books rested on a side table beside a rosary. Over the bed was a painting of a street scene that could be Paris or New Orleans, colorful and dreamy. A similar painting hung in the living room.

It wasn't until I married and left home that my father was banished to the other first floor smaller bedroom, and even then he was an interloper in this feminine domain. His clothes were exiled to the front hall closet where he kept his rifle. On story days the room was a mother-daughter cove of confidences where my mother came as close as she ever would to telling me who she was, dropping clues like bread-crumbs that would take me decades to decipher. As I grew older, she confided intimacies of her marital life best shared with a mother or a sister. I was the substitute for the family left behind in New Orleans.

In its orderliness, the bedroom was a microcosm of the entire eight-een hundred square foot suburban tract house where I grew up. A house she cleaned every day as if it were a jewel that would quickly tarnish if not polished and treasured. Her housekeeping so meticulous, to this day I can see her kneeling in the kitchen like a raven-haired Cinder-ella, her head bowed as she pinched dirt from the green linoleum floor, dirt even the broom couldn't pick up. That only she could remove. In this small house, my mother finally found what she imagined was her haven, her safe place—small and tidy as the life she desired and sacri-ficed so much to have.

To me her stories were magical and transformative. They'd begin with the white jasmine flowers she wore in her black hair as a young woman, illustrated in the black-and-white studio portrait photograph she kept in our living room on a faux marble-topped table as a reminder of that exotic Southern belle she once was. "This was who I used to be in New Orleans before I married your father and came north," the photograph seemed to say.

Sometimes her story would veer and we'd be in the French Quar-ter. The Vieux Carré, she called it, the French words as exotic as she was. She'd describe the iron lacework and the old brick buildings that she said were French. If she felt adventuresome that day, she'd tell the story of the Vieux Carré painter, a story that as a child made me uncomfortable.

"I answered a newspaper ad for a live model. I was nineteen."

I didn't know it then but later I'd understand the circumstances of her decision. She was a young woman with meager skills, poor and adrift with no one to advise her, looking for work, using the gift of her beauty.

"He told me to take off my clothes." She laughed as if she were searching for the humor in her story. "I told him I didn't do that."

"'That's what live model means,' he said, looking me over, studying my face. I started to leave. But he stopped me and said, 'If you want to sit for portraits, I'll give you the name of another painter.' He must have taken pity on me."

"Did you sit for that other painter?" I asked, heat rushing through me at the thought of my mother posing nude for a strange man.

"Oh, yes. You know what the other painter said? He told me he saw these colors in my skin, greens and yellows and peach."

I studied her face the way that painter must have, trying to see what he saw. I couldn't see those colors. Only her warm olive skin, dark brown eyes, her deep dimples and Roman nose. And though all children think their mothers are beautiful, mine was. She never took a bad photo.

Sometimes she'd open the tall dark dresser with the ribbed edges that I liked to run my fingers up and down, and take out her long white gloves with the pearl buttons, carefully wrapped in thin tissue paper, followed by my favorite—the tiny white beaded evening bag with the tarnished clasp and a matchbook inside as if waiting for her to resume her glamorous single life in New Orleans or across the river in Algiers.

Each story contained a lesson at its core. The long white gloves and beaded evening bag were about chastity and being a lady at all times no matter the temptation, no matter the man's promises or his handsomeness. "Gail, men only want one thing. That's just how they are."

The nude modeling story was about maintaining moral standards, knowing your worth, not selling yourself for money, no matter how poor you were.

Sometimes the stories of supper clubs and jazz music, Lake Pontchartrain and The Safari Club would shift as if she were moving closer to the real story that beat under her skin like another self. There would be the way the rain fell only on one side of the street while on the other the sun would beat down relentlessly, a confusion of weather. If I didn't respond with enough awe, she'd tell it again. It was a story she never tired of telling me about a place where the weather was as unpredictable and quixotic as her childhood.

On other days when I sensed a sadness in her, she'd tell me about the old black woman on Canal Street, limping home from her job as a domestic, burdened with groceries, the deep lines of a hard life etched into her dark face.

My mother called the sidewalk a banquette. "Banquette," she repeated the word so I would know the language of the city where she was born and raised, so I would understand how she left that language behind to make a new life in Ohio, and yet it lingered with her like a favorite song she couldn't quite get out of her head, its lilting melody a relic of home. My ear keen to catch traces of her New Orleans accent that sometimes slipped out despite her vigilance. The soft drawl she couldn't totally erase, always there.

"I remember this old black woman walking on Canal Street carrying all these packages. She looked so tired and worn out. This white man was walking toward her and when she didn't move off the banquette, he shoved her off, shouting at her in a nasty voice. 'Get out of my way,'" my mother paused, and then added. "He called her a terrible word. You know what I mean."

I did know.

I never forgot that story or the way she sat on the bed, her hands folded in her lap, her voice full of indignation tinged with sadness, her dark eyes fierce.

"That wasn't right," she said. "But that's how it was in New Orleans back then." She shook her head as if she needed to dislodge the image of the old black woman shoved off the banquette to make way for a white man who called her nigger.

"That poor old black woman fell down, her packages everywhere, and that white man kept walking," she said.

It wouldn't be until after I appeared on *Genealogy Roadshow* that I understood the full significance of that story and why she told it to me.

But even as a child, I knew the story held a special meaning for her and a message for me. This is what it's like to be a black person in the South. Who would want to endure that?

Only later, much later, would I understand she was seeding my life with these clues, hinting at her hidden self or maybe preparing me to accept that part of her she'd left behind in New Orleans and her reason for doing that. Or maybe she was only telling me a story about prejudice and cruelty, teaching me right from wrong as any mother would do.

Once I asked her, "Why don't you have a picture of your father Azemar?"

"I just don't." Her abruptness was a signal to me that the subject was not to be pursued.

She had a scattering of photos of her mother Camille, her sister Shirley, and a few cousins. But in the family photo department, she was bereft. It was as if when she left New Orleans she left all her family archives, if she had any, behind—a clean start free of family and memories.

"Why don't we visit New Orleans," I'd sometimes ask, wanting to see for myself where she grew up, see the scrolled ironwork of the Vieux Carré, walk the banquettes, hear the jazz music of her city, and meet her relatives.

"Because it depresses me to go home."

There was no way to bridge the finality of my mother's reason, a woman prone to fits of depression so acute that for a time she saw a Cleveland psychiatrist. I didn't want to make her sadder and so I stopped asking.

But I didn't stop wondering. There was something about the unknown that I couldn't let rest.

Looking back on her stories of her life growing up in New Orleans, I realize now that she wove a past for me that left out the most important part. The part about her black heritage and what she'd done to hide it.

3

"There's a Nigger in Every Woodshed."

January 1995

THE WINDOWLESS BASEMENT of the Buffalo Grove Family History Center had the feel of an underground bunker—fluorescent lights, cinder block walls, the musty scent of dampness. At the room's entrance sat a gray-haired woman, birdlike and benign. With robotic precision, she meted out instructions on how to use the machines, where the microfilms were located and how to order original documents. She appeared as nondescript and gray as the walls.

I'd come to the family history center in search of my grandfather Azemar Frederic. I was between adjunct college teaching jobs, applying for tenure track teaching positions in creative writing, and working part-time as an assistant editor for a medical journal. The year before, I'd been offered a position in creative writing at a liberal arts college in Tennessee. But I turned it down. Uprooting my life at the age of forty-nine for a position that paid in the low five figures seemed foolhardy. My husband would need to obtain a Tennessee dental license to practice dentistry, and we would have to pay out-of-state tuition at the University of Illinois for our daughter Lauren. So I resigned myself to seeking positions in the Chicago area where the competition was especially rigorous and my chances for success slim.

I had time on my hands and an insatiable longing to find Azemar who over the years had become more and more unreal to me as if he never existed, was a figment of my mother's imagination. Without a photograph of him, I had nothing physical to connect him to me. This need for a physical image of him was primal. It was an aching absence that I needed to fill.

This was 1995, before the Internet, before Ancestry.com. Family research required a journey, was a physical as well as an emotional quest. I'd arrived at 10 a.m. when the center opened. I would stay as long as it took to find my grandfather Azemar Frederic of New Orleans, my mystery man.

But I had little to go on. I didn't know when he was born or when he died. My mother couldn't or wouldn't help me. Her memory faltered when it came to her father.

"He might have died after you were born. I don't remember. Maybe in the 1950s."

What I did know wasn't much, birth and death place—New Orleans and the precise spelling of his first and last name. As a child my mother would spell out her maiden name for me—a school requirement on this form or that. Always stressing that there was no k at the end of Frederic.

"That would make us German. And we're not German," she'd say. "We're French. And your grandmother Camille Kilbourne is English and Scottish." Her tone was fierce and not to be challenged. She took great pride in her French heritage, occasionally throwing out a French phrase to prove her point: *tante*/aunt, *très bon*/very good, *n'est pas*/isn't it so.

Persistent over the years, I pieced together other sparse facts about the elusive Azemar—even his name conjured mystery. My mother had a shorthand way of describing him: hard worker who didn't smoke or drink. He and my grandmother divorced early in their marriage. They both remarried and started families.

My mother never spoke of her father's second family when I asked about them, except to say the oldest daughter resembled her. I didn't know how many other children there were from Azemar's second marriage or who his second wife was. My mother refused to talk about them. The mere mention of them made her go quiet.

"People say I looked like him," my mother would say, placating me as if her face replaced the one I desperately wanted to see. Then she'd add, her eyes far away, "I asked my mother once why she didn't stay married to my father. And she said, 'he was too jealous.'"

And as often happened with my mother's stories, the not telling was the telling. If I'd been older, I might have picked up on her clues. But I was a child. I accepted what she told me. She was my mother.

The morning wore on. Time passed without notice as I scrolled through the microfilm finding Fredericks, Fredericos but no Frederics. Every once in a while I'd have to stop scrolling and close my eyes. The whirling of the microfilm and the low lights were making me queasy or maybe it was the gnawing hunger that I refused to placate. I was a woman on a mission.

It was almost 1 p.m. I'd been there for three hours and hadn't found Azemar. I decided to finish the 1900 Louisiana census record and return next Wednesday.

The surname Frederic happened first. It jumped out at me, spelled exactly as my mother said: C, no K at the end. Then I spotted my grandfather's unusual first name Azemar at the bottom of a long list of other Frederics. In 1900 Azemar Alfred Frederic was three years old and listed as a granddaughter, sex male. Finally I knew when he was born: 1897. A flutter of elation ran through me as I jotted down his information on a legal pad that until now was woefully empty.

There were many family members living in the Girard/Frederic household. Azemar's father was Leon Frederic, his mother Celeste Girard Frederic. I savored the beauty of her name, my great-grandmother Celeste Girard. Azemar was the youngest of five children: Louise, Leon, Leonie, and Estelle. They lived at 379 Ursuline Avenue in New Orleans. The head of the household was Albert Girard, Azemar's maternal grandfather, my great-grandfather. There were also a number of Girards sharing the residence.

As I traced across the grid, I stopped on the letter *B*, perplexed by its meaning, then I scrolled up to find the category: Race.

My mind didn't quite take in what I was seeing. Would the census taker use *B* for black in 1900? It didn't seem likely. Then what did *B* mean if not black? And why would the census taker mark my grandfather and his family black? It had to be a mistake. My grandfather's family was not black.

Aware of the time, I hurriedly searched for Azemar in the 1930 census. When I found him, his race was no longer designated as *B*, now his racial designation was *W*. I was familiar with the one-drop rule, a racial classification asserting that any person with even one ancestor of African ancestry was considered to be black no matter how far back in their family tree. But the *B* perplexed me, as did the *W*. How could Azemar be black in 1900 and white in 1930?

I glanced back at the gray-haired lady. She was shuffling through index cards, keeping herself busy, and looking bored. I got up from the machine and walked over to her.

"I was wondering about the racial designation *B* in the 1900 Louisiana census. Can that be right?" I asked reticently, purposely not mentioning that the *B* was attached to my mother's family.

"Those cards have been copied. *B* means black." She looked me up and down. "You know the saying, 'there's a nigger in every woodshed.'"

I was speechless. Struck dumb.

She laughed, a tight pinched laugh full of malice. "Things were different back then. We had those candies, you know, we called them 'nigger babies.'" She said this with some glee in her voice as if we were sharing the same joke.

The word nigger kept reeling from her mouth like the rolls of micro-film whirling around me. I stood there, stunned, having no idea what the woman was talking about or how to respond. I'd never heard of "nigger babies." And if I had, I'd never be spewing the term out like a sharp slap.

All I could muster in defense of a family whose race I'd just discov-ered and was unsure of was a fact that sounded like an excuse. "In Louisiana," I muttered, "you only had to have one drop of black blood to be considered black." I felt assaulted with an experience I had no way to relate to and that I wasn't certain I could even claim.

She finished my thought for me as if confirming what she'd already said about race and blood. "Yes, just one drop was all that was needed. You know the saying, 'nigger in the woodshed.'"

She seemed to think I agreed with her, that the one-drop rule was correct, leaving no doubt about my race and in her eyes my tainted blood. It was evident to me it would be useless to continue this conver-sation with this bigoted God-lugging woman.

For a long second she stared through her glasses at me as if she was searching for a physical confirmation of my heritage. "Oh," she finally said as if a light bulb had gone on in her head, "You're the one with the slaves in your family."

Slaves? I never said anything about slaves in my family. She'd made her own logical leap—black ancestry equaled slaves. This was a logical leap I was not prepared to accept. This was not how I saw my family or myself.

Shaken, I returned to the microfiche machine, rewound the role of microfilm, placed it back in its box, and refiled it in the steel drawer, avoiding the woman like a contagion, afraid of what other derogatory racial expressions she'd resurrect from her arsenal of bigotry.

Outside, the cold January wind was like a tonic, snapping me back to the ordinariness of winter—snow and cold, the need for shelter. I hur-ried to my car, shut the door, and started the engine. But I didn't leave. I sat staring at the silvery sky, the mottled clouds, the uncertainty of light that made a Midwest January day bearable—when the sun disappears for days.

What just happened? I felt like I'd had an out-of-body experience. In a split second I became someone else, my identity in question. When I walked into the squat, brown building I was a white woman. When I left I didn't know who I was. Was I still a white woman but a white woman with black ancestors? Were Azemar Frederic and his entire family the "niggers" in my woodshed?

Why hadn't my mother told me? Was this the reason she didn't have a picture of her father, fearing I would see the physical evidence of his blackness? That I would see what she'd been hiding? Was this why she never took us to New Orleans to visit her family?

I couldn't get it into my head that I wasn't who I thought I was. I wasn't this white woman. Or I was this white woman who was also this black woman. Or I was neither? Who was I really? And what did my racial mixture mean?

As I pulled out of the driveway, I glanced at myself in the rear view mirror. Nothing had changed. I looked the same. Anyone could see what I was.

4

Getting Proof
1995

"WHAT YOU NEED to do," my friend Linda Andrews said, "is send a letter to the state of Louisiana and request a copy of your mother's birth certificate."

I'd confided in her my need for certainty. How I couldn't ask my mother about her race without more proof than several census records. How reliable were census records anyway if the names weren't even spelled correctly and children's sexes were misidentified?

Linda humored me, going along for the ride. She was the perfect friend for this journey, having found out in adulthood that she was adopted. Her story was as startling and life changing as mine. Toward the end of her mother's life, she suffered from Alzheimer's disease and in a moment of frustration with Linda blurted out, "I should have never adopted you." It was a stunning moment for Linda. Like me, her life-altering event made her question her identity, another secret withheld. Sometimes I think we sense things about people who become our friends, some psychic understanding about each other, like twins separated at birth.

"Why would they give me a copy of her birth certificate?" I wanted reassurances I was doing the right thing. I wanted handholding.

"Here's what you do. You write as your mother. You say you lost your birth certificate and need a copy. They don't know where your mother is living." Linda was a former *Chicago Tribune* reporter, who now worked at the University of Illinois at Chicago where she taught nonfiction writing courses in the English department and ran the internship program. She had the canny, curious determination of a journalist.

"You really think they'll buy it?" I felt a rush of excitement at this ruse. Usually I'd run the charge, fearless and jacked up on adrenaline. But when it came to my mother, I treaded softly, not wanting to displease or hurt her.

"What do you have to lose?"

She was right. "Nothing, I guess."

"Then do it. And call me when you get an answer. This is too juicy."

When the letter arrived, I was prepared to be disappointed. But I wasn't disappointed, only more confused. Inside the envelope was my mother's birth certificate with the official seal of Louisiana at the bottom and stamp dated February 2, 1995. Holding the document was like holding a piece of my mother's life—a piece I knew little to nothing about.

Her parents were living at 2921 St. Ann Street. Camille was sixteen years old and Azemar was twenty-two years old. The midwife Mrs. O'Koenkel delivered my mother Alvera Rita Frederic on October 21, 1921. In parenthesis was written "(col)." It would not be too dramatic to say that I gasped at the sight of those three letters.

No *B*, but "col," which more than likely designated her race as "colored." As stunned as I was by this other piece of evidence, again, I reminded myself that in the state of Louisiana in 1921 there was the one-drop rule.

But my mother didn't look black. Why would she be designated as such? Who made that decision and what was it based on? And does col really mean colored or could it mean other races?

"Write another letter to the state asking them to explain what col means," Linda advised me when I told her my confusion about col on the birth certificate. "Who knows what it meant back then."

"By the way have you said anything to your mother?" I could hear the urging in her question.

"Not until I know for sure about the col." I knew my mother too well. To confront her about her racial designations over the phone would be a mistake. I wanted to see her face when I told her what I found. I needed to judge her reaction. On the phone she could easily change the subject, brush me off, claim ignorance, or worse, become indignant and angry.

The letter from Louisiana Vital Records dated March 15, 1995 explaining the letters col spelled it out for me, leaving little doubt what col meant.

Zelma W. Lombard, Deputy Director of Vital Records wrote: "The letters 'col' is an abbreviation for the designation 'colored.' Our records indicate that during the 1920s and perhaps through the 1940s, 'col' was a term applied to anyone "of color", i.e., Native Americans, Blacks, Asians, Hispanics, etc."

As I read this section of the letter, I thought maybe my mother was of Native American heritage. But then I read on.

"The use of the term 'colored' has been ambiguous over time, however did become more closely associated with the Black race."

The last paragraph threw me.

"If you consider your genealogy different or more specific to one race, you may submit a request for change of racial designation. You will be required to submit information, which shows a preponderance of evidence to support this. We will be happy to review it."

Did my mother ever submit that evidence? I doubted it. And before the advent of online DNA tests how would someone go about disproving a racial designation if a person felt it was erroneous? Later when I delved deeper into Louisiana's racial designations for people of color, I learned of another woman who tried to do this very thing in 1982 with little personal success.

The state of Louisiana had unequivocally designated my mother as colored or black. But still I was struggling with my mother's racial identity and my own racial identity. The initial shock had started to wear off and in its place was denial. My mother was not black. She couldn't be. This was a governmental mistake. You had only to look at my mother to see that she was white.

What did it say about me that I couldn't accept the designation of my mother's race? I wasn't a bigot, of that I was certain. I'd taught my children to accept all people regardless of their color. My refusal stemmed from psychological issues of identity. I identified myself as a white woman. I also couldn't believe my mother could be that duplicitous.

That evening, I told my husband that it was almost certain my mother had passed as white. He grinned. "I always wanted to do a black chick."

"That's not funny," I said, laughing despite myself. Then I realized how his humor was easing my anxiety. That he was telling me that it didn't matter to him what racial blend I was. "Well, maybe it's a little funny."

Black chick? Was that what I was? Was that how people would see me if I revealed my family's racial designation on a 1900 census record and my mother's birth certificate that read "col"? What did it mean to be "colored" in the eyes of the state of Louisiana in 1921 and yet look white? I had to find out. I had to talk to my mother.

5

The Vow
Spring 1997

T<small>WO YEARS WENT</small> by. I let them. I started a new job in the English
Department at the University of Illinois at Chicago, overseeing
the internship program and teaching writing, the job my friend Linda
had had. At the urging of my son Chris who was pursuing a master's
degree in English at the University of Washington in Seattle, I began
writing a mystery novel. Leigh Girard was the name I gave my amateur
sleuth. My grandfather's family still haunted me.

In December 1996, my father died from throat cancer, a protracted,
agonizing death. Even after his death, I didn't say anything to my
mother about her family's racial heritage. I'd told my children and a
few very close friends. It was another fact about me like my dark brown
hair and hazel eyes. I could think of no way to talk to my mother about
this. Though I desperately wanted to.

But certain family mysteries were solved, mysteries my husband
and I accepted and never questioned. Though my husband is blond
and blue-eyed and my skin is porcelain white, our son, Chris, is olive-
skinned with curly black hair and dark eyes. We sometimes joked that
he was switched at birth, because he didn't look like my husband or

me. Our daughter Lauren, on the other hand, is a blend of us, with my husband's straight hair and my fair coloring. Chris related how a friend of his had asked him why he and his sister looked so different, implying that he was adopted. And then there was my mother's affinity for Chris, often saying that he was the only grandchild who looked like her.

Peculiarities about my mother that I'd chalked up to her quirky personality suddenly made sense. Her aversion to the sun, how she'd never go outside without a hat, claiming she didn't want to get wrinkles. Her adamancy about never visiting New Orleans because it would depress her took on a different interpretation. To go home would risk discovery of her racial secret. Though she did suffer from acute depression, she had another equally valid reason for her not to visit New Orleans. Again she was cleverly telling a half-truth, while hiding another truth.

Finally in the spring of 1997 I got my chance to ask her about her birth certificate and the Frederic family's race. My father had been dead for over a year. She seemed stronger, less fragile. And then there was her disturbing admission to me that after my father's death, she was no longer depressed. His alcoholism and subsequent erratic behavior had plagued their marriage. Even after he'd stopped drinking, he was still difficult, still angry. Their marriage had not been a love match.

We agreed that she'd fly to Chicago over my spring break. We'd moved from suburban Libertyville to Wadsworth, a semi-rural area close to the Wisconsin border. The weather would be warm. She was no longer depressed and vulnerable like she'd been for so long. It would be an opportune time to find out the truth from my evasive mother.

After she arrived, I waited a day or two to let her settle in. My husband had left for work and we had the house to ourselves. After lunch we sat in the family room with the TV playing in the background. The dog dozed in a rectangle of light near the north facing windows.

My mother looked so comfortable in the oversized green plush chair that I hesitated for a moment, considering what I was about to do. I knew that once I broached the subject of her racial heritage, there would no turning back. No matter what her response was our relationship would be different. What we knew about each other would change.

I'd waited two years to have this conversation. I took in a deep breath and began. "Mom, I have something to ask you." I tried to sound casual as if I were asking her advice on a recipe or a dress style. But inside I felt as if I were ten years old, anxiety pumping through my body, making me shaky.

"I've been researching your dad, Azemar. And I found something confusing." I plunged ahead. "It said on the 1900 census that he was black. I thought it might be an error. So I sent away to Louisiana for your birth certificate," I paused. "And it said you're colored."

There was a stunned silence into which everything seemed to tumble. Even the TV's drone faded away. Her spine went rigid. She gave me that haughty, angry look I recognized too well. Her dark eyes like arrows aimed at me. "I don't know what birth certificate you were looking at but mine says I'm white."

I couldn't let it go. There was this need to know that overcame the ten-year-old girl who cowered and obeyed her mother out of love and fear. "Well, I wrote a letter to the state of Louisiana and asked them what col meant. And they said it meant black. I don't think it's a mistake. If you'd like to see the letter and your birth certificate I can go get them."

For a long moment, she said nothing. I watched her fingers curl on the chair arms and her shoulders bunch protectively. She seemed to be shrinking into herself. There was a catch in her throat when she said, "How will I hold my head up with my friends." The pleading in her voice caught me off guard. I'd hurt her.

"Mom, there's nothing to be ashamed of. I think it's a good thing."

"You can't tell anyone. Promise me. You can't tell anyone in the family until after I die." She sounded desperate, cornered. Her voice was tinged with fear and shame.

"What about my brother?" I thought he should know. It was his heritage too.

"Not even him. Promise me."

It was a promise I didn't want to make. A promise I didn't fully understand. But she looked so small in the large chair that seemed to have swallowed her. "I won't tell anyone. I promise."

Satisfied she stood and left the room.

We didn't speak of it again during her visit. And this began the longest held secret of my life. A promise made to my mother whose shame and fear were so frightening and painful to witness, my conscience left me no other choice but to honor her wishes.

Not until after her death and after I'd read *The Autobiography of an Ex-Colored Man* did I gain insight into the shame I witnessed that day when I confronted my mother with the truth of her racial heritage.

Near the end of the book, the narrator, so light-skinned he can pass for white, makes a momentous decision after witnessing a crowd of Southern white people burn a black man alive. The narrator catches a train to New York and decides neither to disclaim his own race nor claim the white race. "Let the world take me for what it would." Then he explains what drove him out of the Negro race was shame. "Shame at being identified with a people that could with impunity be treated worse than animals. For certainly the law would restrain and punish the malicious burning alive of animals."[1]

In the silence of the next seventeen years, I began to reexamine, replay all her stories of New Orleans. I started to see them in a different light, shadowed with what was missing, nuanced, and meant to deceive. I began to delve into the mother I didn't know, piecing her together from what wasn't said. Her silence left me reeling.

Who was she? I wondered. Was the obsessively neat woman whose floors you could eat off of, who made a display of entering St. Francis de Sales Catholic Church every Sunday front and center decked out in her veiled hat and white gloves, orchestrating our entrance so we genuflected as a family, insisting we sit in the first pew, was that her disguise or her real self? Did she even know anymore? Had she fallen for her own story?

One neighbor called us the royal family, half jokingly, referring to our dramatic entrances and our Sunday clothes. I squirmed under the spotlight of my mother's theatricality. I longed to sit in the last pew far from the altar. I was a watcher by nature, not a performer.

After the encounter with my mother and the vow, my children bragged to their friends about our mixed race, seemingly unencumbered with the same identity issues and not bound by my vow.

My son took up the mantle of family research. He'd earned his master's degree from the University of Washington and was now living on the East Coast beginning his PhD in English at Johns Hopkins University. In his down time, he combed the National Archives, tracing my mother's family back to the nineteenth century, noting the racial designations, black or mulatto or white—a potpourri of racial fluidity. A gifted researcher, he fleshed out the family tree, stockpiling his research in a binder.

And then we all seemed to let it go. Not that we forgot about the discovery of our racial heritage. It just wasn't central to our everyday lives. We'd done as much as we could do. My mother wouldn't talk. That door was permanently closed. We resigned ourselves to never knowing with any certainty about our mixed-race heritage or what it meant.

Then my mother started to die, slowly but surely, and that changed everything.

As my mother often said to me when I was reeling from some disappointment in life, "When one door closes, another door opens."

That door would be *Genealogy Roadshow*.

But before *Genealogy Roadshow*, I'd make one last attempt to break through my mother's silence.

6

Creole, Anyone?
2012

THOUGH MY MOTHER refused to talk to me about her racial heritage, occasionally she'd appease me by mailing me photographs of her family. I'd been asking her for a photograph of her mother Camille Frederic Romero. The only photos of her I had were mostly black and white, small, and grainy. It would be months, but eventually she found one that she felt she could trust me with, one that didn't give away any family secrets. When I opened the package I was surprised and pleased by her generous spirit in sharing with me this piece of her past. But the seemingly innocuous photograph led to my questioning my own feelings about my mother's racial secret.

The black-and-white eight-by-ten photograph was professionally shot in 1951 at the Safari Room supper club in Algiers, Louisiana. During that time period, it wasn't uncommon for an upscale supper club to hire a freelance photographer to snap photographs of patrons and then offer them an opportunity to buy the souvenir photo to memorialize the occasion.

In the foreground sit my grandmother Camille, her sister, my Aunt Mickey, Mickey's daughter Rhea, and her husband Charles. Camille and Mickey each hold their cocktail glass firmly as if it anchors them.

Rhea and Charles hold hands—his hand over her hand. The leather-quilted circular booth looks lush. Though it must have been a special night, none of them can manage a smile. Only Rhea has a wistfulness about her, her eyes faraway, her mouth relaxed. The photograph evokes another era when men wore suits and ties to supper clubs and women donned their best dresses, silk stockings, and jewelry.

My mother had little information to add to the photograph, no knowledge of the Safari Room, the occasion of the photograph, or where Camille's second husband Arthur Romero was. I took the photograph for what it appeared to be, my mother's close family members having a night out on the town.

I'd met Cousin Charles and Cousin Rhea once as a young child and visited them in California when I was an adult. I don't remember meeting Aunt Mickey prior to 1951. My grandmother had visited us in Ohio on several occasions. I never thought of them as anything but white like me. I was a child. I accepted what I was told.

When my first mystery *Destroying Angels* was released in 2006, I began getting requests from libraries and various adult writing groups to conduct mystery-writing workshops. After all I'd been university trained to teach writing workshops and had taught on the university level for over fourteen years. Often I'd use a photograph as a writing tool to teach characterization in mystery writing. If I knew in advance that the participants might be an older group and not young adults, I'd use the Safari Room photograph.

What I'd tell the writers to do was study the photograph. The only facts I'd give them was the year 1951 and the place the Safari Room, Algiers, Louisiana. I'd jokingly tell them that all the people in the photo were my relatives and to be kind. But I didn't tell them how I was related to them.

One spring, in 2012, I was teaching a mystery-writing workshop at the Women's Exchange (WEX) in Winnetka, Illinois, a posh North Shore Chicago suburb. I liked teaching at WEX. The building was an old mansion with the patina of a former time. As I climbed the stairs to the second floor, I'd smell the heavy scent of lunch being prepared for the day care center on the first floor.

The writing group was small, composed of middle-aged women who had the luxury of taking a morning workshop. We were to meet once a week. So that first day I decided to use the Safari Room photograph for the characterization exercise.

When I handed them the photograph, I could tell by their expressions and the way they studied the photograph that they were intrigued by it. Some smiled, some oohed and aahed. Someone said, "Look at those clothes."

As always, I began with a tantalizing hook. "One of these people will be murdered before the night is over," I paused. "You are to choose the murder victim, the murderer, and the sleuth. Don't think too long about it. Go by your instincts. Then, write a character sketch of the sleuth that goes beyond just that person's physical appearance, describe things like how they hold their drink, how they walk." I paused again while they finished writing down my instructions. "Finally," I said, "give the murderer a dark secret he or she is hiding."

When they finished writing and they discussed their choices and why they made those choices, one of the women asked me about the people in the photo, who were they in relationship to me. After I explained who everyone was, she didn't seem satisfied with my explanation, her eyes searching my face.

"Is your family Creole?" she asked. "Your cousin looks Creole."

A shock of panic went up my spine. My mother's secret raising its uncertain head. Before I knew my mom's secret, I would have shrugged the woman's question off, answering nonchalantly. But I did know her secret. I was stymied how to answer her. I didn't even know what constituted a Creole. But I did know that my mother's birth certificate said she was colored and that she believed she was colored.

Was the woman asking if my cousin was Black, or mixed, or Spanish? Was she asking if the other women in the photograph were also Creoles?

I stumbled around an answer that sounded disingenuous even to me. "He's my cousin by marriage. So I don't know."

She shook her head as if she understood and said nothing more.

"Let's go over next week's assignment," I said, grateful the moment had passed, fairly sure she picked up on my discomfort.

Other than that bigoted woman at the family research center and this nosey writing student, no one had ever suggested to me that I was anything other than a white woman. I was ill prepared for such questions.

Later I wondered what the writing student had seen in my cousin's appearance that made her ask if he were Creole and by extension was my family Creole. To me he looked Spanish or possibly Italian, as did Aunt Mickey and Cousin Rhea. My grandmother looked white.

What surprised me was my own reaction to her question, the fear I felt at being caught out, not wanting to share my bloodline with strangers, who might judge me unkindly, possibly question even my writing accomplishments and educational pedigree. And beating below the fear was anger. What does their being Creole have to do with anything? And if they were Creole, what's it to you?

My vow to my mother was taking an odd toll on me, tamping down the response I wanted to give. "Just like so many of us in America my family is a blending of many different cultures and races, Creole being just one of them." But I couldn't say that. I'd made a promise. I was complicit in my mother's deception.

I didn't stop using the evocative photo. It was too good to give up. Students always responded strongly to it. It inspired their imaginations. But I steeled myself for that question: Is your cousin Creole? My answer next time: What do you mean by Creole?

Ticking away behind that mildly confrontational retort was another question: What was a Creole?

❖

There's little consensus on a conclusive definition of the term Creole. "Most scholars agree that the term creole comes from the Spanish or Portuguese crillo or crioulo meaning created in America, in the New World, as opposed to being created or born in Europe.[1] "The Harvard Encyclopedia of Ethnic Groups explains the word 'Creoles' refers not only to people but also to culture, food, music and language."

In referring to people of Louisiana, it states: "In the United States, in the twentieth century, Creole often refers to the Louisiana Creoles of color. Ranging in appearance from mulattos to European whites, the Creoles of color constitute a Caribbean phenomenon in the United States. The product of miscegenation in a seigniorial society, they achieved elite status in Louisiana, and in the early nineteenth century some were slaveholders. Many, educated in France, were patrons of the opera and of literary societies. . . . Louisiana Creoles of color thus constitute a self-conscious group. Who are perceived in their locale as different and separate. They live in New Orleans and in a number of bayou towns. Historically, they have been endogamous, and until late in the nineteenth century spoke mostly French. . . . Their ethnicity is exceedingly difficult to maintain outside of the New Orleans area. Over time, a great many have passed into white groups in other parts of the country, and others have become integrated as blacks. This latter choice is not based wholly on appearance, for many Creoles who choose to identify as Afro-Americans are white in appearance."[2]

I doubt that inquisitive writing student who asked if my family was Creole had that definition in mind. She wasn't referring to an ethnic identity but a racial identity, possibly a mixed racial identity.

I dug deeper into the history of the Creoles of color, both an ethnic and racial classification, trying to understand the nuances of racial designation, learning of Louisiana's shifting laws on what constitutes a black person.

In a concession to the one-drop rule that dominated the Jim Crow South, Louisiana enacted a less stringent mathematical formula for race in 1970, which was enforced until 1984. The statute read: "In signifying race a person having one-thirty-second or less of Negro blood, shall not be deemed, described, or designated by any public official in the State of Louisiana as 'colored,' a 'mulatto,' a 'black,' a 'negro,' a 'griffe,' an 'Afro-American,' a 'quadroon,' a 'mestizo,' a 'colored person,' or a 'person of color.'"[3]

Surprisingly, this mathematical formula for race was more stringent than the Nuremberg law initiated by the Nazis during World War II that said anyone with one-sixteenth Jewish blood was Jewish. The stringency of the Louisiana statute in comparison to the Nuremberg law says a great deal about governmental bigotry.

Trying to understand the statute's racial classification, I looked up the race terms I was unfamiliar with, terms as archaic as the statue. A griffe has three-quarter black and one-quarter white ancestry. A mestizo is "a person of mixed racial or ethnic ancestry, especially, in Latin America, of mixed American Indian and European descent or, in the Philippines, of mixed native and foreign descent."

I already knew mulatto meant a person with one white parent and one black parent. But I wasn't aware that the word came from the Spanish word for mule, carrying all the negative connotations associated with mules. The offspring of a donkey and a horse, a mule is usually sterile and used as a beast of burden. It rankles me that my grandmother and her parents were listed on several US Census reports as Mulatto. Behind all these designations by Louisiana were fear and the need to keep people of color in their place.

This wasn't 1921 when my mother was born, a period of deep segregation that lasted until the 1960s. This was 1970–1984.

I took out my DNA results to see where I fall in the less stringent racial period. I'm 86 percent European, 4 percent Central/South Asian, 2 percent Middle Eastern, and 9 percent African. My husband works out the mathematical formula. In 1970, I would have been designated as black, a colored, a colored person, a person of color, a Negro. It's almost laughable.

Harvard's definition of Creole also touches on the other question that sits at the heart of my mother's story about passing for white.

"Over time, a great many have passed into white groups in other parts of the country, and others have become integrated as blacks. This latter choice is not based wholly on appearance, for many Creoles who choose to identify as Afro-Americans are white in appearance."

Why does a mixed-race person who looks white choose either to pass as white or not to pass as white? To me it is a "Sophie's Choice" question. I understand the economic and social reasons why a person passes. But there is something else involved in whether a person decides to pass or not to pass, more basic, more fundamental that goes to the heart of identity and family.

W. E. B. Du Bois wrote about the paradox of "two-ness," the ambivalence of people with mixed European and African ancestry.[4] If a mixed-race person is white enough to pass, how does that person deal with the trappings of a racist culture where you're forced to choose a side? Cross over to the white side and gain white privilege but lose family and your authentic self, or remain on the black side and suffer economically and socially.

My mother made her "Sophie's Choice" when she decided to pass for white. In living a double life, never having the freedom to be her authentic self, she must have developed a tolerance for racism, staying silent to the racial barbs she heard at work, and from friends and family. If she spoke out, she risked discovery.

"How will I hold my head up with my friends if they know?" Her words keep coming back to me—her shame, and her feelings of being tainted.

In not answering the inquisitive student truthfully, I kept my vow to my mother, but was keeping that vow tainting me with her shame?

7

Taking Her Secret to the Grave
Avon, Ohio, 2014

THE LAST YEAR of my mother's life she asked me one question over and over, "Why won't God take me?" Then she always added with a wistful smile, "He must have a plan for me. But what that is, I can't figure it out."

Deeply religious, her mind failing her, prone to falls, confined to a walker, she was in and out of hospitals and rehab centers, finally living out her last year in an assisted-living facility in Avon, Ohio, under hospice care, which meant she was always ninety days from death. Every ninety days she was evaluated and if she met the hospice criteria, they let her keep her free hospital bed, drug coverage, and routine visits from the hospice nurse. It was a strange bargain. One predicated on the signs and numerical values of death and dying.

She was beset with one medical crisis after another, but she rallied back from each one as if God was indeed pulling her from death, telling her there were still things she needed to do. That he did have a plan for her. Her blood pressure skyrocketed to 192/92, and then plummeted to 110/90, numbers that would kill most elderly people. Her body swelled with fluid, her mind rattled, little by little turning off. She wanted to die, but her body wouldn't let her.

Whether from the constant urinary tract infections, her medications, or her dementia, she was beset with hallucinations that seem prophetic, full of portents—people climbing the walls, calling her name; my father pushing her down a flight of stairs; ants filling her room. She mumbled to people not there, long dead. The last ten months of her life she lost control of her bathroom functions and couldn't bathe herself. For a woman who prided herself on her appearance and her cleanliness, it was a cruel indignity. I tried to convince myself that her dementia mitigated these indignities, that she wasn't fully aware of what was happening in her body. But there was no way to be sure.

I lived in fear of "the phone call." Every time the phone rang I let out a sigh of relief when it wasn't my brother's phone number on the screen. My mother was still alive. She wasn't dead.

The summer before my mother died, my daughter Lauren and I visited her in the assisted-living facility in Avon, the last place she would reside before being rushed to a hospice unit at a nearby hospital, where she died. Although under hospice care, her care numbers were good enough to keep her in the assisted-living wing and out of the more costly nursing wing. Her room was a private suite with a sitting area, separate bedroom and bathroom. There was a small refrigerator where she stocked her bags of chocolate kisses. A treat she seldom allowed herself before the dementia.

That summer day when I entered her room, at first I couldn't find her. I called out "Mom." No one answered. My daughter waited in the sitting room, while I peeked into her bedroom. I caught a glimpse of her through the open bathroom door, sitting on the toilet.

She looked up startled. "Who are you?"

I was taken aback. "I'm your daughter, Gail."

"Oh," she said, clearly confused. Though she'd been told I was coming that day, her mind had forgotten, and even worse, she had forgotten that she had a daughter and that I was that daughter.

It was a humiliating and disturbing moment for both of us.

By lunchtime, she'd remembered her granddaughter, Lauren and me. But still her mind remained a maze of confusion. When we reached the elevator to the dining room, she couldn't remember which floor it was on though she'd taken that elevator every day for over a year.

At lunch she was chatty and confided in us. "You see that woman sitting at the table behind us. Every time I say something she repeats it. Do you hear her? She's doing it now."

My daughter and I nodded our heads then exchanged looks of bewilderment and helplessness.

It was crushing to witness her mind's deterioration. She'd been a fiercely independent woman who liked to discuss politics with anyone who would listen. At any given time she'd have CNN blaring in her kitchen or living room. She read two newspapers a day. When my husband and I would visit her, she loved to engage my husband in political discussions.

"I love politics. Even as a girl, I loved politics." She prided herself on keeping up with the world around her, politically, culturally, and socially. She prized books and street smarts—her survival skills. When she moved from her home to my brother's house, I cleared out over two hundred self-help books. She was in a constant state of self-improvement.

After that summer visit, our phone conversations became like a Samuel Beckett play, but instead of *Waiting for Godot*, we were waiting for death, parsing it out, as it circled and circled like an eddy around her.

"How are you feeling?" I asked.

"My head feels weird."

"Does it hurt?"

"No, strange. Weird."

"Are you afraid?"

"No, not afraid."

"Do you feel confused?"

"They tell me I was seeing things."

"What things?"

"I don't remember."

"Do you remember falling?"

"No, not falling. My head feels weird."

I mourned the lucidity of our weekly phone calls so reminiscent of those times we sat together in her bedroom, in our cove of confidences. Separated by distance all our lives, those phones calls kept us close, breached that distance. Now in her dementia the distance lengthened. I couldn't reach her.

In those last waning months of her life she had little to say, the conversation one-sided. It didn't matter to me. I just wanted to hear her voice, know that she was still there, the physicality of love. Our conversations dwindled down to the mundane—the weather, what she had for lunch, and the past.

Often she asked the same question I'd answered two minutes prior. Sometimes she drifted off, but she never hung up. I'd have to say, "You sound tired, mom. Get some rest."

I was losing my mother in increments, slowly but surely.

But her dementia had an unexpected upside. She suddenly saw the humor in life. I sometimes thought she used it to cover her failing memory. And whatever made her find fault in me fell away. In her demented state, finally I could do no wrong. It was a stunning realization that this was the mother I'd been longing for all my life. And it took her eroding mind to let her emerge.

About a year and a half before her death, when she was convalescing in a rehab facility after yet another fall, possibly another mini-stroke, I spent an afternoon with her, knitting a scarf and talking. The room was preternaturally dark because she wouldn't allow me to open the window shade, claiming the gardeners were looking at her through the window and watching her. Paranoia was part of her dementia. After some explaining that I couldn't see to knit in the dim light over her hospital bed, she allowed me to switch on the overhead light.

Under the flickering fluorescent light with the faint odor of the bathroom tainting the air, I finally asked a question that I'd wanted to ask for a long time, thinking it might spur her to open up about her family's racial secret.

"Do you have any regrets, mom?"

She paused and considered. "There are some things I'd wished I'd done differently."

When I questioned what those things were. She became evasive. "Oh, just things." She was perched on the side of the bed, eating the institutional food, her frail ankles dangling over the side of her bed. It was the sight of her ankles clad in those pristine white socks that silenced me. And the realization that given her health this might be the last time I saw her. I didn't want to sully my last memory of her with another confrontation, causing her to shrink in fear and shame.

How could I hammer at the wall my mother had so artfully constructed around herself to satisfy my need to know who she really was and by default who I was? She'd created a self that hid the deepest part of her.

In the dim room, with the unpleasant air, I knew at that moment that any chance we had for true intimacy was gone. The nurse had confirmed what I already knew that my mother had mid-stage dementia. As her lucidity continued to fade, there'd be no more chances for revelations. My mother was an ancient woman. I couldn't breach her wall of silence. My mother would take her secret to her grave. Whether out of concern or cowardice, I let the moment go.

Before I left, I said, "I'll miss you, mom."

She looked up at me and said, "I know you will."

Had I really expected her to say, "I'll miss you too"? Probably not.

I gathered the half-finished scarf and knitting needles, stuffed them in my knitting bag, and rose from the hospital chair. This late in life I had no illusions about who my mother was and what she'd done to survive a childhood that I had no doubt contributed to her sister Shirley's early death in 1980 at the age of fifty-seven. To give way to sentimentality was to risk falling apart. She'd never been an affectionate, nurturing mother. To her, mothering was about keeping a clean house, cooking, and honing your children through criticism. Her criticisms had always held me at a wounded distance I was never able to breach. Today was no different. But still I longed for that motherly response. "I'll miss you too, Gail."

I leaned over her, kissed her papery cheek and embraced her. She let me.

As I walked toward the door, she called after me, "Gail, please turn off that light."

I left her in the dimness of a hospital bed light, the window shade drawn against whatever imagined danger waited for her outside.

Though I had other opportunities before her death to ask her about her secret, I never had the heart. The memory of that first and only time I did—the look of fear, panic, and shame on her face, the way she'd shrunk into herself—was so wounding I couldn't do it again. Maybe some secrets should be taken to the grave, I reasoned, knowing the falseness of my logic. Maybe I'm more like my mother than I'm willing to admit, content to live in the convenience and ease of half-truths.

The last time I saw my mother alive was a cold, snowy March day, robbed of all color as if the world could only be white and stark and frightening, full of ice and foreboding. We timed our visit between ice and snowstorms. Finally getting a window of good weather to drive the 360 miles east to Ohio.

Though it was late in the day when we arrived, after quickly checking in at the hotel, we went straight to the assisted-living center. On the way there, I studied the hospice brochure that listed the signs of "active" dying as if the signs were a test I must pass. This was the curse of the child living at a distance. Always at the back of my mind was the thought that this could be the last time I saw her.

When we entered her room, she was sitting in her blue recliner, the television blaring, though she didn't seem to be watching it. Her voice was strangely altered, her head permanently hung to the right, drool in the corner of her mouth, her face and torso bloated, her dark eyes ringed in red, the eyes of a caged animal. There were no traces left of the beautiful, stunning woman she once was. Even her deep dimples had been swallowed by age and disease.

In this otherworldly voice, she told me she didn't like to sleep anymore because she had weird dreams; then she related one that seemed symbolic of a dying wish.

"I was at work and there was a cup with a straw in it that I wanted pushed away. But I couldn't do it myself. When I asked the other workers to push it, they said they couldn't because they'd be fired. Finally one person pushed it away. And he was fired."

On a side table beside her rested a cup with a straw in it. Should I be alarmed? Are aides forcing her to drink, when all she wanted was for God to take her?

The next day she could no longer talk. I sat by her side touching her arm, caressing her shoulder, not wanting to lose her warmth. How trapped and tired and sad she looked with her head listing to the right, all speech gone, the snow filling her window, her shiny black shoes poking out from under the crocheted, multicolored throw, her hands idle, each holding a tissue as if she could raise them and wipe the drool away. I tried to get her to talk but she kept falling back into a labored sleep, her breath raspy and troubled. Was she dreaming me there as she'd done in the past?

I told her she'd led a good life and it was time for her to rest. I told her I'd miss her and that I loved her. I thought, but couldn't be sure there were tears in her eyes. I searched for some sign from her, some word, something. It was too late for that.

Then I reminisced about the time she thought she was 6'5" not 5'6" and jumped into the deep end of a swimming pool on one of our family vacations—one of her favorite stories. I reminded her of the time we saw *Swan Lake* together, one of my fondest memories. I was thirteen and when the curtains parted on the beautiful wintry, glistening scene, I glanced over at her and she was crying. That day I understood something I didn't know about my mother—the depth of her feelings about beauty and how well she hid those feelings.

When I left her I knew that it was the last time I'd see my mother in this life. My sadness was crushing. This woman who had been such a force in my life, I would never fully know her as a person. I would never know why and how she made a life-altering decision that changed the course of her life and my life as well.

That night in the motel, I wrote in my journal: "What will I do without my mom?"

After that visit, she lived another twenty-five days. Agonizing days for all of us. When death is imminent you walk a razor's edge, both wishing for death and wishing it will never come. Nothing can be that final. And yet it is.

In one of my last conversations with my mother, the nurse had to hold the phone to her ear. My mother sounded frail, incoherent, struggling to talk. When the nurse took the phone back she advised me. "She's going down fast. She won't feed herself. We have to feed her. She's going down."

After I hung up, I went over the last phase of "active" dying: deep sleep or sleeping most of the time, hallucinations, talking to dead people, stops eating and drinking, changes in blood pressure, pulse, coloration.

In my journal I tried to understand what was happening to my mother as she actively died.

You prepare to die—
the words go first,
the body follows,

there are signs
and none reliable—
an ebbing reminiscent of a harvest moon,
slung low and orange
over spent fields—
just out of reach
food loses purpose,
sleep sustains,
people visit
none of them alive.

On April 5, ten days after I wrote that poem, my mother died and took her secret with her. I'd kept my vow to her, and now I was free.

8

Serendipity
Summer 2014

THE THREE-MONTH ANNIVERSARY of my mom's death fell on a long Fourth of July weekend and grief had taken a hold of me. The numbing period that gave some measure of protection was gone, the loss now too real.

To console myself, I read *The Art of Losing*, a collection of poems about grief, poets expressing emotions I could find no adequate words for.

W. S. Merwin's poem "Rain Light" sounded like my mother speaking to me: "My mother said I am going now / when you are alone you will be alright / whether or not you know you will know."

Will I be all right? I wondered. *And what kind of all right will I be?* The space grief occupied in me seemed immense with room for nothing else.

One line from a poem by Hal Sirowitz rang too true, again another message from my mother. This time about the secret she took to her grave: "Remember me by the tricks I have taught you."

Wasn't that what I'd been doing? Remembering her by deciphering the tricks she taught me.

On Saturday July 5, in what could only be described as serendipity, my husband spotted an announcement in the genealogical section of our library's newsletter. "*Genealogy Roadshow* is looking for family stories. Do you live in St. Louis, New Orleans, or Philadelphia? Do you have a family mystery?"

"You might want to tell them about your grandfather, Azemar Frederic," he said, testing my interest. He seemed to clock my grief as if it had a time limit. He was all about diversion. I tried to hide my grief from him because he felt helpless against it. One sad person in a household was enough; two would be unbearable.

"Why would they be interested in him?" I was playing devil's advocate because I'd already decided to check out the PBS *Genealogy Roadshow* site as soon as he mentioned New Orleans.

"You can find out once and for all about your mother's race. And wasn't there some Civil War guy who was part of that black unit?"

My mother's race and racial heritage had remained a mystery. Had she been a victim of the one-drop rule? She hadn't look African American so why did her birth certificate designate her as "colored"? Azemar Frederic's race changed from black to mulatto and then in the 1930 census he was listed as white. So what were the Frederics—black, mulatto, or white?

Recently I discovered on Ancestry.com a Leon Frederic, Sr. who may or may not be my great-great-grandfather. He was a private in the Louisiana Native Guards, a black troop who served during the Civil War on the Union side.

"There is that," I said, enjoying the fantasy of an online application to a national TV show, telling myself it would be fun just to apply and there was little chance that they'd choose my story. It's always been my strategy when doing something that frightens me to convince myself it'll never happen. Once it happens then I have to face my fear.

I'd watched the first season of the show and found it entertaining and interesting. My favorite stories weren't the ones where someone discovered they're related to someone famous, but the ones where a personal family mystery was solved. The moment when the show's genealogist revealed the truth was potent with emotion.

For the next hour, I filled out the online form. Most of the questions were fairly easy to answer, except for one. "What is your story and why is it important to you to find out now?" Then the irony struck me. I'm a mystery author who has never been able to solve a mystery in my own family. I'd had four mystery novels published—spent a chunk of my days plotting murder, seeding clues, and red herrings—yet I couldn't solve my own family mystery story.

I wrote: "I'm a mystery author who's never been able to solve a family mystery about my maternal grandfather, Azemar Frederic from New Orleans." I related what I knew about his race, expanding on my story to include Leon Frederic who may or may not be my great-great-grandfather. Then I told the story of how my mother swore me to secrecy.

"I've kept that secret for seventeen years." I finished the application and then pushed it from my mind. The application was a lark, something to do on a Saturday afternoon, something to distract myself from my grief.

Two days later on July 7, while I was out walking at my local forest preserve, a message was left on my answering machine. A person from *Genealogy Roadshow* wanted me to call her back to set up a Skype interview. I played the message twice writing down the details, my hand shaking as I wrote.

Before I called back I told my husband about the message. He looked as stunned as I felt.

When I called, I reached Rachel who worked for a production company in California. We arranged for a Skype interview two days later. Things were moving fast.

"What should I wear?" I asked before hanging up. What I was really asking was what are you looking for, what do you need me to be?

Rachel said, "Don't wear black, white, or crazy patterns, ask lots of questions, and be enthusiastic."

The day before the Skype interview, after several nail-biting days of not being able to get my Skype to work, the show's East Coast researcher Rich Venezia contacted me.

"The show wants me to do more research on your story," he explained. He had a warm, open quality that instantly put me at ease. "Can you send me your mother's birth certificate and the birth certificates of her two siblings?"

Before we ended the call, he said, "If it were up to me, I'd chose your story. But it's not up to me."

"Why do they want a Skype interview?" I was anxious to wheedle any info I could from him about how the show decided who was chosen.

"They want to see how you'll do on television."

"Any advice?"

"Ask lots of questions. They like that."

After I hung up I shared with my husband what Rich said about his enthusiasm about my story. "It's not a done deal but the show must be serious if they have this researcher working on the story."

He smiled a cautionary smile. "Don't get ahead of yourself."

That evening, in what can only be described as another case of serendipity, Isiah Edwards, an amateur military expert from Mississippi, called. A few days earlier I'd sent an online request via a website devoted to the Louisiana Native Guards for information about Leon Frederic.

As I listened to Isiah's New Orleans accent I was reminded of my Grandmother Camille's accent, and for a moment the past rushed around me as if Grandmother Camille and my mom were here in the room with me.

Isiah confirmed that Leon Frederic did serve with the Louisiana Native Guards. He was stationed at Ship Island and Fort Pike. Isiah didn't know if he'd fought in any battles or where he was from. But he was a free man of color. I wasn't familiar with the term free man of color. But I was curious how someone living in a Southern state before emancipation could be free.

It was difficult not to be self-conscious. When Rachel's face disappeared and only my face remained, the interview took on a weird quality because I couldn't get a read on her reactions to my answers and I was too aware of my own reactions. It was like talking on the phone while staring at yourself in a mirror, very disconcerting.

My twenty questions rested on my computer's keyboard. Though I'd gone over them many times, they were there like a prop in case my mind blanked. But mercifully my mind didn't blank. All those years of teaching at the university came to my rescue as I spooled out my questions with as much enthusiasm as I could manage without sounding like a game show contestant.

Near the end of the interview Rachel asked an unexpected question that threw me. "What do you think your mother would feel about you revealing her secret now?"

It flashed through my mind that my mother was beyond feeling. I struggled to answer, saying that she was in a more enlightened place now. And adding quickly that she was never a bigot and was a product of her time.

When it was over, Rachel said they'd let me know in about a week if I made the show. I had no inkling if they'd take my story. Part of me wanted to be on the show and part of me didn't. This lark I embarked on over a Fourth of July weekend suddenly seemed too real.

For a long moment after Rachel logged off, I sat before the blank computer screen flooded with misgivings. What did I just do?

"Are you sitting down?" It'd been almost two weeks since I did the Skype interview, and I'd resigned myself to not being on the show.

I walked the phone into the family room and sat on the sectional already knowing what Rachel was about to say, my heart doing a happy dance.

"I am now," I answered.

"Your story has been selected for the show." There was laughter in her voice. "The taping is in St. Louis. The weekend of August 23. Our production people will contact you with more details."

"So you found something out about my mom's family?"

She laughed. "Much will be revealed."

The next day, Sarah Hochhauser, one of the producers, phoned to explain how this season's show would be different from last season's show.

"This year we want to do backstories on certain stories. So we'll be coming to your hometown to film you for a day." Her Welsh accent made everything she said sound important, crisp, and certain.

My stomach went tight. A day of filming me here where I live? That was not what I expected or wanted.

"We need a shooting venue. Can you suggest some place associated with your books, a beautiful place, a quaint place?"

My head was clogged with a summer cold and things seemed to be moving as if in slow motion. I told her about a local library, the Lake Forest bookstore, and the forest preserve where I walk. She'd check them out and get back to me.

Five days later La Monte Westmoreland, a senior producer, called. He questioned me at length about my story. I could sense he was also gauging my responses, how I'd be on camera.

"The show wants to do a DNA test. Is that okay?" he asked.

"Sure." In for a penny, in for a pound, I thought.

He confirmed that Sarah and the film crew would be here August 7 and would film at my house and at the Lake Forest Bookstore. He gave me the same advice about my clothes.

After he hung up, I said, "Mom, are you working you magic? Is this the ship you always talked about finally coming in?" She'd often say, "One day, our ship will come in." But it never seemed to arrive.

When the DNA kit and the contract came a few days later, everything seemed unreal and too serious as if I was living someone else's life.

Two days before the filming, I located a lawyer who took a look at the contract and advised me not to sign it. "You realize you're giving away all rights to your story? Just keep telling them you're not going to sign the contract."

Suddenly I realized it may have been all for nothing, the application, the Skype interview. I couldn't give PBS my story because I planned to write a book about my mother's family.

I called my son Chris and asked his advice. He suggested I negotiate with them. See if I could convince them to rewrite the contract. "They're not used to dealing with writers," he said. "Explain that this is how you make a living."

We both laughed at that because I'd yet to make a living with my writing. I barely break even. But his strategy was a good one. Much more amenable than saying I'm not going to sign the contract.

After an afternoon of emails between the production company and me, by 6 p.m., I had an amended contract that allowed me to retain my rights to my story. The taping would take place August 7 as planned.

My back ached with tension as I read the taping schedule: 9 a.m.–11 a.m. at the Lake Forest Bookstore, 11 a.m.–4 p.m. my house. Quirky requests were made. "Do I have a typewriter and a spyglass?" Yes, on the spyglass, no on the typewriter.

I told Sarah tomorrow promised to be a lovely day. She said, "That's disappointing." I thought she was joking. But she explained that a rainy, foggy day would add atmosphere to the story. Family photographs and heirlooms were requested as well.

As I gathered the scant photographs and heirlooms, it struck me how these absences in my family's story were what sent me searching nineteen years ago. I managed a handful of photographs mainly of my mother, my grandmother, and one of my Aunt Shirley when she visited us in Ohio. The only heirlooms I possessed were Aunt Laura's engagement ring and the cut-glass rosary I received for my First Communion. I wasn't sure who sent the rosary—my great-grandmother Ada or my great-great-grandmother. Such was the poverty of my mother's family background.

Late in the day La Monte phoned and reassured me that I wasn't the first person to ask for a contract revision and wouldn't be the last. Then he told me with glee that the researchers were even now discovering more things about my family and would continue until the St. Louis taping in three weeks.

"Remember," he said, "You have an A story."

I took a perverse joy in having an A story, as if the A were a grade on an exam I aced.

Adrenaline gushed through me tempered by this feeling of rightness, as if parts of my life had led to this television appearance and behind it all was my mother, that quirky and difficult woman who would not talk about her racial secret, who hid her own shyness in cultivated extroversion, gleaned from books like Dale Carnegie's *How to Win Friends and Influence People.*

A sharp memory from my childhood erupted full of meaning. My mother's scolding me for my awkward shyness: "Speak up, Gail. Speak up." Which meant speak for me. Say what I dare not say.

And wasn't that what I was about to do?

9

Taping Day, Libertyville, Illinois
August 7, 2014

MY LIVING ROOM resembled the backdrop from a *60 Minutes* interview. Window blinds drawn, furniture rearranged, huge photographic light screens strategically placed. A large boom mike dangled overhead, held by Dave, the sound guy from Woodstock, Illinois.

Sarah sat across from me well out of camera range, giving me instructions on how to respond to her questions. In her lap were her interview questions, the sight of them made me jumpy with anxiety.

"Answer my questions fully. Don't use pronouns. Use names. For example don't say 'she' if I ask you a question about your mother. Say 'my mother.' And make sure you repeat my question because my voice will be edited out of the tape."

"I think I can do that." Who was I trying to convince Sarah or me? My only saving grace was that the interview would be edited and any mistakes I made would be fixed. I didn't have to be perfect. But I couldn't quell the roiling in my gut.

I realized that the morning's shoot at the Lake Forest Bookstore—posing before the large water fountain in the town's square, walking the cobblestone pathways between the quaint buildings, pointing to my book inside the bookstore—was the easy part of the taping day. Now it was serious. Now I had to talk. I had to reveal my mother's secret while the camera rolled. I had to be myself on camera—a herculean task for an introverted writer.

And then there were the shards of doubt that kept jabbing at me. Even now I couldn't rid myself of them as ridiculous as that seemed with a camera crew in my living room and a binding contract. My mother was dead. I was free of my vow. But her shame and fear still lingered.

Earlier in the down time between takes, I learned that over a thousand people applied for *Genealogy Roadshow*'s second season. Of the people accepted for the show, about one-quarter were having their backstories told. Seven people were chosen for the St. Louis segment. Sarah bragged that *Genealogy Roadshow* was the most popular show in its category. None of this was helping my nervousness.

Raoul, the cameraman, said, "I'm ready."

Sarah nodded. "Make sure you look at me when you answer my questions. Okay?"

"Okay."

"Why did you apply to the *Roadshow*?"

When the show airs in January, I'm surprised by how little of that interview is used, how our family story is edited and fashioned into a narrative that I'd not necessarily intended but one that leads to unexpected results that change my life.

10

Difficult Beginnings
Genealogy Roadshow, 2014

"For all persons of any known black lineage, however, assimilation is blocked and is not promoted by miscegenation. Barriers to full opportunity and participation for blacks are still formidable, and a fractionally black person cannot escape these obstacles without passing as white and cutting off all ties to the black family and community. The pain of this separation, and condemnation by the black family and community, are major reasons why many or most of those who could pass as white choose not to. Loss of security within the minority community, and fear and distrust of the white world are also factors."

—F. James Davis, *Who Is Black?: One Nation's Definition*

Kenyatta opens the first document. The 1940 Louisiana census appears on the large screen to my right. It takes me a moment to focus as I'm wondering why she begins our family story in 1940.

"Your mother Elvira Frederic is living with a cousin. She works as a maid in a teashop. And her race is listed as 'Neg' for Negro."

I'm stunned. A bevy of contradictions and half-truths course through my mind—the first one about her racial designation in 1940. In the 1930 census she's listed as white. How can she be white in 1930 and Negro in 1940?

But I don't show my surprise, aware of the multiple cameras, how my reaction is being recorded and later will be broadcast on national television. Instead I say that her name is really Alvera not Elvira, not sharing how much she hated when people called her Elvira as if her identity was so fragile even mispronouncing her name could destroy it.

Kenyatta points out that census takers often misspelled names. As I look closer I see my mother's sister Shirley is listed as well. Theresa Spikes is the head of the household and Mary Williams is listed as an aunt. All the women are designated as Neg. They reside on Bienville Avenue, one block from Canal Street. I don't know whom these other women are that my mother and my Aunt Shirley are living with. The chaotic shuffle of my mother's upbringing still playing out in 1940.

Kenyatta opens another document. It's the 1910 census. "In the 1910 census Camille Frederic Romero is designated 'MU' for Mulatto."

I hadn't expected this revelation. My research and questions had been so focused on my mystery man Azemar Frederic, I never questioned my grandmother's race, believing not only what my mother said about her mother's heritage, Scottish and English, but I'd seen photographs of my grandmother and met her several times when I was a child. She was fair-skinned with narrow features and straight fine hair, much like my own hair. How can she be mulatto?

What else don't I know? I wonder as Kenyatta closes the document and opens another document.

My mother, Alvera Rita Frederic, was born at home on October 21, 1921, at 2921 St. Ann Street in New Orleans in an area known as Bayou St. John. The area predates the founding of New Orleans by ten years, making it the city's oldest site. Originally it was a distributary channel of the Mississippi River. In the nineteenth century, St. Ann Street was the residence of the Voodoo Queen Marie Laveau, and it was reputed that she performed many rituals in the area.[1] Census records indicate that in 1921 Bayou St. John was a mixed neighborhood—"colored" and white. And until the 1930s, residents were building houseboats along the bayou.

As picturesque as that sounds, there was nothing charming about my grandmother Camille Kilbourne's impetuous decision to marry Azemar Frederic on January 3, 1921, two days shy of her sixteenth birthday. They were married by a justice of the peace in St. Bernard Parish. Witnesses were Azemar's brother Paul, the justice of the peace's wife Mrs. Gowland, and Frank Nobles. Why did they marry in St. Bernard Parish instead of New Orleans where they both resided? Was Camille avoiding parental interference and censure? Though her mother Ada could hardly object to her daughter marrying at sixteen when she had married Edward Kilbourne at age sixteen in 1900. Perhaps it was a spontaneous decision, borne out by the fact that Camille had no family members as witnesses. Regardless, Camille's flair for reckless, impulsive behavior would haunt her the rest of her life.

At the time of Camille's marriage, her father Edward Kilbourne was already dead. Seven years prior, in 1914, he died from "severe paralysis" caused by an accident that occurred on the dock where he worked as a freight handler. Not long after Edward's death, Camille's mother, Ada McNicholls Kilbourne, married Homer Daste, a carpenter. On the 1920 census, Homer, Ada, and her two daughters Camille and Mildred are living in the St. Ann house where my mother will be born one year later. All the family members are listed as white. Besides the 1930 census, that is the only census where they are designated white. On all the other census records, they are listed as either Negro or mulatto.

Camille gave birth to my mother nine months after her marriage, almost to the day. How eager my grandmother must have been to start her own life and how ill prepared.

Her husband Azemar at twenty-two years of age was more mature and experienced, ready to settle down to a domestic life, working as a shipping clerk in a furniture store. My grandmother was still a child, now saddled with a child of her own. From the onset, theirs was a troubled match.

The vital records clerk who filled out my mother's birth certificate marked her race as colored. Why was she given that designation? Did the midwife have a hand in that determination? If so, in a mixed-race neighborhood what about my mother's physical appearance made the midwife believe that she was "colored"—the olive complexion, her curly hair? Was it only her physical appearance? Whatever the reason for my mother being designated colored, her destiny was legalized and hemmed in by the three letters in parenthesis: (col).

By the time of my mother's birth in 1921, legalized segregation was entrenched in the Southern states. After all the high hopes and optimism of Reconstruction, the South had succumbed to the Jim Crow era cemented by the *Plessy v. Ferguson* decision of 1896, which upheld the Louisiana law requiring railroad companies to provide racially segregated accommodations, thus enshrining the doctrine of "separate but equal."[2]

The name Jim Crow was derived from a minstrel routine performed beginning in 1828 by Thomas Dartmouth "Daddy" Rice and other imitators. Rice was a white man who performed in blackface. As the *Encyclopaedia Britannica* explains: "The term came to be a derogatory epithet for African Americans and a designation for their segregated life." Many of these laws of segregation and racial designation would not be overturned until the civil rights movement of the 1960s.

In *Plessy v. Ferguson*, Homer Plessy, a Creole of color who could pass for white, challenged Louisiana's first segregation law requiring separate railway cars for whites and blacks by boarding a white car and refusing to move. If the stories are to be believed, this was different than Rosa Parks's decision to sit in the white section of the bus because she was tired. Plessy set out to test the separate but equal law and lost his legal case.

These laws of separation were anything but equal. Relegated to the back of the bus, to separate railway cars and separate seating areas in restaurants, and to "Colored" washrooms and drinking fountains that were poorly maintained must have put immense pressure on those people of color in the South who could pass for white. The simplest decisions such as which bathroom or water fountain to use were fraught with psychological identity issues, as well as the fear of being caught passing for white.

The 1920s saw the flourishing of the eugenics movement. Eugenics is the science that seeks to improve hereditary qualities of a race or breed by the control of human mating.[3] Aimed at maintaining white superiority in the United States, the eugenics movement touted the biological and physiological inferiority of African Americans. The fanatical desire to preserve and improve the dominant white race led to laws banning interracial marriage between whites and anyone with even a trace of black blood, leading to the legalization of the one-drop rule.

As Allyson Hobbs points out in her book, *A Chosen Exile: A History of Racial Passing in American Life*, the 1924 passage in the Virginia state legislature of the Act to Preserve Racial Integrity, enshrined the "'one-drop rule' into law by defining a white person as one with 'no trace of other blood.'"[4] Hobbs quotes one eugenicist fear as evidenced in the law, "Many thousands of white Negroes . . . were quietly and persistently passing over the line."[5] Visible whiteness was not to be trusted. And to sully one's pure white ancestry with even a tinge of black blood must not be allowed. How else could the white race retain its superiority?

As outlined in the act: "If there is reasonable cause to disbelieve that applicants are of pure white race, when that fact is stated, the clerk or deputy clerk shall withhold the granting of the license until satisfactory proof is produced that both applicants are 'white persons' as provided for in this act."[6]

The law "required that the racial makeup of persons to be recorded at birth, and prevented marriage between 'white persons' and non-white persons. The law was the most famous ban on miscegenation in the Unites States."[7]

Labeled colored on her birth certificate, my mother's future was defined not by its expansiveness but by its legal and civil restrictions, as well as the economic restrictions of her designated race and gender.

In what can only be described as a defining moment for people of mixed race, the 1930 census removed the category Mulatto that my grandmother Camille, along with her mother Ada Kilbourne, her father Edward Kilbourne, and her sister Mildred Kilbourne, had been designated as in 1910. With the elimination of Mulatto as a racial category, the racial line was now cleanly divided between white and black with no place for people of mixed race like my mother's family. Also, with the category Mulatto removed from the census, there was no legal language to define a mixed-race person, essentially erasing mixed-race peoples' racial identities. In keeping with the one-drop rule of white superiority, people of mixed race were defined racially as black. If there were any doubts about a persons' race, even if they looked white, they would be designated black.

Though the one-drop rule is no longer law, even today mixed race is defined by the minority race. An example is former president Barack Obama. Though his father was black and his mother was white, he is referred to as the first black president, as if his father's blackness erased his mother's whiteness.

Is it any wonder my grandfather Azemar Frederic on the 1930 census declared his race as white? And as Kenyatta explained during the show's taping, census takers were often unreliable sources, if Azemar couldn't visibly pass for white, then he would have been marked as Negro.

Then why had my mother been designated "colored" at her birth? Had the midwife and/or clerk been following the "one-drop" rule when he or she penned "col" on my mother's birth certificate, as well as my Aunt Shirley's birth certificate over a year later, erring on the side of caution? Then how do I understand my Uncle Homer's racial designation at birth? Born in 1924, having the same parents as his sisters, his race was marked as white. Had the midwife been convinced of his race by his blond hair? Even more perplexing is his 1990 death certificate, which stipulates his race as black. How can a person be born white and die black?

This strange fluidity of racial designation for individuals who could pass for white was evidenced in Azemar's subversive act in 1918 during World War I. When he filled out his draft registration card to work at Inland Steel in East Chicago, Indiana, as a pipe fitter, under race he checked white. The handwriting on the card matches his signature. There's no question he was the one who checked the white box. The card bears the stamp of the Local Board of the City of East Chicago.

Was he laughing up his sleeve as he passed for white in a Northern city far beyond the reach of his New Orleans roots and Jim Crow laws? Or was his hand trembling with anxiety as he boldly checked the white box? Regardless, he passed. And on his return to New Orleans, on the 1930 census his race was designated as white. But by the 1940 census, he was once again black.

Without a photograph of my grandfather, it's impossible for me to judge how white he looked. Like my mother, he'd been able to pass as white. But unlike my mother, who died as a white woman in Mercy Hospital in Ohio, he died a black man in Charity Hospital in New Orleans. She had permanently crossed over the color line. He hadn't.

How had she accomplished this audacious transformation undetected? And why had she risked such a high stakes gamble built on secrecy? What sacrifices had she and the people she left behind made so she could live as white? The image of my mother shrinking into herself with fear and shame spoke volumes about the toll she'd paid to pass and had continued to pay.

There were so many unknowns that couldn't be explained or eluci-
dated by a racial designation on a census record or a birth certificate.

As her daughter I had no frame of reference for understanding her
choices. I'd never suffered from racial discrimination except for those
uncomfortable moments in the family history center when the old bigoted woman used the word "nigger" repeatedly. I'd never claimed to be
any other race but white. I'd enjoyed white privilege all my life.

I needed to know more. I wanted to understand why even after she
passed successfully into whiteness, she couldn't shake the shame or the
fear. I wanted to know how and why she decided to cross over the color
line. What about her life in New Orleans made her want to leave it?
And what had leaving her family and denying her true racial heritage
cost her?

Perhaps I also wanted redemption for my mother and all mixed-race
people in this country who, if they'd been white enough to pass, had
been forced to choose one race or another. Forced to decide where they
sat on the bus, whom they married, and whom they could trust with
their secret.

11

Nothing Left to Lose

THE ONLY PHOTOGRAPH that survived from my mother's childhood is cracked and fading to a greenish tint, the three children sitting together in the yard on St. Ann Street blurry with time. My mother, Shirley, and Homer huddle in a semi-circle, only my mother looks angry, impatient with the process of posing, her two siblings sit closer together apart from her. Had the later separation of the siblings already begun?

My mother is perhaps six years old. Her pose is defiant: crossed arms, a knowing expression, lack of a smile. Her dark hair is plastered to her head as if it needed washing or maybe it was my grandmother's attempt to tame her daughter's curly hair. None of the children look happy.

The neglected condition of the aged photograph seems to reflect what was about to happen to the three children on St. Ann Street. The photo would become a relic, one my mother cherished, filled with the longing for a time that would never return and that ended too quickly.

In 1934 after Camille and Azemar were separated for seven years, Azemar Frederic petitioned for a divorce. The petition states that he and his said wife became separated on April 3, 1927, and had never returned to live together. The children were living with the defendant's grandmother.

What strikes me most about the petition is the last paragraph. "Wherefore, petitioner prays that his said wife, Camille Kilbourn Frederic, be duly cited to appear and answer this petition." The word "prays," though commonly used in Louisiana documents, seems particularly apropos of my grandfather's level of desperation, to be divorced, to end the limbo of his marriage.

My grandmother never appeared to answer the petition. It's difficult to comprehend her decision not to appear when the custody of her three children was in jeopardy. On November 5, 1934, my grandfather was granted his divorce. In the divorce decree Azemar was also granted "permanent care, custody and control of the three minor children, Elvera Frederic, Shirley Frederic, and Homer Frederic; costs to be paid by the defendant."

Did my mother know that her father asked for and was granted custody of her and her siblings? If so, she never told me. In a time when custody almost always went to the mother, how had Azemar convinced the court to grant him custody? Was my grandmother an unfit mother? Is that why she didn't appear at the hearing? Was she afraid to answer questions about her competence to raise her children? Or as a poor woman with a seventh grade education was she intimidated by the legal system? An even bigger question, why didn't Azemar retain custody of his children? Why did my mother and her siblings go back to living with members of their maternal family: my mother and Shirley with their great-grandmother Mary Williams or Mama (accent on the second syllable)—who in 1934 was sixty years old—and Homer with his grandmother Ada Daste, his mother, and her second husband?

A story about a kidnapping trickles back to me as if it had been waiting for me to decipher its meaning like an unearthed artifact. When I imagine the children's kidnapping, it's a chilly December night. The day's storm leaves the taste of frisson in the air, everything unsettled. The streets guttered with oak leaves, scattered like so many promises.

"Are you sure about this?" Mickey asks Camille as she parks the pickup truck in front of the Iberville house.

"I can't let him keep my kids. They're mine. I don't want that woman raising them." Camille stares at the house. All the windows are dark. Everyone is asleep.

"You should have gone to the courthouse and fought for them," Mickey whispers. "Why didn't you go?"

"Would it have made a difference?" Camille looks at her sister.

"You'll never know will you?"

Camille can feel her courage wane. "Those are my children in there. It's not right what the court did."

"What if he wakes up?"

"Have you forgotten what a deep sleeper he is?"

"Let's hope she is too."

"You worry too much, sis." Camille pats her sister's hand. "I won't be long."

She opens the passenger door and steps out, feeling the chill night on her bare skin like a warning. I should have worn a sweater. I should have fought for my children.

She doesn't need to look back to know her sister's eyes are watching her as she moves toward the house. She feels the weight of their judgment. Somewhere nearby a dog starts barking and she quickens her pace moving into the shadow of the house and around the back where the children sleep.

Alvera told her she sleeps in a back bedroom with Shirley and Homer and that the room is yellow, her favorite color. She glared at her as if to say I don't need you. That dark glare was what convinced her to steal her children away from their father. Already he was giving them things beyond her. Soon they would forget her, as if they were motherless.

When she tries the back door, she finds it unlocked as she thought it would be. Azemar and his carelessness. Once inside she stands and listens. She hears the familiar snoring of her ex-husband coming from a front bedroom, pictures the woman sleeping beside him. Maybe she can tolerate his jealousy.

The children's room is small, the beds close together. In the soft glow of the bedside lamp, she sees the yellow walls and their sleeping bodies. Gently she wakes them, putting her finger to her lips, signaling that they should be quiet. There's no time for shoes or street clothes. She carries Homer in her arms and gestures to the girls that they should follow her.

As she leads them out of the house, down the back steps and around the side of the house, Alvera lags behind, her usual obstinate self. There's no time to cajole her. She sifts Homer to her other arm and grabs Alvera roughly by her shoulder, tugging her forward. Shirley has started to cry. The dog begins to howl.

When they reach the street, she sees a light go on in the house. She hustles the children into the cab of the truck then jumps into the passenger side.

"Go, go," she tells her sister.

As they pull away from the curb, Azemar is running after them shouting something she can't hear, something she doesn't want to hear.

"Now what?" Mickey asks.

Camille kneels on the seat to look back at her three children huddled together, shivering in their nightclothes.

"I don't know. I haven't thought that part out yet."

After that night my mother would never live with her father again.

What precipitated the kidnapping I can't be sure—desperation, anger, fear? Maybe my grandmother Camille knew about Azemar's marriage and didn't want her three children raised by another woman. Even more perplexing is why she kidnapped her three children and then relinquished two of them to another relative to raise. Was her action one of spite or misguided love?

My mother related the kidnapping story several times to me. And each time she told the story it was as if the kidnapping had happened to someone else. Her light tone and the mischievous expression on her face made her appear detached from what was obviously a story of loss and confusion. Her past seemed to belong to someone else.

"We were stolen from my father, in the middle of the night," she said.

"Weren't you upset and scared."

"No."

She never wavered in her belief that being stolen from her father by her mother was anything but an amusing anecdote.

In 1936 when her mother married her second husband Arthur Romero, the possibility of a stable home was once again dangled in front of my mother and her siblings. But my grandmother seemed to have no knack for picking husbands or keeping her family under one roof.

Four years after her marriage to Arthur, my grandmother was residing in the same house with Arthur, her mother Ada, stepfather Homer, her son Homer from her first marriage and her one-year-old son Warren Romero from her second marriage. My mother and her sister Shirley were living apart from their mother, grandmother, and brother, in a boarding house run by their great-grandmother Mary Williams.

"Wasn't it sad for you not living with your mother?" I once asked her.

She shook her head. "Not really. I could visit her whenever I wanted and if they started drinking I could leave and go home."

Again, I felt she wasn't being totally honest, denying the pain she must have felt as a child not living with either of her parents. But I wasn't able to question her any further because with alacrity she was on to a story about Mr. Arthur, whose name she could barely say without contempt.

"I called the police on him once. I was glad I did. I'm the only one who had the courage to do that." Her back bristled with angry self-righteousness.

"Why did you call the police? Was he beating on your mother?" I'd known for years about the physical abuse my grandmother endured from Mr. Arthur.

"He called me a bastard. I yelled at him, 'I'm no bastard. I have a father.' Then he tried to hit me. No man was going to hit me. There was this talcum can nearby. I picked it up and threw it at his head. That's when I called the police. The police came and took him away. Mother begged me to go down to the station and talk to the police so he could come home. I didn't want to do it. But she kept saying, 'He's my husband. He didn't mean it.' So I got him out of jail. He never messed with me again."

Then she added, almost wistfully, as if she couldn't let the story end here, with an abusive man who was arrested because he called her a bastard and tried to hit her.

"That man loved his job at the A&P. Never missed a day of work in his life. That's all he talked about was that job at the A&P." Her eyes had that far away look of memory. "When I was a child sometimes I visited them, my mother would give me a nickel for a bucket of beer and tell me to go get it. I didn't like that. Because I knew they'd be drinking and I knew where that would lead. I didn't like that at all."

"I asked my mother how she could stay with that man," my mother said.

"Because I love him," she said.

My mother took in a sharp breath as if smelling something foul. "I never understood how she could stay with him."

Though Camille and Arthur remained married until his death in 1973, their marriage continued to be fraught with physical abuse fueled by their bouts of drinking. To my mother's dismay, Mr. Arthur died peacefully in his sleep. My grandmother woke to find his cold body beside her in their marital bed.

I remember with clarity my mother receiving the phone call from my grandmother about Mr. Arthur's death. I listened to the clipped tone of her responses, the lack of sympathy for her mother.

After she hung up, she seemed burdened not by Mr. Arthur's death but what her mother said to her.

"You have to understand Alvera, he was my husband."

My grandmother remained an enigma to me as well. She was always kind and loving toward me, and for a short time when I was in grammar school, we exchanged letters. At the time, she was the only adult who thought a monkey would make a good pet. I loved that about her, her willingness to enter my world.

The few scant photos of her tell me little. In every photo, she struggles to smile, a look of bewilderment on her face as if life has left her stunned, unable to respond.

The photograph I gave the *Roadshow* is dated December 24, 1951, six days after my brother was born. My grandmother had come to Ohio to help care for me while my mother convalesced in the hospital after giving birth. The color photo was taken in the upstairs apartment of my father's cousin's house, where my parents lived before purchasing their first house.

Camille sits on a couch festooned with a flowery, splashy slipcover that she made during her two-week visit. At forty-six she's plump, waist-less with fine thin hair. She gazes down at my brother whom she holds with one hand as if uncertain what to do with him, her other hand grasps me close to her. She's as pale skinned as I am.

My father must have taken the photograph. As he steadied the camera and looked through the lens, he had no idea that his mother-in-law was mixed race. He was seeing a light-skinned woman with European features. As a passable mixed-race person she could visit her daughter who was living on the other side. She was complicit in my mother's deception.

What fascinated me about my grandmother and what I took pride in were her artistic skills. Like me she wrote poetry. No one else in the family on either side wrote poems. She was an extraordinary seamstress who worked for an awning company in New Orleans sewing. Her eye for spatial measurements was so acute she could sew anything without a pattern. She was credited with second sight, which meant she was born with the caul over her face, giving her powers of precognition. Her psychic insights would visit her in dreams.

But whatever gifts she possessed, as I grew older I realized she was her own worst enemy. She seemed the embodiment of the New Orleans motto of letting the good times roll. My mother called her a flapper, a good time girl. The closest she would come to criticizing her mother.

Years before my grandmother was diagnosed with breast cancer, she sold her body to a medical school for fifty dollars. According to my mother, she spent the fifty dollars at the racetrack that day. After her death, I could never locate a gravesite for her, giving credence to her donating her body to science.

Her carpe diem attitude toward life eventually was the death of her. When a doctor cautioned Camille to have a biopsy on a lump she'd found in her breast, she ignored his advice. By the time she returned to the doctor, he recommended a double mastectomy. But she'd waited too long. The double mastectomy only bought her a few years.

While she was dying, my mother resisted going home to see her. The thought of New Orleans, of home, filled her with dread and foreboding. It took my father to convince her to fly to New Orleans to see her mother one last time.

"You'll regret it if you don't," he said.

What emotional barrier stood in the way of my mother seeing her mother before she died? For all her protestations to the contrary, did she harbor resentment toward her? Was it too overwhelming to confront her jumbled feelings about her mother?

Reluctantly she went. It didn't go well. Her mother's cancer had metastasized throughout her body and into her bones. She was in great pain.

When my mother tried to sit on Camille's bed to give her a hug, Camille told her not to sit on her bed, not to hug her. My mother was wounded by what she viewed as rejection.

The sting of her childhood abandonment was evident in her inability to understand that her mother wasn't rejecting her. Sitting on her bed would have increased her mother's pain and hugging her would be torture. In death, mother and daughter were beyond those intimacies.

When my mother returned from New Orleans, she sank into a depression.

My grandmother died in 1982 at the age of seventy-seven. In the aftermath of her death and my mother's subsequent depression, I tried to make sense of my grandmother's life and her relationship with Mr. Arthur in a poem. The violence that underpinned their marriage, that caused my mother to lose respect for her mother, I saw as a violent duet, an apache dance that neither could escape.

Death of an Apache Dancer

In her long thirties when death was a coffin shut
with music, Grandmother sold her body
to the scientist for $50. A sure thing—
the medical school a block from the race track.
She doubled her money that Fat Tuesday,
strutted home down Fortin Street
balancing whiskey and milk, a party jazzing inside her,
to tango with her second husband, Mr. Arthur.

He died in his sleep—a breeze.
Strength gone into drumming a rhythm
on Grandmother's flesh, the metronome

of their cabaret life.
Cancer waltzes with her now
moving deeper inside her
than any man. Hungry
with a gnawing step
making her hips a sliver of space,
her spine a trickle of nerve.

She sways in her bed
weighing the strength to sustain
movement. Washes her hair
avoids the soft spots that thump
between her fingers,
her skull—a baby's head
stretching to release her.
Outside the scientists wait
With their two left feet.

A letter from my grandmother has been sequestered in the secret compartment of my girlhood jewelry box since 1977. I suspect I've kept it because it is her last letter to me. As early as 1977 I was searching for answers about my mother's family. My grandmother's response to my query about her family tree is a masterful blend of truth and evasion.

Dear Gail,

To tell the truth I wouldn't know where to start. My grandmother was born in some country place where they didn't even have a courthouse. They used to write their birth dates in the family bible. My grandfather was born somewhere in England. Now if my mother or grandmother were living I could find all that out from them."

Then she reminisced. "I often think of the fun we had when you were young dressing up in all those old clothes.

Did we do that? I don't remember.

She conveniently left out her father's birthplace, which was Mississippi, choosing instead to concentrate on her white British grandfather. And she had to know just by looking at her maternal grandmother Mary Brown Williams that she was a black woman. That fact is also missing from her sparse family details.

Though I'd never seen Mary Brown Williams, the woman who raised my mother and her sister, I later learned from my mother's first cousin Ula Moret that she was very dark. Adding that she wasn't black, she was Choctaw. Another half-truth passed down through the family.

Perhaps my grandmother's letter to me was her motherly gift to her daughter, atoning for her failures as a mother by keeping her daughter's secret of being mixed race from me and by extension from my father and his family. To the end, she remained complicit in my mother's deception. It was the least she could do for the daughter she abandoned.

What my grandmother's own experiences were as a mixed-race person in New Orleans who could pass as white, it's impossible to know. Her white appearance allowed her to pass out of the racial constraints and segregation of the Jim Crow South. And she was a passable relative who my mother could invite for visits. Even so, Camille chose to live within her own racially defined community and married mixed-race husbands.

The 1940 Louisiana census that *Genealogy Roadshow* used to confirm my mother's mixed-race heritage (Neg/Negro) was the last time my mother was designated as a person of color on a census record. It was also the last time she and her sister Shirley were listed as living in the same household. Working as maids in a teashop, a typical job for a woman of color, and taken in by yet another relative, their choices for a better life in 1940 were limited.

In two years when the United States entered World War II and the first recruits to be trained at Camp Shelby, Mississippi, arrived, the sisters, who both could pass for white, are presented with opportunities to reinvent themselves if they are audacious enough to cross over the color line.

Shirley chose to remain within her racial group. In 1944, she married Alfred Coignet, a mixed-race man from New Orleans. She seemed to have put her unstable childhood behind her, escaping New Orleans, and embarking on an adventurous life while staying true to her racial heritage. Designated as black on his enlistment record, Alfred Coignet rose to the rank of colonel in the Air Force, no small feat.

Perhaps it was the transient nature of her marriage to a career soldier or the pressure of having three children without any family support or the unresolved trauma of her childhood, but sometime during her marriage, according to my mother, Shirley became addicted to prescription drugs. After her divorce she returned to New Orleans by then heavily addicted to drugs. Eventually she was committed to a mental hospital where she died in 1980 at the age of fifty-seven. When my grandmother went to collect her body, she found her bruised and beaten. My grandmother wasn't able to get a satisfactory answer about the cause of her daughter's death or why she was beaten. It was as if Shirley had to fight her way out of life.

My mother made a different choice that I try to understand in all its nuances and consequences. Posed on the brink of womanhood, loosely rooted, barely defined by familial relationships, my mother must have reasoned she had little family to lose if she crossed over to the white side.

Allyson Hobbs posits that the loss of kinship from passing was just as acutely felt by dysfunctional families as it was stable ones. The core issue of passing is not becoming what you pass for, but losing what you pass away from. For Hobbs passing is about loss.[1]

For my mother whose childhood had been rife with familial loss, I suspect she took a different view of the loss passing entailed. Abandoned at an early age, unaware of her father's fight to gain custody of her and her siblings, finding no stable home with her mother and her second husband, eventually living with a cousin, my mother probably thought that losing family was a small price to pay in comparison to what she would gain.

If she decided to pass as white, she could be anyone she chose to be, and all the privileges that accompanied being white were hers for the taking. The influx of recruits from across the United States into the New Orleans area gave her racial anonymity, allowing her to date white men with impunity. The external markers of her skin and features defined her as white. Her only fear was if someone from her community outed her.

Still, knowing my mother as I did, she must have sensed, even if she couldn't or wouldn't admit it to herself, that turning away from her family would leave a psychic wound.

A generation earlier a member of her family had gone north to pass. She was well aware of the toll he and the family he left behind had paid. And yet she was willing to take that chance.

12

Random Acts of Passing
January 2015

> Although it is impossible to determine the frequency of pass-
> ing . . . the two most prevalent forms have been described as
> part-time or discontinuous passing, e.g., passing white at work,
> and continuous passing or "crossing over" the racial divide
> into a new life with a new racial identity.
>
> —Arthé A. Anthony, "Lost Boundaries"

THE USE OF the word *passing* to signify a mixed-race person being accepted as white first surfaced in the American lexicon around the nineteenth century. In Louisiana the French term *passé blanc* was used to describe a person of black heritage who passes for white, and literally means "passing white." The word *pass* comes from Middle English (1275–1325) and is derived from the Old French word *passer*, to cross over, and is derivative of the Latin word *passus* meaning "a step."

In studying the various meanings of the words *pass* and *passing*, I'm struck by how these definitions illuminate the emotional and psychological effects inherent in passing for white. Many of these definitions are associated with death and explain why the term *passing* was used to denote a mixed-race person being accepted as white.

To *pass on* or *pass away* is to die. *Passing out* is a kind of temporary death. There's an irony in my mother begging me not to reveal her racial secret until she passed away. She'd passed out of or passed away from her mixed-race identity. She'd experienced a kind of death.

Then there are the other definitions associated with the word *pass* that suggest reasons for passing. To *pass someone* is to go ahead of them. A *passing grade* means satisfying certain criteria, indicating an achievement. And the list of definitions and uses goes on and on.

The act of passing for white blossomed into other expressions that also connote death and impermanence. To cross over to the other side means to die. It also means to pass into whiteness. There is no stability in the word. Passing by its very definition is transitory.

And when one passes for white, aren't they in a state of instability, having to keep up the pace, to keep moving? Lest someone discovers they've passed over, by passing themselves off as something they're not—which is white.

And when a person passes, crosses over to the other side, when a part of them dies, who do they become?

Two weeks before our segment of the St. Louis *Genealogy Roadshow* airs, I write a letter to my mother's first cousin Ula Moret who lives in Walnut Creek, California. In her eighties she's the youngest of my mother's female first cousins on her maternal side and the only one still living. Her mother Mildred "Mickey" Kilbourne and my grandmother Camille were sisters. I've never met Ula nor have I ever talked to her. She's the last female link to my mother's family.

I'm not sure why I wrote the letter. Maybe to reach out to my mother's remaining family; maybe to get support for my decision to publically reveal my mother's racial secret. I'm still uncomfortable about what I've done, anxious about our segment being viewed by so many strangers. No matter how many times I tell myself my mother would have approved of my going public with her story, that my vow had been fulfilled, I still see her fear and shame when I confronted her with the truth. To me it was as if she felt somehow responsible, had colluded in her mixed race. I couldn't fathom her fear or her shame. It stunk of original sin.

And then there's my own trepidation about backlash. Though it's 2015, I question whether we are living in a post-racial world. News stories abound concerning racial strife. Only days before the *Roadshow* shot our segment in St. Louis, there were protests and civil unrest in Ferguson, Missouri, over the police shooting of Michael Brown.

As an author, I'm easily found through my website. Will I be accused of betraying my mother, of betraying the white race by "coming out" with the truth of my racial heritage? Will blacks see me as disingenuous? Was my mother right in keeping her secret? Am I a disloyal daughter, after all?

A few days before the show airs, Ula calls me. The candor of her conversation surprises and pleases me. As she shares her history as a mixed-race person, I keep thinking why couldn't my mother have been this honest and open with me. But Ula's mixed-race story is vastly different from my mother's.

"I never hid my mixed race," she tells me. "But when I married my husband Roy, who is darker than me, we decided to move to California. There were more opportunities for us in California. I didn't want to be judged by my race."

I recall a photograph of Ula my mother placed on my girlhood dresser after I left home. She looked as white as me. But I don't pursue my observation of skin color with Ula. I feel uneasy. I don't know her yet. The race issue makes me self-conscious and unsure of myself. What experience can I draw on having lived my life as a white woman?

I ask an innocuous question about the racial makeup of the neighborhood where my mother was born.

"I lived on the same street as your mother but in the next block. White people lived across from your mother's house. When those white people moved out, colored people moved in. I call them 'colored people.' I know some people say black. But I always said colored."

Ula's forthrightness seems so contrary to my mother's secretiveness.

"Well, I had a good friend named Leora who had red hair and freckles. You would have never guessed she was colored." She stops for a moment and reflects. "You know it's a mentality as much as a look. People who were brown didn't want to go as colored. And those who were white looking went as black. Some left New Orleans and went on the other side."

She doesn't add "like your mother." But I'm intrigued by why a person who has a choice identifies either as black or white.

"You know about the one-drop rule?" she asks.

"Yes," I answer, letting her elaborate on her own experience of that archaic rule.

"Well, that's how it was in the Southern culture. You only had to have one drop of colored blood. That's the word I use, colored."

Her firm tone reveals her strong character. Her insistence on using colored instead of black says, "This is who I am. Deal with it. This is what one-drop means to me: colored, not black." There's a rightness in her insistence. One drop of black blood doesn't make you black, she is saying. But even so, it still makes you colored.

She changes the subject as if there is nothing left to say about the word *colored*. "I worked for a group of lawyers in New Orleans." I can tell she's leading up to a story about race.

"They never knew I was mixed. I'd get on the streetcar and sit in the white section. There was this screen separating the white section from the colored section. But I had to be careful when I got off that streetcar. I had a friend who had to sit in the colored section. I made it a point to talk to him. 'How are you doing today,' I'd say. You see I was afraid if I wasn't nice, he'd out me."

I'm anxious to push her for more personal details of what it was like being a mixed-race person in New Orleans, but I hold back and we talk instead about our deceased relatives, about Mary Williams, my mother's great-grandmother who raised her and her daughter Ada Kilbourne Daste.

"She was very dark," Ula explains. "But her daughter Ada was very fair."

The way her tongue curls around the *r*'s, these traces of her New Orleans accent are like a balm to me as if it could conjure my mother back. And in some ways it does conjure her back.

"We called her Mama, and Ada was mama, and mother was mother." She pronounced Mama stressing the second syllable.

I edge forward carefully. "So was Mama black?"

"Oh, no, she was Choctaw Indian."

I want to question her more about Mama being a Choctaw Indian since I know that blacks often claimed Native American ancestry. But I don't.

Before we hang up she invites me to visit her and her family in Walnut Creek, California.

"Did your mother ever teach you how to cook red beans and rice?"

I tell her no.

Then she gives me her recipe, which I write down.

"Now I'm going to ask your husband if it was good."

"He knows what to say." I joke.

After our conversation I comb through the Dawes Rolls—the final lists of people accepted between 1898 and 1914 by the Dawes Commission as members of the Cherokee, Creek, Choctaw, and Seminole Indian Tribes—looking for Mary Williams, who I'll discover through her marriage license was Mary Brown. I find no Mary Williams or Mary Brown matching the birth date and birthplace of my great-great-grandmother Mary Brown Williams, of the dark complexion and high cheekbones.

Over the next few months Ula and I will talk more about race and passing and New Orleans. And with each conversation Ula will be more candid, more forthcoming. Or perhaps I'm more at ease asking her the hard questions. Each of her stories lifts the veil on my mother's decision to pass and is another piece of the puzzle.

With some pride, she relates to me how her father Ulysse Duffaut refused to send her and her siblings to a colored public school. And because they were white enough to pass, he was able to send them to the white public school.

Although she sat in the white section on the streetcar, she grew up socializing with the black community. It was a conscious choice on her part.

"My life would have been different if I hadn't done that," she explains ruefully. Then she launches into a bittersweet story of a hard choice she made as a young woman who looked white enough to pass. A story that goes to the heart of the dilemma mixed-race people who looked white faced in the Jim Crow South.

"When I was sixteen and in secretarial school a white lawyer came to my school and selected two girls for his firm of lawyers. Ethel was the other girl. She was seventeen and Jewish. Can you imagine us two girls running a law firm?"

I say, "I can't imagine that." And I can't. Though what I really can't imagine is her audacity in working for a white law firm as a white woman. In that era specific occupations and job sites were defined by race. It was not uncommon to see an employment ad in the newspaper that said, "Colored need not apply."

"While I was working for the lawyers, one of the wives who was a psychologist gave me and Ethel a test. The lawyer's name was George Dryfus. I did so well, George offered to send me to college and pay my tuition and all expenses. He thought I was white. I couldn't do it. I'd have to give up my colored life, my friends and family. I would have loved to go to college."

"Do you regret your decision?"

"I regret the circumstances, not my decision. I would have had to live totally as white."

For her, community was more important than advancement. To permanently pass as white, to leave her family and friends was unthinkable.

"I hated to be segregated. That's why I left New Orleans. I didn't like that I had to sit in a certain section of a restaurant."

"Did you always sit in the colored section?" I use her word.

She chuckles. "Depends on who I was with which side I sat on."

Her ability to sit in either the black or white sections of a restaurant points out the absurdity of segregation and racial categorizations.

"Ethel and I became very good friends. Even after I left New Orleans we stayed in contact. Years later I decided that I wanted her to know who I am. So I told her that I was mixed race. She said, "I've been knowing that.""

Her wanting to tell her friend who she was helps me understand the pressure my mother lived under, never being able to tell anyone who she really was.

She laughs. "But I fooled a lot of people."

Then she tells me the train story, which shows the dangers of racial ambiguity. She was taking a train to meet her husband Roy. Some black friends were going to meet her at the station. When she got on the train, the conductor wanted to put her in the white car.

"I decided it wouldn't be right my sitting in the white car because my friends were colored. So I told him that I was colored. Well, he didn't like that. He decided he was going to fix me. He put me in a colored car filled with burly colored railroad workers."

"Why do you think he did that?"

"He didn't like a colored person who looked white."

My mother's shame blazes up before my eyes. Would her friends and white family have reacted in the same way if after all these years she revealed her mixed race?

And would they, too, become angry and "fix" her?

What angered the railroad conductor? Was his anger related to the mixing of races or that once mixed, there was no way to know for sure what race that person was? In the failure of external markers to define Ula's race did she come too close to being like him? Who was he punishing?

I tiptoe into my mother's decision to pass for white and her ability to live her whole life with no one knowing who she was.

"Your mother totally crossed over when she married your dad. But she had been living as white already, working white as a waitress."

"Do you think he ever knew?"

"I would say he didn't know." Her confirmation supports my own belief that he never knew.

"How do you identify your race?"

"I think of myself as mixed. My oldest son during the period when black was beautiful kept saying, 'I'm black.' When he tried to say I was black, I said, 'Look at me. I'm not black.'"

What Ula is describing is the two-ness, the ambivalence that people of mixed European and African ancestry feel, which is intensified by the lack of racial classifications for people of mixed race in this country, as well as the human tendency to sort people out by external markers. Mixed-race people aren't one thing. They don't fit into one racial category.

Then Ula relates another family story of passing that helps solve a half-century mystery about the disappearance and demise of Aunt Laura.

13

The Case of the Disappearance of Aunt Laura

2015

I HAVE SCANT heirlooms from my mother, a parsimonious woman who'd sit at the kitchen table with the window shades drawn, her ledger book open, while she worked on the family budget. My father's allowance being one of the line items she checked off in her ledger book. Her childhood poverty clung to her like an errant gene.

When I graduated from St. Francis de Sales, a parochial elementary school, my mother gave me a ring and with it the story of Aunt Laura, the ring's original owner. The story was as mysterious as any mystery novel I've ever written. Though in this case it involved a real person, my great-aunt Laura who seemed to have disappeared into thin air sometime in the early 1950s.

The ring is over 110 years old—a delicate proposition of white gold with an intricate European setting surrounding a modest diamond. It was part of a set, passed down through two generations of women in my mother's family. It is one of the gifts I cherish most from my mother. The ring is a gift of family history—mostly unknown.

Aunt Laura lived in Toledo, Ohio, and was the only family my mother had in the North. When I was four years old, many weekends my parents made the two-hour drive from Cleveland to Toledo to visit her. I suspect it was my father's way of pleasing my mother. I distinctly remember the quiet of Aunt Laura's house, its dark and heavy furniture, lacy curtains, and the window seat where I sat looking at the large tree outside. And that's all I remember.

There must not have been anything else for me to do. But I was a child, as quiet and obedient as the house, who could sit contently for hours looking and watching and listening to the hushed voices of the adults.

As soon as we'd arrive Aunt Laura would say to my father, "Son, do your duty." Which meant *go to the store for beer*. If she had lived longer, if she hadn't disappeared, I think I would have liked Aunt Laura. She retained a bit of New Orleans—that loose, casualness that my mother worked so hard to rid herself of. I don't remember if Aunt Laura kept her New Orleans accent, which my mother washed from her mouth like dirt.

But Aunt Laura was not blood. She married my grandmother Camille's only uncle, Edward Nichols. Both Laura and Edward were born and raised in New Orleans. What I was told by my mother, clearly an unreliable narrator, was that Edward worked for the railroad and that he and Laura left New Orleans for a railroad job in Ohio. By the time we were visiting Aunt Laura, Uncle Eddie, as my mother referred to him, was already dead.

When my mother became pregnant with my brother in 1951, we didn't go see Aunt Laura for about a year or so. I don't think they talked on the phone. Maybe they exchanged Christmas cards. They must have been close. Why else would she have given my mother her engagement ring?

One Saturday when my brother was old enough to travel the two hours to Toledo, we drove north again to visit Aunt Laura.

I can see my father standing on the porch of the old house, his startled expression as a black man answered the door.

When he returned to the car, my mother asked, "Where's Aunt Laura?"

"She's not there," my father answered as perplexed as my mother.

"Well, where is she? Did that man say?"

"He doesn't know. He thinks maybe she died."

And then we drove away. We drove home to Cleveland.

After my mother gave me Aunt Laura's ring, I questioned her about what happened to her, stunned by the story.

"She probably died. And those people bought her house from the state."

Her response only added to my curiosity. "But why didn't you or Dad try to find out what happened to her?" Something wasn't right here. I could feel it.

My mother answered sheepishly, "We should have. But things were different back then. I think we might have called the police. But they didn't know anything." She paused. "Aunt Laura always said she'd leave us something in her will." There was regret in her voice. I wasn't sure if it was for Aunt Laura or the inheritance.

Over the years whenever I wore Aunt Laura's ring I considered the transitory nature of my mother's family—how easily people passed in and out of it as if they'd never even been here. It wasn't until Ula mentioned Uncle Eddie in one of our conversations about passing that part of the mystery of their story became clearer to me. And I realized that once again my mother had told me another story of our family that left out the most important part.

"Uncle Eddie lived as white," Ula told me. "He went north like your mother and passed. Laura did too. They both lived as white. He never went back. Though he did send his mother money. But he never went back home. Never saw his mother again."

Fellow travelers, I thought, sharing a common journey away from family toward a better life. But in Uncle Eddie's case he never returned home.

The facts of his life as recorded by state governmental documents provide the outline of his life, giving me no depth. Edward Joseph Nichols/McNickel was born in New Orleans in 1883 to Joseph McNickel and Mary Brown, the woman who raised my mother, the woman Ula called Mama and described as a Choctaw Indian. She was born in Louisiana in St. James Parish in 1866. On every census record Mary Brown/McNickel/Williams is listed as black. Joseph McNickel, Edward's father, was born in Ireland.

Laura Baker Nickels/McNickel was born in 1884. Her father Pat Baker was born in Germany. Although they both had white fathers, their mothers were women of color.

By the time of their wedding in 1905, decades after Reconstruction, people of color experienced increased violence, segregation, economic exploitation, and denial of citizenship rights, forcing many to pass for economic reasons.[1] If the census records are to be believed Eddie achieved a seventh grade education and Laura only a third grade education.

In 1910 they are living on Chartres Street in New Orleans' Fifth Ward, which at that time was one of the wards at the heart of the mulatto community. However, Eddie and Laura are designated as white on the 1910 census, as are their neighbors. His occupation is plumber. In the prior 1900 Louisiana census, Eddie, who was living with his mother Mary Williams, was designated black.

Residing in a city where race was scrutinized and escaping your racial community difficult, his opportunities for upward mobility were limited. As a person of mixed race, he couldn't drive a bus, work for the telephone company or the public service.[2]

What finally made them decide to leave New Orleans and move to Ohio and live as white? Most likely their decision was based on economics. They had no children that might tie them to their families, and they would remain childless. Possibly economics outweighed family. Or maybe like Ula, they were tired of being hemmed in by race and segregation, judged at every turn.

The fact that Uncle Eddie never returned home to visit his mother but sent her money indicates the permanence of his decision. Maybe the money mitigated his guilt. Other than the money he sent his mother, he might as well have been dead. He truly passed on from his family.

By 1920 Eddie and Laura are living in Adams, Ohio, on Oak Grove Street. He's working as a plumber and owns his home, no longer renting as he did in New Orleans. By 1935 Eddie attains a position of advancement as a steam fitter for the railroad. In the 1940 census Eddie works as a plumber for a private concern. They no longer own their home and are living on Woodland Avenue in Toledo, most likely the house I visited as a young child. Even today large oak trees line the street. The neighborhood is modest, clearly in decline. The houses date from the late 1800s to early 1900s.

For reasons I can't explain my mother sent me a photograph of Uncle Eddie years after I questioned her about her mixed racial heritage. With no photo of her father to share and my continued silence about her racial heritage, maybe she wanted to give me some visual proof of one man in her family, a visual reward for keeping her secret.

He's a striking man with white features, high cheekbones, a deeply dimpled chin, and dark wavy hair. He looks Native American. But he could easily pass as white.

Ula described Eddie's mother Mary Brown as very dark. Based on Mary Brown's marriage certificate, which names her mother as Elizabeth Johnson, born in 1832 in South Carolina, there's a possibility that Elizabeth Johnson was born into slavery.

My curiosity about Uncle Eddie and Aunt Laura isn't satisfied. The mystery remains: what happened to Aunt Laura? Tracking down details about Uncle Eddie proves easier than I anticipated with the help of Ancestry.com, Family Search, and the Ohio death records. Uncle Eddie died at home in 1948 of a coronary occlusion at the age of sixty-four. His death certificate reads white for race. Laura buried him at Calvary Cemetery in Toledo, a Catholic cemetery.

When I call the cemetery to ask which church they might have belonged to, the woman tells me they don't keep records of the churches. I also ask if his wife Laura Nichols is buried in the cemetery. It takes her a scant few minutes to tell me no. Another blind alley in my search for what happened to Aunt Laura.

From the Find A Grave website, I discover his headstone. A volunteer had kindly taken a photograph of it. The headstone reads "Edwin J. Nichols, 1883–1948." In death his first name is misspelled. But he fared better than his wife Laura, who died without family to properly bury her. At least that's what I assume since I can't find a record of her death yet.

With no clear death date for Aunt Laura, I search Ancestry.com, Family Search, and Ohio vital records in vain. Relying on my mother's story of what happened to Aunt Laura, I guess at her death occurring a year after my brother's birth, which would be 1952. All my searches are fruitless. In my mind, I see her dying alone in the dark house with the side bay window, her body discovered by neighbors, the county disposing of her body and her possessions. She becomes for me a cautionary tale of passing and loss.

As if I can redeem her story, I take her ring to a local jeweler and have it appraised. Perhaps its antiquity, over one hundred years old, might be valuable, adding a gloss over her lonely death. When I get the appraisal, I'm disappointed. The ring is valued at 435 dollars. "One bead-set, Old European cut diamond. Diamond weight is 0.19 carat," the appraisal reads.

In my initial enthusiasm when I dropped the ring off to be appraised, I told the jeweler the story of Aunt Laura who disappeared and was never found. Now I realize that the ring's value is the story, which I'll pass down to my daughter along with the ring and she'll pass it down to one of her daughters. In this way Aunt Laura will live on through the women in my family who will know this piece of my mother's family history of passing.

But I can't let the story end here. In a last-ditch effort to find out what happened to Aunt Laura, I enlist the aid of two librarians. Sonia Schoenfield is the genealogy librarian at Cook Memorial Library in Libertyville, Illinois, who offered her services after I gave two presentations about my appearance on *Genealogy Roadshow* and my mother's story at the library. The other librarian is Becky Hill, Head Librarian at the Rutherford B. Hayes Library in Fremont, Ohio. Though I ask for their help a week apart, their discoveries come within a day of each other. And what they discover is a surprising ending to the disappearance of Aunt Laura.

Initially, Sonia locates an obituary for a Laura Nicholas in 1968 in the Toledo Lucas County Public Library. I tell her it can't be my aunt. The death date is wrong, and I'm certain she was buried in a pauper's grave and her estate was turned over to the state of Ohio. Sonia also finds Edward Nichols's obituary, and I order it, thinking it may hold clues to Laura.

The next day Becky Hill's email arrives solving the sixty-three-year-old mystery of Aunt Laura. Mrs. Laura Nichols died in Perrysburg, Ohio, in 1968 at the age of eighty-five. At the time of her death she was living in a Perrysburg nursing home. She was buried at St. Rose Catholic Church Cemetery.

I'm stunned. Because I'd relied solely on my mother's account of Aunt Laura's disappearance, I rejected Sonia's finding of a 1968 death date. But there's no denying the obituary in the *Daily Sentinel Tribune*, dated April 29, 1968.

Questions race through my mind all leading back to my mother's conviction that Laura died alone in her house in Toledo in the early 1950s. I order the obituary, which may contain more information about Laura. What I want to know is her mother's name. The marriage license says her father was Pat Baker. I know he was from Germany. But I can't decipher her mother's first name.

When the obituary arrives in the mail, it provides no new information about Aunt Laura. It ends: "She was born in New Orleans, but spent most of her life in the Toledo area."

The solution of the mystery of Aunt Laura's disappearance is bittersweet. All those years lost I could have visited my New Orleans aunt, gotten to know her, learned about her and my Uncle Eddie. I could have had a window into my mother's family.

Other questions that will never be answered trouble me. Why didn't my mother, who claimed she was in Laura's will and who was given her engagement ring, ever try to find her? Was there a falling out? Why wouldn't Aunt Laura tell my mother that she was moving? There's a missing piece.

Or was my mother following the familial pattern that had been established so early in her life? Family slipping in and out, not to be relied upon or sought after, the rejection too deep to matter, better to let them go, consider them dead.

I reject out of hand any notion that my mother feared Aunt Laura would reveal her secret because in doing so, she'd be revealing her own secret. They were complicit in each other's deceit.

With what slyness they must have sat in the shadowy living room among the heavy furniture, the lacy white curtains, chatting while the oblivious husband contentedly drank his beer.

Or was their transformation so complete, so a part of their psyches, it never occurred to them that they were anything but what they appeared, what they were playing at: two white women from New Orleans who made good by coming north to Ohio.

I'll never know why my mother lost touch with Aunt Laura or why she didn't try to find her. But I find consolation in knowing she didn't die alone in her house and wasn't buried in a pauper's grave—which would have been a terrible price to pay for permanently passing as white. Someone had looked out for her. Someone had stood in for family.

As I place the ring back in the turquoise velvet box where I keep it, I wonder if Laura or Edward ever regretted their decision to live as white and turn their backs on their families. Or like Ula they regretted the circumstances. One thing I'm certain of is they served as trailblazers for my mother. They showed her a way to escape her "one drop" of African blood, how to capitalize on her white appearance, and how to disappear into whiteness.

14

Gens de Couleur Libre

"Neither Black Nor White, Neither Slave Nor Entirely Free."
—Mary Gehman, *The Free People of Color of New Orleans.*

G ROWING UP IN New Orleans' mixed-race and black neighborhoods, my mother lived the color-caste system. There's little doubt that she knew of the paper-bag skin test: if your skin color was the color of a brown paper bag or lighter then you were allowed to join certain social organizations, fraternities, and sororities. Dr. Audrey Kerr in her book *The Paper Bag Principle* notes that in New Orleans there were "paper bag parties" where you had to be a certain complexion to attend. I don't know if my mother attended paper bag parties, but if she did, she would have passed easily.

The closer one's skin tone was to white, the higher one's status was in the mixed-race and black communities, making stepping over the color line to sit in the white section of a street car or a restaurant acceptable if one knew how to act white. Such hyper vigilance to subtleties in skin tones, requiring comparisons to an item as arbitrary as a paper bag seems biblical to me in its search for a stain like the unseen stain of original sin that permeated my Catholic education. And what did it mean when you couldn't pass the paper bag test? Were you undesirable, less of a person, tainted?

Though my mother was aware of such distinctions and meanings about skin color, what she didn't know was she was from a long line of free people of color, stretching back to colonial Louisiana.

This racial designation, free people of color, was one I wasn't aware of until I began digging deeper into her ancestry. Like many Americans, I learned about slavery in American history classes, which presented a simplistic view of slavery. The Civil War was in part fought to free the slaves. All people of African descent residing in the Southern slave-holding states were slaves until after the Civil War when the Emancipation Proclamation freed them. That there was a racially designated classification in Louisiana (most heavily concentrated in New Orleans) known as "free people of color" was left out of my history lessons. Though I was well aware of free black people and free black communities in the Northern cities such as Philadelphia, Boston, Providence, and New York. A group of people designated as free people of color in a Southern state was a revelation to me.

Michael Taylor, Curator of Books at Louisiana State University Libraries, discusses the perplexing absence of free people of color in American history in his article, "Free People of Color in Louisiana: Revealing an Unknown Past."

> "The fact that free people of color, particularly in the South, never made it into the mainstream narrative of American history is extraordinary considering their status were one of the most talked about issues of the first half of the nineteenth century. Even where their numbers were small, they made significant contributions to the economies and cultures of the communities in which they lived, and, as a group, exerted a strong influence on government policy and public opinion at a time of increasing polarization over the issue of slavery."

The article refers to the free people of color as "forgotten" people, which is an apt description.[1]

The derivation of the designation "free people of color" dates back to Louisiana's colonial period (1718–1768) when sexual relations among European settlers, African slaves, and Native Americans resulted in a third race of people, the *gens de couleur libre*, free people of color.[2] The history of how these mixed-race people attained freedom is varied. From the beginning of New Orleans there were free blacks who came either from the Caribbean or from France.[3] Others were born into freedom in Louisiana as second generations of free blacks and as such didn't identify with an African identity or slavery. Still others won their freedom through military service during various times of war. And then there were the instances when a slave owner would grant manumission to an individual slave or entire families upon his or her death. And after the Haitian Revolution (1791–1804) thousands of free blacks poured into New Orleans, doubling their population by 1810.

But what prompted free women of color to have interracial relationships with white men as opposed to free men of color who they could legally marry and thus enjoy the privileges that accompanied marital status? As mistresses of white men, they were legally barred from those privileges and were socially ostracized.

Demographic numbers offer insight into their reasons. In 1777 white male New Orleanians outnumbered white women—175 males per one hundred females and free black females outnumbered free black males about two to one.[4]

Left with limited options, women of color sought protectors in long-standing, formalized relationships with white European men, who were only too willing to oblige them. This system of formalizing sexual relationships between women of color and white men was called *plaçage*. The term comes from the French word *placer*, which means "to place with." The people of color referred to these arrangements as *mariages de la main gauche*, "left-handed marriages." This practice existed in

Louisiana and other French and Spanish slave holding territories from the late seventeenth century through the nineteenth century.[5]

Some scholars consider the system exploitative of women of color, others view the system as beneficial to both parties: giving the women "economic security for themselves and their children with the possibility of manumission during the colonial and slavery periods or, later, the possible legal transfer of wealth from the father to the woman's children through wills and other testaments." For men during the colonial period, "*plaçage* allowed men to enjoy the benefits of marriage without worrying that their territorial holdings would be divided among their heirs," and later they could distribute their wealth among all their heirs if they so desired.[6]

The mystique surrounding the white men's choice of a consort at formalized quadroon balls, which began in New Orleans in 1805, is rife with the stuff of romance novels. Books and movies abound with the tragic tale of the sultry quadroon kept as a mistress only to be cast off later when the white man marries a white woman. The implication was that the sultry quadroon who broke with social and moral codes has made the fatal mistake of falling in love with her white consort and can't live without him. That narrative not only suggests her powerlessness but also her immorality and self-loathing.

In reality, this blending of African, European, and Native American blood in New Orleans created women described as "hauntingly beautiful," often seen as temptresses. Their beauty and refinement so angered white women during the time of Spanish colonial rule that Governor Miró enacted the "*tignon* law" on June 2, 1786. The law made it a criminal offense for women of "pure or mixed African blood" to give excessive attention to their dress.[7] The absurdity of the law attests to Miró's fear that the women of color needed to be controlled. These women had become too light-skinned, too European in appearance, or dressed too elegantly and thus disturbed the social order.[8] Their beauty was its own kind of power.

What I find compelling about the *placées*, or "kept women of color"—who by today's standards would be considered immoral—was their ability to undermine the harsh oppression of their everyday lives and, in the process, protect themselves and the children who were products of these relationships. Historian Joan Martin calls their actions not only moral and ethical but also courageous within the framework of a society whose normal moral and ethical codes didn't apply to them.[9]

It's not a huge leap for me to view the circumstances surrounding my mother's decision to pass in the same light of oppression and the need to mitigate that oppression even if it meant breaking the strictures of that oppression by marrying a white man. Though in her case she broke no law since her marriage took place in Ohio and not Louisiana.

Ironically, the *plaçage* system, which created people who could pass for white but were genetically mixed race, became the impetus for such laws as the 1924 Act to Preserve Racial Integrity enacted to guard against "white Negroes passing over the line." Numerous scholars point out how patriarchal institutions sanctioned mixed-race relationships when it was beneficial for white European men and then instituted laws against mixed-race marriages when "white Negroes" threatened the purity of the white race.

Regardless of one's viewpoint on *plaçage*, it created a third race in Louisiana that over time accumulated wealth and power. These free people of color occupied a unique position being "neither black nor white, neither slave nor entirely free," French-speaking, and mostly middle-class.[10] Over time the free people of color would be seen by the white community as a threat to their own way of life because of their unique position and their wealth and power, ushering in stricter laws against them, culminating with the Jim Crow laws and the one-drop rule, which defined the racial designation of black as having any trace of black ancestry.

Whether or not my ancestor's mixed-race unions were formalized under the *plaçage* system, they contributed to that third race in Louisiana. Their stories are woven into the fabric of mixed race in this country.

15

Leon Frederic, Light Enough to Fight
1838–1905

"You wanted to know if Leon Frederic is your great-great-grandfather, and if he was a member of the Louisiana Native Guards during the Civil War," Kenyatta states. "Take a look at what we found."

So it's true, I think to myself, examining the documents as they appear on the screen. Leon Frederic, my great-great-grandfather, was a private in the Louisiana Native Guards. A shiver of excitement runs up my spine at the confirmation.

Then Kenyatta brings up a newspaper article. Her voice hesitates as she looks into my eyes, gauging my reaction, almost apologetic. She launches into an explanation of the *Times-Picayune* newspaper article. Leon's story holds yet another surprise, one that my mother would have found if not shameful, then distressing, supporting her decision to hide her black background.

❖

Several years before appearing on *Genealogy Roadshow*, I traced the Frederic line to Leon Frederic (1838–1905) using Ancestry.com. Though

I wasn't absolutely certain he was my great-great-grandfather, what I discovered about him presented me an opportunity to break through my mother's silence. It would be the last time I'd directly confront her about her racial background.

I was excited to share with her what I considered amazing news about Leon Frederic, linking him to the Civil War and a little-known, but important, piece of American history. Naively, I believed that if she felt pride about her racially mixed heritage instead of shame, she'd finally open up about her experiences as a mixed-race person.

"Leon Frederic who I think is your great-grandfather is part of the African American Civil War Memorial in Washington," I told her. "His name is on a plaque."

She went quiet on the phone and I knew that rather than breaking through her wall of shame, I'd only fortified it by breaching my agreement not to talk about her racial heritage. Quickly she changed the subject, asking about my children.

Never again did I share with her any research my son Chris and I found about her family. We continued searching into the family genealogy, comparing notes, following paths that sometimes led to dead ends. Ancestry.com made my search easier, though sometimes it presented more questions than answers.

Chris, on one of his solo trips to visit my mother, broached the subject of her racial background by bringing up his research about her family. But she refused to discuss it with him, politely but firmly changing the subject as she'd done with me.

The need to uncover the unknown, to know the truth burned inside of me. But all I could find were dates and places, tied to records and documents, without dialogue or setting or characterization, like an outline for a scene, waiting for something to happen, for someone to speak.

❖

On September 2, 1862, my great-great-grandfather Leon Frederic enlisted as a volunteer soldier in the First Regiment of the Louisiana Native Guards. From his enlistment document given to me after the St. Louis taping but before the show aired in January 2015, along with 163 pages of other genealogical documents, I learned that the examining surgeon, Robert Smith, described Leon as having black eyes, black hair, fair complexion; five feet, six and a half inches tall. Other than his gender, the surgeon could be describing my mother, including the height. The skin description seems an odd identifier to my twenty-first-century sensibilities. But in 1862 enlisting as a free person of color, Leon's light complexion was important to the Union war effort in Louisiana.

When Leon signed his name with a firm, artistic flourish, he had no way of knowing that his action marked a momentous historical moment. The First Regiment of the Louisiana Native Guards was the first black regiment in the history of the United States Army.

I trace his signature with my index finger as if I could know what he was feeling as he put pen to paper, enlisting for a term of three years in the Union army.

La Monte Westmoreland, *Genealogy Roadshow*'s producer, told me months after the show aired that the genealogist, Rich Venezia, didn't conclude that Leon Frederic was my ancestor until days before the show taped, comparing and studying Leon's signatures on various documents. To my untrained eye, there's no mistaking the similarities in Leon's various signatures.

Even before the *Roadshow* verified that Leon was my direct ancestor, I contacted Isiah "Ike" Edwards, an amateur military historian and expert on the Native Guards whose ancestor had also been a Native Guard. I learned that Ike is the keeper of the flame of these forgotten men to the extent that he's petitioned the city of New Orleans to honor the men with a plaque, which the city has yet to do. He explained with a touch of pride in his voice that the Native Guards preceded the "Glory Boys," as he called them.

"You know," he said, "the ones they made the movie about."

I knew of the movie and the famous poem "For the Union Dead" by Robert Lowell, an ode to "Colonel Shaw/and his bell-cheeked Negro infantry." But prior to discovering Leon Frederic I'd never heard of the Native Guards. As I listened to Ike, I wondered how much of black history is buried, shoved aside, considered unimportant to the American narrative.

Though technically, the Native Guards weren't the first black troops to enlist, they were the first black troops to be mustered into the US Army. The famous Fifty-Fourth Massachusetts, immortalized in the movie *Glory*, weren't completely organized until May 13, 1863, eight months after the Native Guards were already part of the Union troops.

As the first black troops in the US Army, serving in a Southern state, the Native Guards faced enormous obstacles both from the Southern whites and the Northern soldiers and officers, including General Benjamin Butler, commander of the Department of the Gulf.

Initially Butler was hesitant to enlist blacks as soldiers. Only necessity made him change his mind. Once New Orleans fell to the Union, the War Department wanted him to hold the city at all costs but gave him no additional troops. He was tasked with obtaining recruits from Louisiana. After failing to enlist enough soldiers from the Irish and German immigrants, he reached out to the free men of color of the Native Guards, who had reluctantly served in the Confederate Army.[1]

To assuage his own mind about the men's loyalty to the Union, he questioned one of the captains from the Confederate Colored Brigade, Charles S. Sauvenet, a free man of color and a translator in the Provost Court of German, Spanish, and French.

"How came you, free colored men, fighting here for the Confederacy, fighting for slavery?"

Sauvenet answered that if they hadn't volunteered they would have been forced to join. "We have property and rights here, and there is every reason why we should take care of ourselves." Then he went on to explain their treatment by the Confederate Army. Although they had participated in drills, they were not allowed to use arms and never given muskets.[2]

Butler must have seen the truth in what Sauvenet said. When New Orleans fell, the Confederate Native Guards hadn't run as the Confederate white soldiers had. They stayed in New Orleans protecting their property and families, waiting to see which way the wind would blow.

Satisfied with Sauvenet's explanation, Butler wrote Secretary of War Edwin Stanton of his decision to use colored men if he didn't receive reinforcements. "I shall call on Africa to intervene. I have determined to use the services of free colored men who were organized by the rebels into the Colored Brigade . . . They are free; they have been used by our enemies, whose mouths are shut, and they will be loyal."[3]

Butler fully understood the political ramifications of taking such a bold and politically unpopular move not to mention his own misgivings about black troops. From the onset of the occupation of New Orleans, he had been hesitant to enlist fugitive slaves as soldiers. He harbored a prejudice against the military ability of blacks, believing they were afraid of firearms. And he was aware that President Lincoln feared turning the border states of Missouri, Maryland, and Kentucky against the Union if black troops were armed.[4]

But if he wanted to hold New Orleans and the valuable waterway of the Mississippi River, he needed additional troops.

By August 1862, Butler could wait no longer for the government's sanctioning of colored soldiers. He issued an appeal for men of color to join the Union Army.[5] Within three weeks, he had one thousand Native Guards ready to fight for the Union.

On September 1, 1862, Butler wrote to Stanton, asking that the War Department sanction his recruitment of Negroes under the Militia Act of July 17, 1862. "My Native Guards, one thousand strong are to be filled up in the next ten days, the darkest of whom is about the complexion of the late Mr. Webster."[6]

Butler's comment about Mr. Webster's complexion was meant to reassure Stanton that the regiment was composed of lighter-complexioned soldiers, who would not arouse fear among the white Southern population when they appeared in uniform bearing arms. These men weren't slaves nor were they interested in leading a slave rebellion. In fact, some of these free men of color were also slave owners.

Leon Frederic—a fair-skinned, free man of color, shoemaker by trade, with a pregnant wife, mother, and two sisters to support—was among those one thousand strong.

And possibly, he shared another commonality with some of the free men of color of the First Regiment of the Native Guards. On the US Military Index of the First Regiment of the Confederate Native Guards, a Leon Frederick is listed. Though the Confederate Native Guard Leon Frederick's name ends in a *K*, it is likely that this Leon Frederick is my great-great-grandfather, the same Leon Frederic who enlisted in the Union Native Guards. He'd been a soldier in both the Confederate Native Guards and the Union Native Guards.

Butler's emphasis on the First Regiment's skin color goes to his belief not uncommon at the time of the connection between the lighter skinned free men of color and their status in the color-caste system. Upon Butler's arrival in New Orleans, he commented in an earlier letter to Stanton about the free men of color's appearance. "In color, nay, also in conduct, they had much more the appearance of white gentlemen than some of those who have favored me with their presence claiming to be the 'chivalry of the South.'"[7]

In his letter Butler was acknowledging the relationship between skin color and status among the free colored people.

"Eighty per cent of the free black population in New Orleans in 1860 had European blood, fewer then ten per cent of slaves in New Orleans had evidence of white ancestry. Because skin color and free status were highly correlated, many free blacks identified more closely with Southern whites. In this color-caste system, the closer one's skin tone was to white, the higher the status."[8] Leon Frederic with his light complexion held a high place of status in this color-caste system.

Clearly, for Butler the men's color was a political bargaining chip in securing the sanctioning of a black regiment.

For all Butler's reassurances to Stanton about his colored regiment, he was wrong on two accounts. He hadn't approached the Native Guards about serving in the Union Army; they approached him. And the one thousand men weren't composed "altogether of freed men."[9] More than half the regiment was composed of fugitive slaves.[10] These fugitive slaves, sharing little if any European ancestry, were dark skinned. And their appearance would indeed alarm the Southern whites.

On a bright fall afternoon in New Orleans, Leon Frederic and the First Regiment paraded down Canal Street. The city turned out to see the military parade led by the regiment's commanding officer Colonel Stafford. A band played "Yankee Doodle" while flags flew and drums beat. Leon's wife Philomene, his two sisters Rosa and Hermina, and his mother Roxelane Arnoux cheered him on. Brilliantly turned out in his Federal Blues, musket at the ready, Leon must have felt the stirrings of change on the horizon, the possibilities of equality that military service in the Union Army might afford.

An Englishman named Task observing the parade commented on how the white Southerners turned away in disgust at the display of fugitive slaves among the regiment's aristocratic free men of color. Word would spread quickly through the white community that slaves were armed and fear and hostility would follow.[11]

Watching the parade Philomene must have heard the derisive comments made by the white Southerners. Herself, a light complexioned, free woman of color, she could have been standing with the white Southerners if she'd chosen to, her fair skin protected from the intense Louisiana sun by a silk parasol.

Did a shiver of dread run up her spine that warm afternoon, newly pregnant with their second child, my great-grandfather Leon Frederic, Jr., realizing the true danger her husband was in? After the parade, had she pleaded with him to resign? After all her own brother, Jules Lanabere, who'd been a private in the Confederate First Native Guards Militia, opted not to join the Union Army.

"Why do you have to do this?" I can hear her asking him. "I need you here with me when the baby comes. I can't go through this without you. What if something happens?" There would be no need for her to say more, the loss of Emile, their first child, still raw.

Or perhaps she'd said nothing, understanding that her husband was a risk taker, a man who liked to gamble, whose own father, Ursin Frederic, was a veteran of the Battle of New Orleans. There was a tradition to be upheld. Like so many free men of color who'd won their freedom through military service, was Leon banking on full American citizenship if he and the other Native Guards distinguished themselves in battle? Once and for all they would prove that blacks were heroic, brave, and deserving of being citizens with full rights.

By January 1863 when Leon's First Regiment reached Fort St. Leon on the west bank of the Mississippi River at English Turn, fifteen miles below New Orleans, they'd yet to engage in battle. They'd already endured prejudice at Camp Strong, located outside New Orleans near the Louisiana racetrack, from some of the white soldiers. When they left Camp Strong, they were subject to taunts and jeers in the streets. Not because they were Union soldiers but because they were black men who were Union soldiers. Even the fairer-skinned, free men of color were treated with scorn and hostility. After the parade on Canal Street, as expected, word had spread through the city that black soldiers had taken up with the enemy, and were armed with guns.[12]

Not allowed to fight, they were used as laborers. "In the six days since leaving Camp Strong, the First Native Guards and the Eighth Vermont

Regiment opened fifty-two miles of railroad, built nine culverts, and rebuilt the bridge at Bayou des Allemands, which was 435 feet long."[13]

The harassment and hostility from the white population in the surrounding area continued, and white officers refused to salute the black officers. Despite their ill treatment, their morale remained high. They were ready to fight; they wanted to fight. They hadn't joined the Union Army to build culverts or rebuild bridges. There was no glory in that. By engaging in battle, they would prove they had the right to be American citizens.

Their commander, Colonel Spencer H. Stafford, agreed with them and on January 3, 1863, he wrote to General Nathaniel Banks, the new Commander of the Department of the Gulf, requesting that his men be allowed to fight.[14]

But notions that black soldiers were not fit for battle and could best serve as laborers prevailed. General Banks believed, as was common in that time, that Negroes were only capable of hard labor, sometimes comparing them to mules and horses in their usefulness. Also, there was an erroneous belief that blacks were immune to tropical diseases.

After leaving Camp Strong, Leon must have written to his wife Philomene of his frustrations at the Native Guards' treatment. Though no letters have survived, I imagine his words.

February 6, 1863

My Dearest Philomene,
Your letter arrived by the evening train and put my mind at ease. To hear you are well is all I need to sustain me. You need not fear. I've been in no battle only a skirmish, which by now you may have heard about. We protected the rail and drove out the Rebs. The officers seem pleased with us. The only thing your husband may die of is hard labor and frustration. I know not how many miles of railroad we opened, how many culverts we built. The locals being none too happy to see us hurled slanders our way. But I am heeding your advice and kept my temper though I was hard pressed to do so seeing how quick I am to anger when

the cause is just. But I'm a soldier now and must keep myself in line or so I'm told. But contrary to what your father may think of my foolishness in enlisting, my spirits remain high.

I share with you a rumor that ran through the camp you may find of some humor. The white officers think Negroes are not susceptible to swamp diseases. I can hear you laughing at that. Maybe that is why they use us so poorly, digging and building. Not letting us fight. When all we want to do is fight, really fight in a battle.

There is a young colored officer that I've become acquainted with. His name is Lieutenant John Crowder. I have engaged him in conversation and have learned of his humble beginnings, being born a slave. He's a smart one having taught himself to read and write. He abides no liquor and does not smoke but can be persuaded to partake of a game or two of cards.

Listen to no rumors that the colored soldiers are not to be paid. You must free your mind of that. They are sure to pay us.

Kiss Mama for me and tell my sisters that they are to be of help to you when your time comes. I know you favor Bernard if it's a boy seeing as that's your father's name. Sometimes I think you abide him too much. In this one thing I will not bend. Grant me this necessity, that the child if it is a boy bear my name. It is a good name and has served me well. Say you will grant this wish to your husband.

It is very cold here and the light goes.

Your loving husband,
Leon

On February 12, 1863, Leon is reported on the muster roll as a deserter from Fort St. Leon. On March and April's muster roll he is present. A "RETURNS" card appears in his file as well. From the explanation given in "Compiled Military Service Records," a returns card was issued for a soldier upon his return to his regiment. For his desertion, his pay was stopped and he owed the US government one hundred dollars.

Puzzling over his desertion and return to his regiment the following month, I can only posit theories as to why he was marked as a deserter. His wife Philomene Lanabere Frederic had given birth to their first child, a son Emile, in October of 1861. Seven months later on May 21, 1862, Emile died. The death record erroneously identifies Emile as a daughter and gives no cause of death. But the record does state that Emile was the legitimate daughter of Philomene Bernard with Leon Frederic, "f. m. color" (free man of color). His wife heavily pregnant with their second child, was Leon worried about Philomene and decided to take a temporary leave from his unit to see her, to reassure himself that she was in good health?

Ike Edwards, the amateur military historian, provided another, less complex explanation. "You were marked 'Deserted' if you were not there for roll call."

Whatever the reason, whether he missed roll call or left to visit his wife in New Orleans, Leon returned. By March 1863, he was back with his regiment, soon to be tested in a battle that amounted to a massacre for the men of the First and Third Regiments of the Native Guards. This little-known, yet historic battle, would rival the heroic assault of the Fifty-Fourth Massachusetts at Fort Wagner in July 1863.

From the onset the Native Guards were treated poorly, given obsolete rifle-muskets and cast-off uniforms. Wood floors for tents were given to the white soldiers, while the Colored Native Guards had to be content with dirt floors. By April 1863, they had yet to be paid.[15]

Finally in March the First Regiment was moved from Fort St. Leon to Baton Rouge, where they joined the Third Regiment. But they weren't called into service. Their idleness, of course, bred discontent among some of the soldiers leading to infractions. One incident of particular note involved Lt. John Crowder.

Baton Rouge
April 27, 1863

My dearest wife,
Mama's letter arrived with the good news of our son's birth and your good health.
That you honored my wishes and named him Leon brings me much joy and good
spirits. Tell me, does he thrive? Who does he favor? Just as soon as I can I will
come home.

By now you've heard of the colored officers who resigned. Fret not about this.
We men are staying strong and will not desert. That officer that I told you about,
John Crowder, stays the course and vows never to resign. Though I had to warn
him to be careful. I overheard Captain Lewis say he wants to get John out. He
dislikes him greatly because of an incident that occurred.

Young though John is he had the grit to have a soldier arrested who did a lewd
expression in front of a visiting lady. Captain Lewis who viewed this despicable
action did nothing to discipline the soldier. So John took it upon himself to handle
the matter.

When I told John to be wary of Lewis he says he wants to fight him in a duel.

I had to contain myself not to laugh at his notions of chivalry. He is only
sixteen and will soon learn the foolishness of such ideas. Were we not so young
once and so foolish.

With all my heart and love,
Leon

Baton Rouge
May 6, 1863

My darling Philomene,
I pen you good tidings today we were paid for five months. As soon as I can I will
send money your way. Tell your father that he need not worry about your needs.

I will send money by Mr. Johnston who I expect to come. Let me know that you have received such. How does my son? Does he thrive?

Lt. Crowder was by my tent earlier for a game of cards and something in his presence makes me think we may finally see fighting. He showed me a talisman that he wears under his coat. He sent for it from home. He kept touching it from time to time, and I asked what he had there. He informed me that it is his good luck talisman. I need no such thing for luck. I make my own luck.

Your loving husband,
Leon

In 1863 all that remained to getting control of the Mississippi River and cutting off rebel supplies via the Red River were the Confederate troops entrenched at Port Hudson, which was fourteen miles north of Baton Rouge. The Confederate troops had been driven to the Port Hudson garrison by the Union troops. In advance of an all-out assault, on May 23, the First and Third Regiments of the Native Guards joined Banks's army at Port Hudson.[16]

The Wednesday morning of the assault began with Brigadier General William Dwight, Jr., the Union general in charge of the Native Guards, getting drunk before breakfast. Dwight hadn't studied the maps and knew nothing of the terrain where the black troops would advance.

When questioned by General Nelson what the ground would be like, he said the approach was "the easiest way to Port Hudson." There was nothing easy about the approach or the terrain. The Native Guards were being sent on what amounted to a suicide mission. Well fortified, the garrison at Port Hudson had earthworks along the brow of an elevated bluff and twenty siege guns and thirty-one field pieces inside.[17]

The surrounding area provided additional protection from advancing soldiers with natural gullies and felled trees. Dwight ordered the

First and Third Native Guard Regiments on the extreme right. They formed a line of battle in a willow tree swamp.

Ordered to move forward, their advance was covered by two brass guns from the Sixth Massachusetts Artillery. But the Confederates answered with a vengeance and the Sixth Massachusetts retreated leaving the Native Guards on their own.

The Native Guards made six to seven charges under heavy fire and were slaughtered. It was reported that Captain Andre Cailloux, one of the remaining black officers, continued to charge. Though his shoulder was shattered by grapeshot, he carried his saber in his one good arm. The flag bearer was shot down and another man picked up the flag and charged on, when he was shot, another picked up the flag.[18]

Confederate soldier Walter Stephens wrote in his diary of the battle, "There were also several charges made on the Fifteenth Arkansas and First Mississippi, and on the extreme left were two negro regiments, who charged us. We drove them back and cut them all to pieces."[19]

An account from P. F. DeGourany, a Confederate soldier, appeared in the *New Orleans Weekly Times*. "How many of the poor wretches perished in the fatal trap into which they had been so unwisely driven I cannot say. During that day and the next we could hear the groans of the wounded that had fallen among the willows, and the dead lay festering in the hot sun, creating a sickening stench. Unable to stand this, some of our boys started the next morning on a blackberrying expedition, as they styled it with grim pleasantry."

The ill-fated and impossible assault by the Native Guards—who after leaving the shelter of the willow trees, had to cross a marsh littered with fallen trees and in some places six feet deep and then charge up an incline, all the time the rebel sharpshooters sitting high on a bluff, picking them off—was dismissed by Dwight.

When told of the casualties and impossibility of the task, Dwight would not rescind his orders. "Charge again."

Nelson knowing the foolishness of the order told the Native Guards to remain in their positions in the willow trees and continue to fire on the rebels even though there was no possibility of them hitting any of them. He reasoned that since Dwight had no intention of leaving his tent, the sound of the rifles would make him think that his order to charge again was being obeyed.

As the afternoon wore on, the Native Guards continued to fire from the willow trees, though they were out of range of the sharpshooters, the Confederate guns continued to shell the willow grove shattering limbs.[20]

None of the Union assaults were successful. Finally at 5:30 p.m. someone raised a white flag to call a temporary cease-fire so that the wounded could be treated. More than 450 Union soldiers were dead, thirty-six were Native Guards. The number of Union wounded and missing was over fifteen hundred. In the First Regiment, Leon's regiment, three officers and ninety-two men were wounded. One of the officers killed was Lieutenant John Crowder who refused to resign and believed he could move up in rank if he held steady. The Third Regiment reported thirty-eight wounded.[21]

All the Union dead and wounded soldiers were taken from the battlefield except the soldiers along Telegraph Road, where the Native Guards had begun their attack.

The day after the battle (May 28, 1863) Walter Stephens Turner recorded in his journal: "The enemy have buried all their white men and left the negroes to melt in the sun. That shows how much they care for the poor ignorant creatures. After they are killed fighting their battles, having done all they can for the Federals then for them to let the bodies of the poor creatures lie and melt in their own blood and to be made the prey of both birds and beasts."

Turner's entry is a blazing criticism of the Union officers, illustrating the total disregard the Union officers had for the colored troops who'd given their lives for their country.

When the stench became unbearable, Colonel Shelby of the Thirty-Ninth Mississippi sent a message to Banks asking permission for his men to bury the dead. Reportedly Banks said there were no Union soldiers in that sector. Maybe he thought Shelby's message was a trick or maybe he was that heartless.[22]

Leon Frederic survived the assault at Port Hudson and was not among the wounded. What must he have thought that evening and the days to come as the rotting stench of his fellow Native Guards lay open to the elements? Did he still think his military service would move him and his race toward citizenship? Was he still betting on beating the odds?

Dearest Philomene,

That I live to pen you this letter is no small miracle. By now you know of Port Hudson. But do you know of the trap we were led into? I think the old Veteran my father looks out for me. I have sad news. Lt. John Crowder that I wrote to you of perished. His death and the treatment of his body have made me more determined to see this through. Pray for me.

Your loving husband,
Leon

The day after the battle at Port Hudson, Captain Lewis, who had failed to report the soldier for exposing himself to a woman, was arrested for cowardice—a small measure of justice.

Leon finished his three years of service and was never again listed on a muster roll as "Deserted."

Ike Edwards emails me Leon's service record. After the Battle at Port Hudson, he was stationed at Port Hudson until May 1864 when the First and Third Regiments were reassigned to Morganza, Louisiana, for the next eight months.

Because of the increased enlistment of black troops, the Bureau of Colored Troops created a new designation for the colored troops, United States Colored Troops (USCT) and renumbered the regiments. Leon's First Regiment was renamed the Seventy-Third Regiment.

In February 1865, the Seventy-Third Regiment is picked by Major General Edward R. S. Canby, who replaced General Banks as commander of the Department of the Gulf, to help capture the last rebel stronghold on the Gulf Coast—Mobile, Alabama, with its two fortified positions at Spanish Fort and Fort Blakely. The Seventy-Third is one of only two black regiments chosen from Morganza.[23]

In a scenario similar to the assault at Port Hudson, the Seventy-Third led the charge on Fort Blakely. Although this time, the ground was level but cut up by deep ravines. The men had spent a week before the charge doing what they'd become accustomed to doing, digging approaches to the Rebel position under the constant fire of the sharpshooters.

Within five hundred yards of the main line was a Rebel rifle pit. The Seventy-Third was able to reach the rifle pit and capture several Rebel soldiers before they could escape back to their own lines. As the Seventy-Third rushed toward the Rebel fortification under heavy fire from the fort, within minutes they captured seven pieces of artillery and some prisoners.

In the last casualties of the war, the Seventy-Third suffered three killed and twenty-four wounded. These would be the last casualties the regiment would suffer. April 9, 1865, the same day as the assault, General Lee surrendered to General Grant at Appomattox in Virginia.

In writing of the regiment's valor during the assault, Brigadier General William Anderson Pile said: "To the Seventy-Third US Colored Infantry belongs the honor of first planting their colors on the enemy parapet."[24]

Mustered out of the army in September 1865, the Seventy-Third celebrated their discharge with a welcome home parade down Conti Street with fife and drum. No longer a soldier Leon settled back into civilian life. But it was an uneasy transition.

On July 30, 1866, two years after the end of the Civil War, blacks still didn't have the right to vote. But the black veterans of the Louisiana

Native Guards who fought so valiantly during the war would not let go of their belief that their service entitled them to full citizenship. Although the Louisiana Constitutional Convention of 1864 had granted greater freedoms to blacks, the delegates didn't grant them the right to vote. In a backlash to the blacks' new freedoms, early in 1866 the Louisiana state legislature, consisting mostly of former Confederates, passed a series of restrictive laws amounting to legalized slavery. Blacks needed to find a strategy to gain the vote quickly. Delegates in favor of giving blacks the vote decided to reconvene the convention on July 30, 1866, at the Mechanics Institute in New Orleans.[25]

While the delegates met inside the hall, outside a procession of black men neared Canal Street about one-half block from the Mechanics Institute. The parading men were demanding their civil rights. Leading the procession were three drummers and a man with a fife carrying a tattered American flag. Many of the men were army veterans who like Leon Frederic had served three years in the army and believed that entitled them to the full rights of American citizens.[26] If Leon wasn't among the marching Union army veterans, he was well aware of what was happening that day.

On the corner of Common and Dryades streets, across from the Mechanics Institute, the procession was met by a group of armed white men. This group was composed of Democrats who opposed abolition, most of whom were ex-Confederates.

No one knows who fired the first shot. But within minutes there erupted a battle in the streets. Most of the black men were unarmed; some sought refuge inside the Mechanics Hall. The battle lasted two and a half hours. In the melee the police were joined by hundreds of white men and boys who chased down blacks wherever they could find them.[27] The police stormed the building and hunted blacks, shooting unarmed men huddled in corners with their hands in the air.[28] By the time the riot was over, approximately thirty-eight people had been killed and 148 wounded, most of them black. "At least one of the dead and nine of the wounded were veterans of the Native Guards."[29]

Similar riots in Memphis strengthened the determination of the Radical Republicans in Washington who captured control of the US Congress and subsequently passed a series of Reconstruction Acts in 1867, imposing federal military control over the ex-Confederate States. The Reconstruction Acts also gave black men the right to vote.[30]

But the victory would be short-lived. Within five years the whites regained control of Louisiana and by 1889 blacks would lose "all the political gains they had achieved, including the right to vote, when the state adopted a new constitution."[31]

"For the first time since the war, we've got the nigger where we want him," boasted a white New Orleanian in 1888.[32]

For Leon Frederic, who'd fought for the Union, the loss of the right to vote must have been a crushing blow. He'd taken a gamble on freedom through service to his country and lost.

From census records, it appears that he was adrift. Five years after the war, he's no longer plying his trade as a shoemaker. Historian Loren Schweinger points out that after the Civil War, Creoles of color in the Fourth, Fifth and Sixth wards, the heart of the free mulatto community, "experienced losses" or "lost everything," and this included the skilled craftsmen.[33]

In 1870 Leon works as a saloonkeeper, living in the Fifth Ward, and for the first time his race is listed as white. By the 1880 census he's a cigar maker, race Mulatto. The cigar-making trade was a typical trade for free men of color.[34] In the 1886 and 1892 city directory he's a grocer living on St. Philip Street, possibly working for his father-in-law, Bernard Lanabere, who owned a grocery store. Then in 1891 his wife Philomene dies.

Six years later he's arrested. The 1897 newspaper headline reads: "A Police Spurt to Catch Gamblers." Under the subhead—"French Market Gambling"—Leon Frederic's name appears.

"Last Saturday night two negro laborers Charles Brown and George Banks reported to Captain Walsh that they had been swindled out of about thirty dollars in a gambling game that was going on at the corner of St. Philip and Decatur streets. The captain, Corporal Driscoll and Officer J. Roach went to the place and arrested Leon Frederic, a collector, and Antonio Juan, a fish dealer, and locked them up on a charge of gambling. The negroes were also arrested and held as material witnesses."

Perhaps gambling was a lifelong vice for Leon who was first arrested for gambling in August 1878. The *Roadshow*'s genealogist's research notes confirm that the Leon Frederic who was arrested for gambling in 1878 and 1897 is our Leon Frederic.

Whether gambling was a lifelong problem for Leon or whether after the war he was damaged and broken like so many soldiers and turned to gambling as an outlet, it's impossible to know. Without question my mother would have viewed her war hero ancestor in a less than favorable light because of his gambling and arrests.

But what cheers me is that by the time of Leon's death in 1905, his life is back on track. He's working as a clerk, living at 2207 Ursuline Avenue, and designated colored. The last mention of his occupation of collector is in 1900. When a severe bout of bronchitis takes him, he's residing with his daughter Rita Philomene and her children.

His obituary in the *Times-Picayune* is as brief as his life was full.

16

The Vagaries of War
1941–1943

O<small>N</small> D<small>ECEMBER</small> 8, 1941, one day after Pearl Harbor, when the United States declared war on Japan, my father, Harold John Kalina, must have felt like the unluckiest man alive. On the advice of his father, Stephen Kalina, he enlisted in the National Guard on January 29, 1941. Though Congress had passed legislation the previous August to order the National Guard into active duty, it was for no more than twelve months and confined to the Western Hemisphere.

"It's just a year," his father assured him. "And you'll learn a trade."

The economy still hadn't fully recovered from the Great Depression despite Roosevelt's best efforts. A skilled trade not only would provide him with a viable income but also put him squarely in the Kalina family lineage of skilled workers. Since arriving in Cleveland, Ohio, in the late 1880s most of the Kalina men worked in one of the skilled trades from carpentry to welding.

Then the dominoes started to fall. In August 1941, by a narrow margin, Congress passed another legislation to extend the National Guard service from twelve to eighteen months and allowed for transport outside the Western Hemisphere.

By this time my father had been training at Camp Shelby, Mississippi, for eight months. He must have felt the noose tightening around his neck as his dream of one year and out was snatched away.

I imagine him writing home to his family putting a good spin on his extended enlistment that they saw right through.

Dear Folks,
By now you've heard the news. It's only three more months, and I'll be home.

Love, Hal

Whatever he said or didn't say in that letter prompted his younger brother Stephen to write a letter of his own to the *Cleveland Plain Dealer* expressing his frustration about the injustice of the extension. The letter is a snapshot of the country's sentiments just prior to our involvement in World War II, demonstrating that the scars from World War I still were not healed.

The letter is titled "Feels that Draft Extension is Mistake." Stephen quotes a silver-tongued orator, who I can only assume is Franklin Delano Roosevelt, who had assured the mothers and fathers of these young men currently in camps that there wouldn't be an extension of their service.

"Your boys are not going into war, they are going to a year's training and after twelve months will be home again and back at their jobs. I say it again and again, your boys are not going to be sent into any foreign wars."

Stephen ends his letter by recalling a similar situation that occurred at the beginning of the US's involvement in WWI. With bitterness, he says that the men in WWI called to serve their country had but twelve weeks training before they were shipped to France. He calls for the leaders of the country to be honest.

"Well, now, if we need these men for any other purpose than training. Why don't our leaders come out and tell . . . the boys and we will be better Americans and better soldiers." He points out that some of these men had high draft numbers and left good jobs to serve in the National Guard, trusting the government's pledge of one-year service.

In a surprising close to his letter, he asks the reader, "Have you any idea how these men feel today? Don't be surprised if we have civil war in some of these camps after January 1942."

On the precipice of war, before Americans knew the full extent of what lie ahead, from the perspective of my uncle, my father was getting a raw deal and had been lied to by his government. What comes through to me is my uncle's plea for honesty. Tell us why these men are in these camps. Tell us if they'll be sent into war as ill prepared as the men who served in WWI with eight or twelve weeks training.

I don't know the date of my uncle's letter that appeared in the newspaper. He probably wrote it shortly after my father's draft was extended. Did my father have a high draft number? He never said, and I never asked.

When my father related this story to me of bad luck or bad timing, the irony was still with him twenty years later. But he always added, as if afraid I wouldn't understand, the importance of duty to one's country. "I never regretted it, being in the war. It helped me mature."

After my dad's death, my mother asked me to go through his dresser drawers in his bedroom. By then my parents had been keeping separate bedrooms for decades.

When I found my Uncle Stephen's letter scotch taped in an old photo album, the yellowing tape its own comment on time and memory, I felt that old pang of sorrow I always felt when I thought about my dad and WWII. With a daughter's longing, I wished I'd known him before the war, if not destroyed him, then altered him drastically. I wished I'd known that dad, not the one who came home shell-shocked and suffering from bouts of malaria, determined to ease his pain with alcohol.

But if he hadn't been stationed at Camp Shelby, Mississippi, from January 31, 1941, to March 31, 1942, he would have never met my mother.

In my dad's photo album are a number of newspaper articles all connected to the war in some way. Though I can only guess *where* my parents met, one article reveals *when* they met. The article bears the poignantly awkward heading, "October Wedding Offsets Sadness Month Once Brought to Soldier."

"It was three years ago, in October, 1941, that I met Alvera in New Orleans," the sergeant said. "Before I went overseas the following April, we were engaged to be married."

The swiftness of their courtship (six months) still stuns me. When my parents became engaged, they barely knew each other. In what could only be described as facile optimism, the reporter states that my father's war experiences, as dire as they were, would be offset by his upcoming nuptials. "The ledger will be evened up on the side of happiness."

I'll never know with certainty where my father met my mother. Though two scenarios are possible. Each giving a historical glimpse into New Orleans during the war years and how the city accommodated the soldiers before they were shipped off to war.

While stationed at Camp Shelby, Mississippi, my father was given a plum assignment as a truck driver, which allowed him to make deliveries and transport men for R & R from Camp Shelby to New Orleans. He was in the Thirty-Second Division, Company E, 112th Engineers (Red Arrow Division), part of the engineer truck drivers who supplied canteen routinely in New Orleans in half-ton trucks. He was also part of the Red and Blue armies who participated in the "Louisiana Maneuvers," which were the largest war games held in the US. One of his duties was to set up tents at the Lake Pontchartrain area for the troops to billet in as temporary quarters.

He had set hours of work and could go into New Orleans, staying overnight as long as he returned by 8 a.m. to base camp. On one of these overnight jaunts into New Orleans, he could have met my mother.

New Orleans hosted a series of chaperoned dances for the troops arranged by various organizations such as the Council of Catholic Women, Young Women's Christian Association, St. Mark's Community Center, New Orleans Junior League, and Veterans of Foreign Wars. The organizations supplied the women for the dances.

A *Times-Picayune* article dated July 5, 1941, and titled, "5127 Soldiers Storm City in 3-Day July 4th Holiday" describes the arrival of the soldiers. "Military convoys, composed of about fifty motor vehicles each, started arriving at the army recreation center at the lake near Elysian Fields Avenue . . . until a total of approximately six hundred vehicles had been parked." Without question my father had driven one of those vehicles into the city.

The pre-war festivities sparked with innocence, hospitality, and humor. A shrimp and crab boil was held in the City Park Stadium for a thousand soldiers. "This will be a new experience for many of the men and a number of chaperones will be on hand to show the soldiers how to 'operate' on the seafood."

The day ended with a dance at 9:30 p.m. at the Jung Hotel for fifteen hundred soldiers with partners furnished by an inter-organization volunteer committee. Was my mother at this dance? If she was, she didn't meet my dad that evening.

All I know about their meeting is my father was too shy to approach my mother and sent his army buddy over as his emissary. Or was their meeting more casual, less orchestrated by a city accommodating the large numbers of soldiers soon to be shipped off to war?

The other possible scenario is they met at the Meal-a-Minit at 1717 Canal Street, where my mother was a hostess. The restaurant's name was purposely misspelled to make it quicker to read, just as Joseph Gruber's meals were served quickly. Gruber advertised in large print Seating for 1,000, and at the bottom of the sign in small print was the catch phrase TEN AT A TIME.[1] As Ula explained to me, at this time my mother was working as white and was transitioning into her white identity.

Over the six months of their courtship my mother learned of my father's tightly knit family on the west side of Cleveland, his two sisters, and one brother, and the extended family all clustered together in their Eastern-European neighborhood. The promise of family stability that my father represented must have been alluring to my mother.

There's an autumnal photo of them at Camp Shelby dated 1941. I can tell by their clothes—my father in full dress Army uniform, his cap sitting jauntily on his head; my mother wearing a plaid suit and a white open-collared blouse—that an occasion has brought them together this day. They stand at the junction of two tents, in the background a tall fir tree as delicate as the moment. Already my father wears the red arrow insignia of his unit.

In all the years to follow, in all the years I'll witness them together, I'll never see my mother stand so softly beside him, so shyly, both so hesitant with feeling, a moment gentle with promise, never to return.

Everything worked against my father from start to finish. In April 1942, his unit—the Thirty-Second Division, Company A, 114th Engineers— was ordered to go to Camp Edwards in Massachusetts, where they were to be trained for combat in Europe. Later in the year, they were scheduled to participate in Operation Torch in North Africa.

Those orders were altered when the Australians alerted the United States that the Japanese were attacking New Guinea and nearing the Northern Coast of Australia. Australia only had militia defending their homeland. The bulk of the Australian troops were fighting in North Africa. Fearing the Japanese would invade Australia, the Australian government appealed to the United States for troops. General McArthur decided that the Thirty-Second Division would be sent to New Guinea even though they were not prepared to go to there.

As his brother Stephen feared, the men of the Thirty-Second Division were ill prepared for war in the South Pacific. The soldiers lacked proper equipment and uniforms, were not trained in jungle warfare, and knew little about Japanese fighting techniques. At the time, the United States had the sixteenth largest army in the world. Italy had a much larger army. The United States had no air force, outdated weapons, very little artillery, and few tanks. Because my father's division was originally slated for Europe, they shipped out from San Francisco with winter clothing. They would be the first troops to make contact with the Japanese and would suffer the consequences.

In September 1942, my father's unit was flown from Amberly Field in Brisbane, Australia, to Port Moresby, Papua New Guinea, then from Port Moresby over the Owen Stanley Mountains to the village of Buna where they were to attack the Japanese who were entrenched there. The plane never made it to Buna.

In the *Plain Dealer* article, my father described the crash: "The crash was in the Owen Stanley Mountain Range. Part of our wing was clipped off. We got out and started toward Buna. When we reached a point thirty miles from Buna, we boarded a ship, which Jap dive-bombers promptly sank two hundred yards from the coast. One-quarter of the men exhausted by fever and marching drowned."

What he neglected to mention is the arduousness of that march out of the mountains. Even when I pushed him for details, all he would say was, "We walked twenty days, and got supplied by air drop every third day."

Other veterans' accounts of that twenty-day hike out of the mountains are more forthcoming, calling the experience "a living, wide-awake nightmare," from the unrelenting rains to the eerie ghost forests to the waist-deep channels of mud.

Tropical diseases flourished among the men, including malaria, dengue fever, dysentery, athlete's foot, and ringworm.

When my father's unit reached Buna, they were in poor physical shape. The battle of Buna began in earnest in November. American Historian Stephen Ambrose described the Allies condition as "hollow-eyed with jungle fever and hunger."[2] Casualties were severe. The Buna campaign was an army show and didn't get as much notice as Guadal-canal, but the fighting was every bit as savage, and the cost in dead and wounded was even higher.

During the Papuan campaign my father would build bridges under Japanese fire, watch a friend get shot in the head sitting beside him, be wounded by shrapnel, almost lose vision in his right eye, and contract malaria and jungle rot.

"I made friends," he explained. "But not too close, since they may get killed quickly. I was not afraid to die. If it happened, it happened. Those who were afraid to die became too careful and made mistakes." He paused and added humorously, "When your number's up, it's up. There's nothing you can do about it."

The Army would be victorious in the battle of Buna, which lasted from November 16, 1942, until January 22, 1943. Allied losses in the battle were at a rate higher than that experienced at Guadalcanal. Overall, about sixty thousand Americans fought on Guadalcanal, suffering 5,845 casualties, including sixteen hundred killed in action. On Papua, more than thirty-three thousand Americans and Austral-ians fought, and they suffered 8,546 casualties, of whom 3,095 were killed.[3]

US Army Lt. General Robert Eichelberger in his memoir, *Our Jungle Road to Tokyo*, written in 1950, stresses the losses suffered in the battle of Buna, "Buna was . . . bought at a substantial price in death, wounds, disease, despair, and human suffering. No one who fought there, how-ever hard he tries, will ever forget it. Fatalities," he concludes, "closely approach, percentage-wise, the heaviest losses in our Civil War bat-tles." He also commented, "I am a reasonably unimaginative man, but Buna is still to me, in retrospect, a nightmare. This long after, I can still remember every day and most of the nights."

My father was awarded a Presidential Citation for action against the enemy in Papua New Guinea. He won another Presidential Citation for putting up a bridge under Japanese fire during the fall of 1942, as well as a Silver Star. His effort nearly cost him his sight in his right eye.

While my father was fighting the Japanese in New Guinea, my mother was in training as a cadet in the Women's Army Corps (WACS). On November 9, 1942, in a flourish of patriotic fervor, she enlisted in the WACS, which had been newly created in July 1942. On her enlistment record she is an Aviation Cadet and her race is listed as white. Her term of enlistment is for the duration of the war or other emergency, plus six months. She lasted a few months, injuring her back lifting a heavy pot during kitchen patrol duty. That back injury would dog her off and on for the rest of her life.

Medically discharged from the WACS, she was once again back in New Orleans living with her cousin Theresa and her great-grandmother Mary Williams. All her patriotic dreams of serving her country were shattered.

In February 1943, a letter from my father offered her another option that would allow her to escape New Orleans.

"Why don't you live with my folks in Cleveland until we get married," my father wrote her. "It's a big house with lots of room. You could share a bedroom with my sister Delores. She's a good kid. You'll like her."

What did she have to lose? My mother accepted his offer. She'd already decided that once married she would live in Cleveland.

On her train journey north, whatever trepidation she felt must have been outweighed by the excitement of the road. Every mile moved her further and further away from her community where her identity was known and moved her closer and closer to a new place where her identity could be re-created.

Gazing out the window watching the landscape change as the train chugged north through Mississippi, Tennessee, Indiana, and Illinois did she feel changes inside her? Were there moments when she questioned her deception and vowed to tell my father the truth when he returned from the war? Or had she convinced herself that her mixed race didn't matter? When clearly it did.

Like her stint in the WACS, her time with my father's family only lasted a month or two. Insular, tribal, and entrenched in working class mores, my father's family must have viewed my mother with suspicion and alarm. Her independence threatened their notions of female subservience.

To them she was as exotic and perplexing as a tropical flower. A flower they couldn't name, had never seen before, with her curly, lush black hair, olive skin, and eyes as black as ink drops. Her Southern accent made them uncomfortable, putting them on edge.

And then there was my father's mother, Mamie Kalina, a woman who ran roughshod over her passive husband. She was a hellion of a woman, with blazing strawberry blond hair and a stout, determined frame. My mother had met her match.

"They kept telling me what to do, where I could go, when I should be home. I wasn't used to that. They treated me like a child. I felt like a prisoner. I couldn't even go see a movie," my mother complained to me. "They treated Delores like a servant."

My father's younger sister, Delores, obeyed their rules even though she was of age. My mother bristled under such parental restrictions, as foreign to her as another language. Her life mantra had always been "No one tells me what to do."

And yet, she was uncertain how to handle the tightly knit Kalina clan. Uncharacteristically, she called her mother in New Orleans who told her to come home.

When my mother threatened to leave, Mamie said, "If you leave here, you leave that engagement ring. That's what Harold would want." It was Mamie's way or the highway.

My mother left her engagement ring and headed home to New Orleans. All her hopes of finding a stable family dashed. Restless and depressed by her broken engagement, she resumed her job as a hostess at the Meal-A-Minit restaurant on Canal Street. Once again working as white.

Though her foray in the North under the scrutiny of my father's white family had bolstered her confidence in passing for white, the specter of discovery in a place where she was known as a mixed-race woman must have continued to cause her distress.

No longer engaged, she began dating again. But she saw no opportunities for herself in New Orleans. When Margaret, the cashier at the restaurant, invited her to accompany her to California, my mother didn't hesitate. California offered her the kind of anonymity that she'd been seeking.

She would be part of the Second Great Migration, an influx of African Americans from the South to the North and California beginning in 1940. Though to most outside observers, she was a well-dressed Southern white woman pursuing her California dream.

17

California Dreaming
1943–1944

E VEN DURING THE war years California must have seemed like a place of dreams, especially to my mother who was seeking economic opportunities and racial anonymity. California benefited from the wartime economy. The coast became the primary focus of military-industrial production. "During the war years the federal government spent a total of $35 billion in California—one-tenth of the total amount spent on all domestic wartime projects."[1] With the wartime economy booming in California, millions of Americans sought better and more prosperous lives. My mother was one of them.

It was commonly known in the Creole community in which she lived that California was the "promised land." Porters and train workers told of this place where jobs were plentiful, and if you were white enough, you could easily pass.[2]

In late 1943, she and Margaret took the Sunset Limited train from New Orleans to Los Angeles, California, a two-thousand-mile journey. As she boarded the train did she feel a twinge of unease when the black porter asked if he could take her luggage and then escorted her to the cars reserved for whites?

The dark, olive-green train with the black roof passed through Texas, Arizona, the Mexican border, and California. As the train chugged west, even the heat and grit blowing in from the open windows added to her adventure of crossing from one place to another.

Toward the end of her life, she talked about her train trip and her time in California, sometimes wistfully, sometimes with regret, a lost opportunity she would never admit to losing. But that train trip remained a vivid memory for her.

"It wasn't air conditioned and it was so hot we left the windows open. Dust and dirt covered everything."

I listened quietly, watching the play of emotions on her face, disgust at the heat and dirt, and excitement at the unknown that awaited her in California.

When I asked her about why she went to California in 1943, she insisted that she'd gone there to meet my father who would land in California when he was discharged from the army. There are so many holes in her story.

It's difficult to know when my parents reconciled. But I doubt that it was prior to her leaving for California in 1943. Even if they were reconciled, my father wasn't due to be discharge until December 1944. Nor was it likely he would land in California.

No matter how many times I questioned her about why she traveled to California, she stuck to her story. Looking back now, I realize she was hiding her real reason for going to California, one she couldn't tell me without revealing her racial identity.

In my mother's life, it's almost impossible to untangle dysfunction and race, truth and untruth. In crossing over to the white side, my mother took to the road, which has traditionally been a way to pass. The road offers freedom from discovery. Everyone you meet is a stranger, who doesn't know you or your family.

In the physical distance that my mother put between New Orleans and Los Angeles, she created a space where she could re-create herself, a place where she could create a new identity, a white identity.[3]

❖

My mother kept a secret photograph album of her time in Los Angeles. The album was sequestered from my father and given to me in trust prior to her moving out of her house and moving in with my brother and his family.

"I want you to keep this for me," she instructed, handing me the fifteen-by-twelve tattered album, which was rubber-banded and wrapped in a Sears plastic bag.

I was honored. This album had special significance for her. She didn't want it lost in the melee of moving or stored in a basement, forgotten and moldering in dampness.

"Promise me you'll keep it safe," she said.

By that time I'd proven myself a tacit torchbearer of her family history. The album would not only be kept safe with me but also cherished. She didn't say so, but I believe she was also giving me another piece of her mysterious puzzle, a glimpse into the past she'd kept hidden from my father. She was eighty-nine years old and showing signs of dementia and failing health. She understood that her time was limited and I'd soon be free of my vow.

The album first appeared when we visited her after my father's death. I never knew of its existence. When she produced the album, it unleashed a plethora of stories, all centered on California. Slowly leafing through the black felt-like pages with the white lettering and the photographs held in place with four black corners, she was finally able to share with us the life she created in California before she married my father.

The black-and-white photographs are revelatory of her transformation from a mixed-race identity to a white identity. In every group photo every person is visibly white. No family members visited her in California.

During her eight-month sojourn in California, she rented a room in a boarding house in Los Angeles run by Mrs. Jackson. It must have been a commodious house because in the photo titled "Jackson Household Picnic," I count ten adults and one child. Under the photo's title my mother printed: "A swell bunch of people." Her childhood in her great-grandmother's boarding house must have prepared her for sharing quarters with strangers. She was adept at courteous distance.

In the picnic photos, besides my mother, one other woman stands out from the other boarders. My mother identified the woman as Doris. In one photo Doris poses in the foreground clad in a halter-top and shorts, meant to show off her slim figure. The other lodgers are lined up after her. In three short years, Doris Jensen from Nebraska will star in the film *Kiss of Death* opposite Victor Mature. It will be her breakout role. By then her name will be Coleen Gray and she'll go on to star in a string of film noirs in the late 1940s into the 1950s.

Thinking Coleen Gray might remember my mother and cast light on her time in Mrs. Jackson's boarding house, I write her a letter after the *Roadshow* airs and enclose a copy of her in her picnic attire, hoping the photo jogs her memory. She doesn't respond. She must have been ill because a few months later in August 2015, she passes away at the age of ninety-two. And I'm left with only the photographs to tell my mother's California story.

The theatricality of the LA photographs attest to the masquerade my mother was creating. Only Coleen Gray outdoes my mother in projecting a memorable image, her shoulders back, her chest forward, making sure she's prominently seen.

In many of the photos my mother sports her signature white flowers in her carefully styled dark hair. In every single photo one foot is slightly lifted as if she's imitating a fashion model. Had she seen that pose in a fashion magazine? All the other women look ordinary in comparison, except Coleen Gray. What better place than Tinseltown for her to try out another persona, a place where the line between real and unreal was blurry if not nonexistent?

Besides the soon-to-be famous Coleen Gray, other show business people rented rooms from Mrs. Jackson—a nameless Disney animator and Horace, a film studio stuntman. My mother couldn't remember Horace's last name or the name of the Disney animator.

Horace seemed to have taken a personal interest in my mother: not only did he take her on location during the filming of a war movie but he arranged a screen test for her. She didn't seem all that upset when she related how she'd missed the phone call for the screen test. Her one shot at movie fame gone. She claimed she was too shy to be a movie actress.

But I think she realized that under the glare of a camera she would be seen for who she was. At that time period, women of color roles went to the Italian-looking starlets. Was she fearful that someone back home would see her in a movie and recognize her? "Isn't that Alvera Frederic? You know she's mixed."

The souvenir photographs of her and her dates, all soldiers and all white, taken at Los Angeles nightclubs attest to the white identity she was forging in California. In the 1944 Zamboanga nightclub photo, Eugene Landon has his arm around my mother and she leans into him. A postcard she saved from the Zamboanga South Sea Nite Club describes the Polynesian nightclub as a rendezvous of Hollywood stars and celebrities, as well as the home of the tail-less monkeys.

In the other souvenir photograph, from the Hollywood Palladium, my mother leans back against Mark J. O'Connell, who writes above his photo: "Please, I'm not drunk!" Though he does look drunk. Across the table from Mark and my mother are Eugene Landon and Corrine Jordan. Apparently there was nothing serious between my mother and Eugene. But if these August 1944 photographs are any indication, my parents still hadn't reconciled.

To the delight of my children she told us about the midnight California beach party where she met Lloyd Bridges before he became famous, starring in the TV series *Sea Hunt* that launched his acting career.

"Lloyd Bridges could have been your father," my children teased me. Were we all uncomfortable with this mother and grandmother who bore no resemblance to the one we knew?

An undertone to all these stories and all her dates and adventures in California is a kind of boastful pride: "See, what I got away with. No one knew. Not even the boarders at Mrs. Jackson's boarding house. I fooled a lot of people."

Of all her stories of that time period, there was one that had particular poignancy and made me question my mother's commitment to my father. The soldier's name was Michael, whose last name she could never remember but whose words she could never forget.

From Chicago, Michael was dark-haired and swarthy, the kind of looks my mother gravitated toward. Probably he reminded her of the men from her neighborhood who she'd grown up with, the ones she determined never to marry. Though Michael was Italian not mixed race.

After her broken engagement and before leaving for California, she met Michael in New Orleans.

"We'd have these discussions about God. He said he didn't believe in God. I told him I'd pray for him," was how she explained their relationship, philosophical and deep.

When he was shipped overseas, they continued corresponding even after she was living in Los Angeles. He was stationed in England and from there he was to be shipped to Normandy, France, to fight in the D-day invasion on June 6, 1944.

In his last letter to her he told her he was motorcycling around England enjoying the sights. He ended the letter saying, "I was in a room full of people and I was lonely without you."

Michael died before the invasion. A few days before being sent to France, he was killed in a motorcycle accident in England.

My mother received a telegram informing her of his death.

"When I got the telegram I fell to the floor and wept."

By September my parents were engaged again, their wedding scheduled for October 25, 1944.

❖

Toward the end of my mother's life, she talked about Michael with such yearning as if his death had robbed her of happiness, as if she wished he'd lived so she could have married him instead of my father. Would her life have turned out differently if she had married Michael from Chicago? I doubt it. As I knew too well, it was impossible for her to fully reveal who she was. And Michael, like my father, would always have sensed something being held back, some part of her that she would not share. But she had a way of denying what she did not want to see, a way of living in the fantasy she created and re-created every day. Sometimes I envied her ability to live in a world of denial.

After my father's death, I visited her and we went for a walk around the suburban neighborhood where I grew up. It was a late summer day when the afternoon light seemed to hold its breath, making everything look better than it was. Even the patches of lawn appeared misty with light.

We set off from the green house weaving our way through the middle-class streets, the tract houses, and the older homes. As we walked past John Muir Elementary School where I used to play as a child, my mother said, apropos of nothing, "No man will ever love me again."

She was newly widowed, still struggling with losing her husband of fifty-two years. Though she admitted to me that since my father's death she no longer felt depressed. That his death had freed her from the weight of his anger usually directed at her. I still knew she missed him if only the habit of his presence.

I kept walking, keeping pace with her fast stride. Taken aback by her brutal honesty, her regretfulness and loss, I said nothing.

An immense sadness welled up inside of me as I turned to look at her as if I needed to verify the truth of her words. Would no man ever love her again?

She still wore her hair as she did in the 1960s—teased and sprayed into a dark halo around her head. Her eyebrows had thinned and were penciled in. Her beige slacks were shapeless with an elastic waistband that pouched out her stomach. She'd given way to comfort foregoing vanity. Even her shoes were white Keds so pristine in their whiteness as if she'd just taken them from their box.

But most striking was her face—the softening of her skin that teetered on the brink of sagging. For all her creams and face exercises she was visibly aging. Yet, her gait was vigorous and quick, as she'd shared with me an intimacy I didn't think her capable of. For those few moments walking the old neighborhood, she'd let me see a sliver of her real self.

For a woman who'd prided herself on her beauty, who used her beauty to her advantage, was she mourning her loss of romantic love or was she mourning what she traded for that love?

18

Antebellum Love and Sex
The Cabinetmaker and the French Grocer

Kenyatta brings up on the screen Leon Frederic and his wife Philomene Lanabere Frederic. She explains that Philomene's father was Bernard Lanabere who was born in France. So my mother didn't lie. We are French. In the nest of half-truths and deceptions, she told the truth about her French heritage.

Then she brings up another screen that sends a quiver of excitement up my spine. Ursin Frederic, born in New Orleans, 1790; his wife/consort, Roxelane Arnoux, born in 1808 in Santiago de Cuba. Ursin and Roxelane are Leon Frederic's parents.

In the whirlwind of the moment with the cameras running, the low buzz in the Grand Hall, and my family surrounding me, it hits me: the Frederics have been in this country since 1790. My mother's family has deep roots in Louisiana. Ursin Frederic, born 1790.

I wait for the next revelation, Ursin's parents. But it never comes. It will be up to me to find his parents. My search will prove to be more difficult and astonishing than I could have anticipated, elucidating the complex story of race in America.

My hunt for Ursin Frederic begins with the baptismal records of the Archdiocese of New Orleans Office of Archives and Records. But the archives turn out to be the first of many stumbling blocks in finding Ursin Frederic and his parents. There's no record of Ursin Frederic in the baptismal records for 1784–1795. The researcher/archivist, Jack Belsom, who I'll become friendly with over the next six months, writes: "The early records of the Archdiocese show references to the Frederic family in St. Charles Parish, on the so-called "German Coast." Then he adds that the baptismal records were destroyed in a fire in the nineteenth century.

I puzzled over the German Coast Frederics. Who were they? Are we related to them? If so, could my mother have gotten it wrong? Were the Frederics German and not French?

Ancestry.com offers no link between the German Coast Frederics and Ursin. I'm at an impasse and realize that I have two choices: go to Baton Rouge where the archives are stored or hire an onsite genealogist.

I reach out to Rich Venezia, the *Roadshow*'s genealogist who did our family research. Rich and I have kept in contact since the taping of the show. He's an affable and generous man who once was an aspiring actor. I've written a testimonial for his website, Rich Roots, lauding his research skills. He suggests several genealogists, one of whom is Judy Riffel, a Baton Rouge genealogist who specializes in Louisiana records and research. She's also done genealogical and historical research for numerous television shows including *Genealogy Roadshow*. She is the perfect fit for my research project. For the next four months she and I will travel a genealogical road together full of bumps and turns and surprises, emailing and talking on the phone. Though she makes many amazing genealogical discoveries about the Frederic family line, one discovery eludes her: Ursin's parentage.

The first surprise concerning Ursin comes from the War of 1812 pension applications at the Louisiana State Archives. Roxelane Arnoux, Ursin's consort, applied for a pension as Ursin Frederic's widow. Judy reconfirms that Ursin Frederic is my third great-grandfather and that Roxelane Arnoux is my third great-grandmother.

Ursin was a private in the company of Captain Saint Gems, Colonel de la Ronde's regiment, under the command of General J. B. Plauche. From Powell Casey's book, *Louisiana in the War of 1812,* Judy pinpoints that Colonel P. Denis de la Ronde of Plaquemines Parish commanded the third regiment of the General Militia of uniformed men.

"In light of this," she writes, "I believe Ursin Frederic was most likely a white man."

Her conclusion destroys the narrative I've begun to construct about Ursin and Roxelane, as both being free people of color. I stare at her revelation experiencing in reverse my initial surprise at discovering that Azemar Frederic was mixed race.

In a follow-up email, I ask for clarification of her belief. Her answer is clear. "The regiments in the General Militia on the list I sent you were white. The free men of color were organized in separate battalions. I checked those and none of them matched the description Roxelane Arnoux gave for Ursin's service. The Third Regiment under P. de la Ronde was the closest match."

If Ursin Frederic was indeed a white man, as it appears he was, then that explains why he never married Roxelane Arnoux, making her his consort. At that time, marriage between whites and free people of color was illegal in Louisiana. Although Ursin and Roxelane never married, they have four children together: John Frederick born 1829, Rosa Frederick born 1834, Gustave Leon Frederick born 1836 (my second great-grandfather), and Hermina Frederick born 1843.

I examine more closely Roxelane's legal application for a widow's pension and receive another jolt. Near the end of the document, the clerk notes: "Personally appeared before me Bernard Lanabere and Simon Picolle, which are creditable persons." The document states that these two men attest to Roxelane Arnoux being the widow of Ursin Frederic.

Bernard Lanabere (my third great-grandfather) is the father of Leon Frederic's wife Philomene Lanabere Frederic. Bernard, like Ursin, is another white man in my mother's paternal family tree who had children with women of color. Their stories converge and merge, demonstrating the closeness of the family's two branches.

"Papa, you have to help Leon's mother obtain her widow's pension," Philomene must have pleaded. "You have standing in this community and you are a white man. The court will listen to you."

That April day in 1873 Bernard Lanabere, a white man, appeared in court before the clerk of the Supreme Court in New Orleans and attested that Roxelane Arnoux, a free woman of color, was the widow of Ursin Frederic. The term widow throws me. How can Roxelane be a widow if she and Ursin were never married? Clearly, the clerk who approved her right to receive Ursin's pension accepted Roxelane as his widow.

Whatever the definition of Roxelane's cohabitation with Ursin Frederic was, the Frederic lineage of free people of color can be traced back to the union of Ursin Frederic and Roxelane Arnoux. Their story is embedded in Louisiana's history of sexual relationships and racial blending during the early American and antebellum years. Their interracial union, like so many others of the time, contributed to Louisiana's three-tier caste system: white, free person of color, and slave.

When Roxelane Arnoux applied for a widow's pension, she was acknowledging her place in that caste system as a free woman of color and relying on the status that accompanied her place. Inherent in that caste system, as races blended over time, was the light skin and European features that would be the outcome of some of these relationships, creating people like my mother who could pass for white if they desired to cross over the color line and rejoin their white ancestors, breaching the racial barriers that Louisiana and other Southern states chiseled into law.

Armed with the knowledge that Ursin was a white man and using New Orleans city directories and the 1798 census of Faubourg Sainte-Marie,

Judy fleshes out Ursin's life, compiling evidence that he may have descended from the German Coast Frederics, as Jack Belsom suggested.

The German Coast Frederics were one of the first families of Louisiana. In the early 1720s, about eighty years before Louisiana became a part of the United States, Johann Conrad Friederich, his wife Ursula Freyen, and their three children immigrated to Louisiana's German Coast, most likely lured there by the Company of the Indies who brought Rhenish, Palantine, Alsatian, and Swiss German expert farmers to feed the starving, fledgling French colony. They settled on the right bank of the Mississippi River in the German village of Hoffen, ten leagues above New Orleans. Conrad was from Rothenberg, Germany, and was Catholic. The German Coast was one of the earliest settled areas of the Louisiana territory.

At the time of the 1724 census, Conrad was fifty years old, had a wife, Ursula Freyen, and three children. Sebastian, the youngest, was five years old (born 1719). The census describes Conrad as "a good worker."[1]

The Friederich name throws me until I talk to Jack Belsom who explains that French officials often "frenchified" German surnames. An amusing anecdote explains the changing of the German surname Zweig. In the marriage contract between Jean Zweig and Susanna Marchand, the French notary changed Zweig to Labranche. Probably the French notary found the German surname difficult to pronounce and write and asked what the name meant. The marriage contract noted that Jean Zweig wasn't able to write. When Zweig told the notary that Zweig meant *branch*, the notary wrote Labranche as his surname. And the name Labranche was never changed back to Zweig.

In my search for German Coast Frederics, I find another Friederich listed in the 1724 census, Mathias from Wingersheim, Alsace. It's unclear what the familial relationship is between Conrad and Mathias or whether there is one or if Ursin is descended from either line.

According to Richard Stringfield's book, *Le Pays de Fleurs Oranges*, in 1750, Jean Adam Frederic, Johann Conrad Friederich's grandson and possibly Ursin's grandfather, left the German Coast at the age of

ten and went to live in Plaquemines Parish.[2] Whether Jean Adam was
sent away to learn a trade or was a recalcitrant boy, ten seems a young
age for a child to leave his parental home, suggesting the strictures of
the time when children often died young and were expected to grow
up fast to assume adult responsibilities. Even portraits of children of
the period show them dressed in adult style clothing as if they skipped
childhood altogether.

Jean Adam Frederic married Genevieve Millet, whose parents emigrated from France to Louisiana prior to 1745. When the hurricane of
August 18, 1793, hit the area, Jean Adam and the extended Frederic
family, numbering forty-one people, sustained significant losses. Crop
losses included rice, corn, indigo, and oranges. Livestock such as sheep,
chickens, turkey, and pigs were also lost in the devastating hurricane.

Spanish archival documents show that a collection was taken up
in New Orleans for the family's benefit. The documents refer to the
Adam (Frederic) family as unfortunate, describing their circumstances
as "reduced to the utmost distress having lost everything in the hurricane." The direness of their loss is evident in two charitable gifts: various types of fabric from Mr. Lisle Sarpy and seven red coats from Mr.
Colin L'Anve. The hurricane had literally taken the clothes off their
backs. The hurricane was a turning point for many of the extended
Adam Frederic family. Some of the family decided to leave Plaquemines Parish and try their fortunes in New Orleans.

In the 1798 census Jean Adam Frederic (age fifty-eight) is living in
the Faubourg Sainte-Marie. In that same census, a Jean Frederic, carpenter, is living just two households away from Jean Adam Frederic at
the corner of St. Philip and Rampart. Considering their proximity of
residences, ages and same last name, it's possible Jean Fredric is Jean
Adam's son. But is Jean Frederic Ursin's father?

Adding to the evidence that Ursin is related to the German Coast
Frederics, in the 1811 city directory there is a J. L. Frederick residing at
the corner of St. Philip and Rampart, the same address that Ursin will
reside at in 1822. Most likely J. L. Frederick is Jean Frederic who lived

two households away from Jean Adam Frederic in 1798. The 1822 city directory lists Ursin as a cabinetmaker. Perhaps he learned the trade of cabinet making from Jean Frederic, carpenter, who may have been his father. That the building at the corner of Rampart and St. Philip was a carpenter's shop is supported by an 1828 advertisement for the sale of several lots at auction, one of which is between Rampart and Phillippa Street, where the carpenter's shop was lately burnt.

But neither Judy nor I can find any direct link between Ursin and the German Coast Frederics through legal documentation.

Even the verifiable fact that Ursin—who was living in New Orleans at the time of the Battle of New Orleans—chose to enlist as a private in the third regiment of the Louisiana militia, all of whom were from Plaquemines Parish where Adam Frederic had resided, is circumstantial evidence at best. His decision could reflect his desire to fight with his friends and family from the parish where he might have grown up. Or it could not.

Judy and I both come to the conclusion that Ursin may have been illegitimate and was never acknowledged by his white father, thus explaining our inability to find a birth or baptismal record for Ursin.

"Is there nothing else we can do to find his parents?" I email Judy.

Judy suggests I search the Historical Notaries Indexes, by Notary, which are available online. She cautions, "This is a very slow and time-consuming undertaking, but it might be worth it."

To hire Judy to search the Notarial Archives would be quite costly.

I groan aloud when I click on the site and view the full page of notarial archives for the Parish of Orleans. Each notary has volumes and volumes of records, beginning in 1739. But the notary archives are my last hope to find Ursin Frederic's parents. Among other transactions, notaries recorded inheritances. If Ursin was left an inheritance from his father, then I would know who his father was. It's a long shot. But I have one clue that might make the task easier. Narcisse Broutin was the notary of record for the sale of the lot in 1822 where Ursin had his cabinet making shop.

Overwhelmed with the amount of research I still have to do for the book, I sheepishly ask my husband Jerry, who is a retired dentist, if he would search through the archives.

He agrees, reluctantly and with provisions. "An hour a day at the most. And not every day."

Other discoveries give me a glimpse into Ursin's life and the period in which he lived. As unexpected as the possibility that the Frederics may have been of German descent and that they came to the Louisiana Territory in the early 1720s, what wasn't unexpected was that they owned slaves. Once I learned how early the family came to the Louisiana Territory, I anticipated finding slave owners in the family tree. They were farmers who owned plantations. I would have been more surprised if they hadn't owned slaves.[3]

There is solid documentation that not only did white Europeans own slaves but also free people of color were slave owners, indicating that free people of color did not identify with Africans, even though African blood was mixed with their European blood. Their free status and the three-tier caste system allowed them to identity more with Southern whites than African slaves even though as free people they did not enjoy all the privileges of whites. Their psychological profile of identifying with their oppressors is not surprising and all too familiar.

Ursin also owned slaves. There's a record of him selling a slave named Saturin, age thirteen, to Joseph Lenoir in 1814. He also had a slave named Elizabeth Frederique who died in 1835 at the age of eighteen and is buried in the same cemetery as Ursin Frederic, St. Louis No. Two. The name Frederique suggests the relationship between Elizabeth and Ursin might have been more intimate than slave and master. Was she the daughter of a sexual dalliance with one of his slaves or was she his consort? Either scenario is feasible and neither one is palatable.

In January of 1822, before Ursin cohabitates with Roxelane Arnoux, he has a daughter, Marie Armande Frederic, with Marie Polline, a quarterone (a person whose one parent was white and the other mulatto). Marie Armande's baptismal record names Marie Polline as her mother and Ursin Frederic as the child's natural father, indicating that the parents weren't married. The baptism is recorded in the register for baptisms of free people of color. Traditionally mixed-race children took on the race of the mother and were treated accordingly.

Marie Armande's godparents offer clues not only to the importance of the role of godparents but also the fictive kinship interrelationship between the mother and the godmother. Often parents sought godparents of equal or higher status in order to gain privileges for their child.[4] This was the case with Marie Armande's godparents: Jean Marie Armand and Seraphine Andry. Both godparents were white and Seraphine was from a prominent New Orleans family. After a cursory online search of Seraphine Andry, I discover in the Louisiana Digital Library that Seraphine Andry petitioned in 1829 to free three of her slaves: Marie Pauline, Marie Amanda, and Marie Louise Victorire. This is seven years after the birth of Marie Armande.

I ask Judy Riffel if she thinks Marie Pauline could have been the Marie Polline listed on Marie Armande Frederic's baptismal record. After all, the names are very similar: Marie Pauline/Marie Polline. The birth date of the freed slave child Marie Amanda is 1822, the same birth date of Marie Armande Frederic, and their names are nearly identical.

Her answer confirms my hunch. "I'd say that's a pretty good match."

When Marie Armande Frederic's certificate of baptism arrives from the Archdiocese of New Orleans Archives, there's a note from Jack: "Seraphine Andry recognizes the child as free." By selecting her mistress as godparent, Marie Pauline/Polline obtained freedom for her child and eventually herself.

My imagination spins wildly and the fiction writer emerges creating scenarios concerning how Ursin became sexually entangled with Marie Polline, the "quarterone" slave of Seraphine Andry. Their relationship wasn't a *plaçage* arrangement since Marie Polline wasn't a free woman at the time of her daughter's birth. Did the wealthy Seraphine Andry send Marie Pauline to Ursin's carpentry shop on a personal errand and they were drawn to each other? Did Ursin suggest assignations? Did Marie Pauline see a relationship with Ursin as a path to freedom for subsequent children and possibly herself? I'll never know.

But none of this information gets me any closer to learning who Ursin's parents were. My husband has begun scrolling through the notarial archives but its very slow work. He complains that some of the entries are illegible, names are spelled phonetically or misspelled, and then there's just the overwhelming volume of entries.

In desperation, thinking I might be able to save him this laborious task, I call the Cemetery Department of the Archdiocese of New Orleans and ask for Ursin's internment record, thinking his parents or siblings might be interred with him. But I come up blank.

Adding to my confusion and uncertainty about Ursin's parentage, Jack Belsom phones me with what he considers a breakthrough in finding Ursin's parents.

"Are you sitting down?" Jack Belsom teases me.

Holding the phone, I hurry up the stairs to my home office, close the door, and grab a pad of paper before sitting. I can hear the excitement in his voice. "I am now," I answer.

"We may be cousins."

A week ago I contacted Jack about the sacramental records for Ursin Frederic, giving him alternative birth dates for Ursin. According to Ursin Frederic's tombstone in St. Louis Cemetery No. Two, he was born in New Orleans on August 1, 1792, and died September 15, 1856. In addition to the 1792 birth date on Ursin's tombstone, other documents gave a range of birth dates. Jack graciously searched the records from 1784–1790 and 1791–1795. But he'd found no baptismal record for Ursin. I am leaving no stone unturned.

"I talked to my friend who is an expert on the German Coast," he says. "And he found a Ursin Celestin Frederic. Now here's the exciting news. Ursin Celestin Frederic married Elosie Duvernay. I'm descended from the Duvernay family. We may be cousins."

Then he tells me a story of how he's been a friend of Greg Osborn and it was years into the friendship before they discovered they were cousins.

"You have to understand if you're descended from one of the early families of Louisiana, you probably are cousins. That's how it is in New Orleans, two degrees of separation."

Though I'm excited by the possibility that we're cousins, I'm almost certain Ursin Celestin Frederic is not my Ursin Frederic.

I thank him for the information and tell him I'll look into it. After I hang up I reread Judy's early research on Ursin. Sure enough, Judy eliminated Ursin Celestin Frederic as a relative. But still I email her and request a copy of Ursin Celestin Frederic's widow's application for a War of 1812 pension, the document she used to rule out Ursin Celestin. When it arrives, it's clear from the information that Ursin and Ursin Celestin are two different men. I'm back to square one and continue constructing Ursin's life from what I do know.

By 1829 Ursin is living with Roxelane Arnoux, a free woman of color, in the suburb of Marigny, on Greatmen Street (now Dauphin Street) between Frenchman and Champs Elysees Streets where their first child, John Frederick, is born in 1829. On his birth record, John is described as the "child of their cohabitance" and his race is designated as colored. On the same document, Ursin's age is given as thirty-nine years old and Roxelane's age as twenty-five years old. Their fourteen-year age gap lends credence to this being a *plaçage* arrangement.

As to what happened to Marie Polline is only conjecture. Perhaps she died or Ursin became tired of her. Regardless, Ursin moved on to another woman. As to Ursin's daughter by Marie Polline, in 1851 Marie Armande has a son Joseph and she is residing on St. Phillip Street near

Rampart, the same street on which Ursin had his cabinetmaking shop in 1822. It's unclear if it's the same building that housed his carpentry business.

In subsequent birth records dated August 1835 and March 1837, Ursin and Roxelane's children are described as "natural" or "from the cohabitation of" Roxelane and Ursin. The children of these *plaçage* unions were known as "natural" children as opposed to "bastard" children, an important distinction in many ways, but especially in terms of inheritance. Bastard children couldn't inherit from their fathers, but natural children could inherit.

Like many *plaçage* liaisons, Ursin lived with Roxelane monogamously, dispelling the notion of the tragic quadroon, and his "natural" children were his heirs.[5]

For the majority of their lives together, Ursin and Roxelane resided in the Marigny area. In the early nineteenth century when Ursin and Arnoux established their residence, "New" Marigny, the area away from the river near Claude Street, was where the white Creole gentlemen set up their *plaçage* households.[6] During that time, Marigny was composed of single and double Creole cottages. Many of the inhabitants were tradesmen, in occupations such as shoemaker, carpenter, blacksmith, butcher, and tailor. As a cabinetmaker Ursin's trade was typical of the population.

By 1811 there were over 150 households living there. In 1830 when the city was divided into three municipalities, Marigny was included in the Third Municipality and all business was conducted in French. Reunification took place in 1851 and the Third Municipality became the Third District. By the 1840s with the influx of German immigrants, shotgun cottages were built with more frequency and became the dominant nineteenth-century New Orleans–type house.[7]

Though the houses may have looked charming, living in Marigny during the early nineteenth century was anything but charming. Because the ground water in the city had high mineral content making it unusable for drinking and washing, water had to be brought in by cask and cart. An open gutter served as the sewage system, and at night soil wagons collected human waste from the gutters, which was deposited into the river creating an awful stench.[8]

Another group of immigrants to the Marigny area in its early days were refugees from Santo Domingo. Roxelane Arnoux and her family might well have been one of those refugees. She was born in Santiago de Cuba, where many of the refugees fled first before coming to New Orleans.

My friend and colleague English Professor Emerita Nancy Cirillo whose area of specialization is Caribbean studies educates me about the Haitian Slave Revolt (1791–1804), which was led by Toussaint L'Ouverture, a free black. Not only was it the only successful slave revolt in the Americas, but also the black rebels who won control of Santa Domingo, located in the western part of Hispaniola, established the first independent nation of former slaves, renaming the island "Haiti."

In 1803, the largest mass exodus from the island took place when about thirty thousand people, including whites, free people or color, and some slaves sailed to Cuba after the revolutionaries defeated the French army sent by Napoleon. Roxelane's family might have been among those fleeing to Cuba.

When Cuba deported many of the refugees in 1809, Roxelane's family remained in Cuba.[9] According to ship records, not until 1825 does Roxelane Arnoux, age seventeen, arrive in New Orleans. That would put her birth year as 1808, which matches the birth year on her death record witnessed by her son Leon Frederic. On the ship's record she is listed as a passenger on the schooner *Thom* disembarking at the port of New Orleans in the third quarter of 1825, four years before the birth of her first child with Ursin.

The schooner *Thom* departed from St. Jago, Cuba. What is of particular interest on the manifest is the captain's name: Jean Arnoux. His death record lists his birthplace as Jeremie on the Island of Santo Domingo around 1774. He was the legitimate son of Jean Arnoux and

Margdeleine Arnau. What his exact relationship to Roxelane was is unclear. If Jean Arnoux was a white man and Roxelane's father, then Roxelane was a child of a mixed-race relationship. On the 1860 census her race is designated as Mulatto. But if he wasn't her father, he certainly was related to her.

Prior to enlisting the services of Judy Riffel, I'd mentioned to Ike Edwards that Roxelane Arnoux was born in Santiago de Cuba. He explained to me that many of the men who won their freedom as a result of the Haitian slave revolt, when they came to New Orleans, participated in the War of 1812 as part of the free men of color militia. He was suggesting that Ursin Frederic's family might have originally been enslaved in Santo Domingo and took part in the slave revolt. Since Leon Frederic, Ursin's son, had served in the Native Guards as a free man of color during the Civil War, it wasn't too far a leap, though an erroneous one.

Every so often I ask my husband how it's going.

"Slow," he says.

"Did you find any Frederics?"

He shows me the scant list, a few John Fredericks, no Ursin.

But one mystery concerning Ursin is finally solved. I've pondered over the word *(Lours)* in parenthesis after Ursin Frederic's name in his obituary, wondering if as Rich noted on the *Genealogy Roadshow* packet that *Lours* might indicate that Ursin was born in Lourdes, France.

Judy Riffel has a different idea, one that makes perfect sense. Because the obituary was written in French, and *Lours* is the French word *l'ours*, meaning "bear," Lours might have been his nickname.

Judy writes: "It could have been his nickname, many soldiers had them. Since there were two Ursin Fredericks, he could have gone by 'l'ours' to differentiate himself from the other one." Or it could be a play on Ursin's name from the Latin *ursus*, "bear."

Her interpretation delights me. Ursin "The Bear" Frederic seems to embody his fierceness and strength. Ursin was a bear of a man with a big appetite for life, especially when it came to women. He was a man of complexity: a slave owner, a womanizer, a father who supported his family, and a war veteran who risked his life for his community. Though there is no justification for slavery, I don't feel the need to apologize for him or hide what he did. The mist of history comes between us just as it did with my mother and me.

In trying to piece together ancestors lives, I'm acutely aware that we're separated by the experiences of our individual times and places. And for every ancestor who made choices I wished they hadn't, there are other ancestors who made choices I celebrate.

Bernard Lanabere, my third great-grandfather, was born in Serres-Castet, France, on September 18, 1811. The nearest town to Serres-Castet is Pau, which boasts a castle that was the birthplace of Henry IV of France, who reigned from 1598 to 1619. Bernard's father Jean Lanabere was a farmer. His mother's name was Marie Liben.

Bernard had the dubious distinction of bearing the name of his older brother, the firstborn son, who was born in 1807 and died before Bernard's birth. Though at the time it was not uncommon to name a child after a deceased child, I can't help but think he must have endeavored all his life to escape the shadow of that older deceased brother. In contemporary psychology Bernard would have been the replacement child. Perhaps his leaving France for America was in some ways to escape the specter of his dead brother. How could Bernard ever hope to measure up to the idealized dead brother who forever would be perfect?

In *The Foreign French: Nineteenth-Century French Immigration into Louisiana: Vol. I 1820–1839*, I find a record of a Lanaber (Lamber?) of France arriving in New Orleans, November 4, 1836, on the ship Louisiana. He is thirty years old, occupation not given, and has departed from the port of Bordeaux. Putting aside the misspelling of his last name, this Lanaber is five years older than my ancestor Bernard if the ship record is accurate. Also, my Bernard arrived in New Orleans in 1838 according to his death certificate. However, the 1836 arrival of Lanaber from

France is the only ship record I can find of a Lanabere arriving in New Orleans during the time period when Bernard would have immigrated. Considering the inaccuracies in reporting ages at the time, the Lanaber who disembarked in New Orleans in 1836 is probably Bernard Lanabere. Also, the port of Bordeaux was the closest port to Serres-Castet for vessels sailing to America. Though passenger manifests after 1834 were less fragmented and appeared to be more complete, the embarking French passengers were underreported, so it's not surprising that the only listing I could find was for a Lanaber. Though the law of averages tells me Lanaber is Bernard Lanabere.

When Bernard immigrated to New Orleans, he was part of a French migration pattern. Prior to 1832, annual patterns of immigration from France that passed through New Orleans were about one thousand. After 1832 until the Civil War there was an increase of French immigrants in New Orleans from three thousand to seven thousand, with the French being the third largest group after the Irish and the Germans in the city.[10] Interestingly, New Orleans ranked among the six leading American ports between 1820 and 1839 for French immigration.[11]

What motivated Bernard to leave the tiny hamlet of Serres-Castet? Perhaps he was frustrated by the area's growing economic stagnation, which prompted many young men, particularly peasants, to leave France in search of economic opportunity.[12] If he stayed in Serres-Castet, he most likely would have followed in his father's occupation of farming, bent to a plow, eking out a substandard existence. Maybe he traveled to Bordeaux thinking the city would offer him better options, only to discover that other rural artisans, peasants, and workers, displaced by France's recession, sought refuge there between 1830 and 1840, creating shanty towns, which were breeding grounds for cholera outbreaks.[13] Faced with such grim prospects but determined not to return to Serres-Castet, Bernard booked passage on a sailing ship in steerage (between-deck).

Likely he would have had to pay the exorbitant fare that was being charged at the time by unscrupulous European ship owners.[14] It's possible he heard of the New Orleans French community and its booming economy, incentives for a young Frenchman compelled by difficult economic circumstances. Like many of the immigrants, he traveled to New Orleans in a seasonal pattern, timing his arrival in November to avoid the summer season rampant with hurricanes, yellow fever, and malaria.[15]

Traveling in steerage was not for the faint of heart. Bernard would have been required to bring his own bedding. Though food was provided, passengers had to cook it. And if it was a rough crossing, they had little time in the fresh air, confining them below deck. Steerage was crowded, dark, damp, rat infested, and rampant with insects and disease. There was limited sanitation, which made it a dirty and foul-smelling place. Passengers slept, ate, and socialized in the same spaces. Certainly steerage was a breeding ground for sickness, accounting for many deaths at sea.[16]

By 1841 Bernard is living with Felicite Meyronne, a free woman of color, and they have a daughter, Philomene Lanabere, born in New Orleans in 1841. His occupation is listed as coffeehouse. Because he is a white man and Felicite is a free woman of color, they could not marry legally in New Orleans, suggesting this may have been a *plaçage* relationship. The same Louisiana Civil Code that prohibited free people of color from marrying slaves also banned marriages between whites and free people of color, an indication of the racial barriers in Louisiana.[17] Bernard faced the same barrier to marriage as Ursin did.

Possessed of an entrepreneurial spirit, in January of 1854, Bernard applied for a license for a cabaret at the corner of Bayou Road and Johnson. Later that year he sailed to France, returning to New Orleans October 28 on the ship *Lemuel Dryer*. Unlike his first voyage to New Orleans in steerage, this time he is one of only twelve cabin passengers. His occupation is listed as merchant. In eighteen years, the poor farmer's son from Serres-Castet has turned his life around and become the immigrant success story. On the manifest his name is spelled correctly though his age is off by one year.

By the 1860 census Barnard is a successful grocer with real estate valued at $8,000 and personal property valued at $5,000. He and Felicite have four children: Philomene, age twenty; Jules, age eighteen, who works as a clerk in his father's grocery store; Eugenie, age fourteen; and Azemar, age twelve. That peculiar and unusual family first name, Azemar, came from Bernard Lanabere and Felicite Meyronne.

Not until 1870 during Reconstruction is the ban against interracial marriage lifted for a brief time. In what I consider a testament to their love and devotion Bernard at age sixty-three and Felicite at age sixty marry in 1873. They will have only five years together as a married couple. Felicite dies in 1878 of bronchitis, possibly as a result of yellow fever. In 1878 a yellow fever epidemic swept through New Orleans and the first recognized case of the disease was noted in the Charity Hospital of New Orleans. That year 4,046 people died of yellow fever. It's likely Felicite was one of them.

By 1880 Bernard is a retail grocer living on Orleans Street. At the time of his death in March 1883, he's residing at 163 N. Claiborne Street in the Second Ward city of Tremé.

Reading through the list of his movable effects is a step back in time, painting a picture of middle-class life in the late nineteenth century: one mahogany hair-bottomed parlor set, one French mirror, one old piano, one dining room set composed of six cane-bottomed chairs, one mahogany bedroom set, and silver spoons and forks. The total value of his movable effects, cash, and real estate is $3,770, the equivalent of $95,000 in today's money. However, his debts nearly exceed his assets.

Still Bernard has to be admired for his sense of adventure, entrepreneurial spirit, and dedication to family. Though I have no way of knowing if Ursin Frederic would have married his consort Roxelane Arnoux if he'd been able to, the fact that Bernard legalized his union with Felicite Meyronne speaks volumes about his regard for her and their children.

When Bernard's daughter, Philomene, and Ursin's son, Leon, marry in 1861, both free people of mixed race, they are the forerunners of a pattern of endogamous marriage, which continued in a direct line through generations of the Frederic family until my mother broke that pattern in 1944 by marrying a white man and stepping outside her ethnic and racial group.

19

Interracial Marriage Hidden
Cleveland, Ohio, 1944

O N A WARM, breezy October day, my parents were married in Cleveland, Ohio, at St. Boniface Catholic Church. My mother wore a borrowed white dress and veil. No one from my mother's family attended the ceremony. Her two bridesmaids were my father's sisters, Bernice and Delores. All the men in the photographs, except my grandfather and Uncle Stephen, are dressed in military uniforms.

Though passably white, my mother's mother didn't attend the wedding of her oldest daughter. Maybe she wasn't invited. Maybe my mother feared her mother would drink too much, or worse, bring her husband, Mr. Arthur, or maybe it just wasn't important to her? My father's insistence that they marry in Cleveland, Ohio, must have delighted my mother, allowing her to keep her race hidden.

If she had any qualms about her deception, her brief stay with my father's family must have convinced her that they would never approve or accept her mixed race. Nor could she come clean with my father who was devoted to his family and would never go against their wishes. But social stigma was only half of the problem my mother faced, making marrying in Ohio her only option.

In 1944, the year my parents were married, intermarriage between a white person and anyone with even the slightest drop of racial mixture was still illegal in most Southern states, including Louisiana. The law stated: "If any white person intermarry with a colored person, or any colored person intermarry with a white person, he shall be guilty of a felony and shall be punished by confinement in the penitentiary for not less than one nor more than five years."[1] That law wasn't overturned until 1967.

Had my mother and father married in Louisiana, there is every possibility she would have been required to produce a birth certificate, which would have shown her race as colored and they would have been prohibited from marrying.

Though couples were rarely legally prosecuted, they were socially shunned. The case of Richard and Mildred Loving was an exception and became a landmark case for the Supreme Court. Though from Virginia, the Lovings were married in 1958 in Washington, DC, to evade Virginia's Racial Integrity Act. Mildred was of African American descent and Richard was white. Upon their return to their home in Virginia, three armed police officers burst into their bedroom and arrested them. Mildred, who was pregnant with their first child, spent several days in jail. They were found guilty. The presiding judge told Mildred, "as long as you live you will be known as a felon." The Lovings with the help of the American Civil Liberties Union were able to have the law overturned by the Supreme Court who ruled in 1967 that laws prohibiting interracial marriage were unconstitutional.[2]

On my parents' marriage certificate from St. Boniface Church there was no mention of race. In marrying my father whose complexion was so white it seemed translucent, my mother genetically assured herself that her children would not be dark skinned. That whatever percentage of African blood she carried, it would be diluted enough not to be visible. She'd crossed over permanently.

But still she must have worried. Ula told me that they used to wait and see what color the baby would be. Always there was that fear that a distant gene would suddenly rear its dark head and appear, visually proclaiming racial heritage.

In Nella Larsen's book *Passing*, published in 1929, Clare Kendry, who's been passing and is married to a white man who thinks she's white, explains to her girlhood friend, Irene Redfield, why she's decided to have only one child.

"After taking up her own glass, she informed them: 'No, I have no boys and I don't think I'll ever have any. I'm afraid. I nearly died of terror the whole nine months before Margery was born for fear that she might be dark. Thank goodness, she turned out all right. But I'll never risk it again. Never! The strain is simply too—too hellish.'"[3]

I once asked my mother why she had only two children. She answered vaguely, blaming God. "That's all God gave me."

It would take her two years after her marriage to conceive me, then five years before my brother was born. Those five years between my birth and my brother's was she calculating her risks, watching my skin color, assuring herself that she could chance a second child?

Though I'm as porcelain white as my father, my brother favors my mother, his skin more olive toned like hers. After my brother's birth, perhaps she thought she'd better not risk another child, whose skin might be darker and might give away her secret, causing my father to question her race.

Her sister Shirley's first child, Margaret, was a "throwback," dark skinned with flat features but "good" hair. I'm sure my father accepted that Margaret's skin and features were from her father, Alfred Coignet, who lived openly as a mixed-race person.

Even contemporary novels deal with this issue of a throwback, as Toni Morrison calls her character Lula Ann in her novel *God Help the Child*. Lula Ann is "midnight black, Sudanese black." Her mother, Sweetness, and her father, Louis, are light-skinned with good hair. Sweetness asks the question: "Can you imagine how many white folks have Negro blood running and hiding in their veins? Guess. Twenty percent, I heard."

Alvera Frederic, New Orleans, Louisiana, possibly 1942.

The Safari Room, Algiers, Louisiana, 1951. From left to right: Aunt Mickey (Mildred Kilbourne Duffaut), my grandmother's sister; my grandmother, Camille (Kilbourne) Frederic Romero; Rhea Cruzat, Aunt Mickey's daughter; Charles Cruzat, Rhea's husband.

St. Ann Street, New Orleans, Louisiana, possibly 1927. From left to right: Shirley Frederic, Homer Frederic, and Alvera Frederic.

Camp Shelby, Mississippi, 1941. Alvera Frederic and Harold Kalina.

Jackson household picnic, Los Angeles, California, 1944. Coleen Gray, the noir film star, is in the foreground. My mother is fourth in from the right.

My parent's wedding photograph. Cleveland, Ohio, October 25, 1944.

Photograph of my parents taken by a *Cleveland Plain Dealer* photographer to accompany the October, 1944 article, "October Wedding Offsets Sadness Month Once Brought Soldier."

Edward Kilbourne, my mother's maternal uncle, New Orleans, Louisiana.

Homer Frederic, my mother's brother, and Ula Duffaut, my mother's maternal first cousin. New Orleans, Louisiana, 1946.

I, *Léon Frederic* born in *New Orleans* in the State of *Louisiana* aged *twenty three* years, and by occupation *Shoe Maker* do hereby acknowledge to have voluntarily enlisted this *Second* day of *September* 1862, as a Soldier in a Volunteer Regiment of Louisiana, to serve the United States for Three Years, or during the War, with persons owing allegiance to and in open rebellion to the United States Government, unless sooner discharged by proper authority, and to be subject to orders from the Federal Government ; do also agree to accept such bounty, pay, rations and clothing, as are or may be established by law. And I, *Léon Frédéric* do Solemnly Swear, that I will bear true faith and allegiance to the United States of America, and that I will serve them honestly and faithfully against all their enemies or opposers whomsoever ; and that I will observe and obey the orders of the President of the United States, and the orders of the officers appointed over me, according to the Rules and Articles for the government of the Armies of the United States. *Léon Frédéric*

Sworn and subscribed to at *New Orleans* this *3d* day of *Sept* 1862.

Before Me *Lt Col S A Nelson*

I CERTIFY ON HONOR, That I have carefully examined the above named Recruit, agreeably to the General Regulations of the Army, and that in my opinion he is free from all bodily defects and mental infirmity, which would, in in any way, disqualify him from performing the duties of a soldier.

Rob A Smith Examining Surgeon.

I CERTIFY ON HONOR, That I have minutely inspected the Recruit *Leon Frédéric* previously to his enlistment, and that he was entirely sober when enlisted ; that to the best of my judgment and belief he is of lawful age ; and that in accepting him as duly qualified to perform the duties of an able-bodied soldier, I have strictly observed the Regulations which govern the Recruiting service. This soldier has *black* eyes, *black* hair *Dark* complexion, is *five* feet *six 1/2* inches high.

H. Louis Stey Recruiting Officer.

DIRECTIONS.—This enlistment must be signed and acknowledged in triplicates, one copy to be sent to the Adjutant-General, one to the commander of the Regiment, and one copy to be retained by the recruiting officer; the copy to the Adjutant-General must be sent immediately after being signed; the oath must be sworn and subscribed to before any commissioned officer.

Leon Frederic, Sr.'s enlistment document for the Union Army, First Regiment of the Louisiana Native Guards, September 3, 1862, New Orleans, Louisiana.

STATE OF LOUISIANA

THIS RECORD IS VALID FOR BIRTH ONLY

1003420

Be it Remembered, That on this day to wit: the _Ninth of November_ in the year of our Lord, One Thousand, Nine Hundred and _Twenty One_ and the One Hundred and _46_ of the Independence of the United States of America, before me, JOHN CALLAN, M. D., Chairman of the Board of Health, and Ex-Officio Recorder of Births, Deaths and Marriages, in and for the Parish of Orleans, and the City of New Orleans, personally appeared _Mrs. O. Koeckel a midwife_ native of _this city_ residing _No Urmanic St_ who hereby declares that on _the Twenty First of October this year_ _(Oct 21, 1921)_ at _No 298 Flann St_ was born a _female_ child, named _Alvera Frederic_ (_col_) Lawful issue of _Azema Frederic_ a native of _this city_ aged _22_ years, occupation _Clerk_ and _Camille_ _Kilbourn_ a native of _this city_ aged _16_ years.

Thus done at New Orleans, in the presence of the aforesaid _Mrs. O. Koeckel_ as also in that of _F. H. Lanauzs and H. J. Robinson_ both of this city, witnesses by me requested so to be, who have hereunto set their hands together with me, after due reading hereof the day, month and year above written.

John Callan
Chairman Board of Health and Ex-Officio Recorder

Mrs. O. Koeckel
F. Henry Lanauze
M. Robinson } Witnesses.

Sworn to and subscribed before me, this _9_ day of _Nov_ 192_1_
F. Henry Lanauze

FEB 0 2 1995

Alvera Frederic's birth certificate, October 21, 1921, designating her as "colored."

Alvera Frederic, Meal-A Minit restaurant, Canal Street, New Orleans, Louisiana.

Harold Kalina, Technical Sergeant, United States Army, Co. A, 114th Engineer Combat Battalion, WW II.

Camille (Kilbourne) Frederic Romero, New Orleans, Louisiana.

Because of Lula Ann's skin color, Louis abandons the family. Sweetness is embarrassed by her daughter's dark color and distances herself from her child. The novel isn't set in the 1920s or 1930s. It's set in the 1990s. As Sweetness explains, "Back in the nineties when Lula Ann was born, the law was against discriminating in who you could rent to, but not many landlords paid attention to it."[4]

After their wedding my parents honeymooned under Army sponsorship in Miami, Florida, for a week. Even now the photographs of their honeymoon make me uncomfortable. Their slim bodies clad in bathing suits as if those were all the clothes they could manage. There's a humorously awkward photo of my father attempting to throw my mother into a water fountain. I have a vague memory of mother saying they didn't leave the room very much during their honeymoon.

The Saturday after their wedding, my father reported to his army unit for reassignment. He was assigned to a new outfit, the 1526th SU in Australia. V-J Day was ten months away. The war was not over yet for him.

On November 21, 1944, less than a month after my parents' wedding on October 25, 1944, my father was hospitalized at Billings General Hospital, Fort Benjamin Harrison, Indiana. He'd found a way out of his personal hell.

20

War's Aftermath
2015

SEVEN MONTHS AFTER I'd written my father's war years section of the book, his military personnel records arrive. I don't expect any additional information about his time in combat, mainly because a fire destroyed most of his records that were kept at the National Personnel Records Center in St. Louis, Missouri. Even the letter informing me that there is information regarding my father's service record warns me that because of the fire the records may be incomplete. Even though I don't know what is in the surviving records, I can't leave any stone unturned. If there's a chance that I could learn something about my father's combat service during World War II, other than what he told me and what I'd read, I have to take it. What I'm hoping to find are the battle reports that his commanding officers filled out after major incursions.

Why this is so important to me is because what happened to him in the war might explain his descent into alcoholism.

The packet I receive from the archives is thick and bolsters my confidence that the battle reports are part of the packet. But as I page through the contents, my hopes are deflated. Instead of battle reports, there are pages and pages of my father's medical records, beginning with his honorable discharge from the army dated December 18, 1944.

At the time of his discharge the records state that he was in poor physical condition. The reason for his discharge was medical. His diagnosis was "psychoneurosis, anxiety-type, severe." The clinical record's final diagnosis, signed by a doctor, was "combat exhaustion, severe, cause undetermined, following duty under enemy fire in New Guinea, July to November 1942, manifested by tremors, restlessness, irritability, battle dreams, and insomnia."

Prior to his medical discharge, he'd been hospitalized for a month. The precipitating factor for his hospitalization was an incident involving his newly assigned first sergeant. He complained to an army doctor about the first sergeant.

"I am so disgusted with my new outfit and the First Sergeant I feel like going AWOL," he complained. "This guy will either be a changed man within a week or else dead were he put in a combat area."

It's not mentioned in his medical records but I suspect this first sergeant was the man he punched in the face in order to be termed "crazy," his words. He'd taken this drastic action to get help for his severe psychoneurosis.

I'm not surprised by his diagnosis. But what I am surprised by and not prepared for are the details of his medical condition, casting my father, if not in a new light, then in a different light, glaring and troubling, sapping some of my anger at him for his years of alcoholism and the damage it did to our family.

For weeks afterward I'm haunted by what my father told the doctors and the doctor's observations. My father died overseas and his ghost returned, a ghost as disturbed as he was disturbing.

Other than recurrent bouts of malaria, my father had no other discernable physical maladies. He entered the hospital complaining of frequent headaches, nausea, blurring of vision in the right eye, restlessness, irritability, startled reaction to sudden noises, and nightmares.

The doctor wrote that his history revealed that he spent two and a half years in the South Pacific, of this period over six months in front-line combat. He also had, during this time, twenty-one admissions for recurrent malaria. "Interview with soldier indicates that he is extremely tense, apprehensive, and confused about his own physical and mental states. The headaches, nausea, and general malaise he dates from the onset of his malaria. Since his removal from the overseas theater, his symptoms have remained constant in severity."

But what devastates me is my father's description of his own mental state—nervous, tense, and jittery—which he attributes to his time in combat.

"I'm so irritable, I can't get along with no one. I feel like going over the hill," he said. "Since I've gotten back to the states in November, I have a lot of trouble concentrating and I lose my head at sudden noises."

He described to the doctor several "narrow escapes" that he experienced during the six months and two weeks he was in combat as an infantry squad leader. On one occasion a Japanese bomber sank a corvette that his unit was being transported on as it moved up the New Guinea coast. After the ship was torpedoed, he had to swim ashore. Only one-third of the men survived. On two occasions he was almost buried alive in his foxhole by shell explosions. While on reconnaissance patrol, he fell twenty feet off a log injuring his right ankle. At the termination of his combat duty, of the initial 126 men, only thirteen survived.

He told the doctors that he has nightmares, which are described to him by others, but he does not recall. He gets a nauseated feeling, which comes and goes without apparent reason.

"Sudden noises make me lose my head completely and my entire body has a queer but real feeling of being a dish rag," he stated. "Some afternoons, I get this chill and blurring in my right eye and headaches. That's when I think the malaria is coming back. I've gotten very irritable and I have these temper outbursts that leave me shaky and nervous."

And in what I consider the most telling of my father's observations of himself, he said, "I'm fed up with the army and all through with it. I find it hard to understand myself now because I worked so hard overseas and was promoted from private to technical sergeant while serving in the South Pacific. I guess I'll never be the same anymore."

The doctor's progress notes dated December 1944 concluded: "The impression conveyed by the solider was that he scarcely understands his own conduct. He obviously realizes that he is not the man he was."

While hospitalized he was given Nembutal capsules, ephedrine, and phenobarbital, all addictive drugs. On his discharge form the doctor wrote, "Maximum benefit from hospitalization has been attained. Further care in an army hospital is not indicated since after prolonged hospitalization the soldier cannot be restored to a duty status. Further institutional care is not necessary and the soldier can be released to his own care without danger to himself or others."

"Cannot be restored to a duty status" turns my stomach. Of course, this was before posttraumatic stress disorder (PTSD) became a symptom of a severe psychological condition often associated with being in combat.

Once fully discharged from the army, the war would not leave my father who suffered from persistent bouts of malaria and shell shock (PTSD).

In the first years of my parents' marriage, they lived with my father's parents in the small upstairs apartment, conducive neither to my father's recovery or their marriage. It would take my parents almost two years to conceive me.

My mother painted a bleak picture of their early marriage. "He'd wake in the night screaming. He'd shiver and sweat from the malaria." She put her hand to her throat. "One night he tried to strangle me. He thought I was the enemy."

The war had psychologically crippled my father. Whatever he had seen, whatever he had done had changed him forever. He would never fully recover. As he said, "I wasn't the same man." And he never would be.

Seven months after my father returned to civilian life, after nearly four years in the army, an article appeared in the *Cleveland Plain Dealer* detailing my father's struggle to secure his GI Bill of Rights.

"Three times he has sought benefits supposedly available to qualified veterans under the bill. Three times he has been denied." The article calls him a hero of Buna, listing his two Presidential Citations and the near loss of his vision in the right eye.

Unable to attend college for a degree in architecture because of his inability to secure his GI benefits, needing to earn a living to support a wife, and still tormented by the war he turned to alcohol for relief, to erase the memories that crept in at night and the bitterness that would not leave him. His would be a life-long addiction that nearly killed him in 1979 and caused years of havoc for our family.

Some memories stay with me as well.

The late afternoon sun blazes the window over the kitchen sink, sending shards of light around the room. The radio plays *Blue Moon*. The radio plays from morning to night as if the music can take away my mother's loneliness. I sit at the gray Formica table coloring leaves on a tree, the leaves are different shades of green: olive green, dark green, yellow green. I am seven years old. It is important to stay inside the lines. It is important to be obedient.

My mother stands at the sink holding up my father's bottle of sweet sherry that she found hidden in a cabinet, screaming at him, "Choose, choose. Me or the drink." When he doesn't answer, she tips the bottle and lets the sherry pour into the sink.

His hands are by his side. He stands helplessly watching her, making no attempt to stop her or reason with her. He appears stunned by her rage, the audacity of what she is doing.

I'm wishing I could run away and hide. I'm wishing I could escape into the tree of the many shades of greens. But I can't. Instead I concentrate on the sherry's amber color as it streams from the bottle, the way the liquid catches the light from the window in the green kitchen of the old house on West 98th Street where the night we moved in a tornado hit, stranding us in the dark house where no one now is happy.

When the bottle's empty, she smashes it to pieces, marring the porcelain sink, glass flying everywhere. My father leaves the kitchen. I hear the front door close and the car rumble away. My mother doesn't cry. She takes the broom and dustpan from the closet and bends to her task of broken glass, of what she has done, of her rage that has no end.

Somewhere in the house my brother wakes from his nap crying.

21

Hiding in Plain Sight
Parma, Ohio, 1950s/1960s

S EVEN MILES SOUTHWEST of Cleveland, Ohio, the suburb of Parma was the bastion of whiteness in 1954. After World War II when my parents bought a tract house in Parma, the suburb was experiencing tremendous growth as part of the nationwide post-war housing boom. Between 1950 and 1960, its population grew from 28,897 to 82,845. By 1956, one year after we moved to Parma, it was the fastest growing city in the United States with a heavy first-generation Polish American population.[1] The GI Bill and the population's move out of the cities and into the suburbs fueled its growth. War-weary soldiers flocked to the green suburbs wanting a fresh landscape where they could put the war behind them.

Our lower middle-class neighborhood was composed mostly of blue-collar workers and nuclear families where the women stayed home to raise the children and the men went to work. There was one exception to the stay-at-home mothers on our street: my girlfriend's mother who worked as a secretary in Cleveland. Her life away from home was exotic and alluring to me, made more so by our forays into her closet where her business suits and tailored dresses were shrouded in garment bags. We'd unzip the bags one by one releasing the stale scent of her perfume and sweat, then we'd select suits and dresses to try on, every one as somber and quiet as her mother with tightly permed, fawn-brown hair. When I asked my friend, an only child, why her mother worked, she told me a doctor said she had to or she'd be too depressed.

There were no people of color on our street, except for one family, two houses south of us, the Nakaos, a Japanese American family, who kept mostly to themselves.

Parma, specifically Lincoln Avenue, at least our block of Lincoln, was the kind of neighborhood where when a heavy summer rain fell, causing the sewers to overflow, we'd take off our shoes and wade in the water, splashing each other.

One summer I started a neighborhood newspaper, gathering news from the other stay-at-home moms and typing up the news on the old Underwood typewriter in the basement, then sending my brother out to deliver copies to the same neighbors who'd given me the news, charging them a modest dime for the paper.

We stayed up late on the cool Ohio summer nights catching June bugs in glass jars, their fluorescent glow flickering like some magic trick, until we were called inside for bed. It was very Ozzie and Harriet, at least on the surface, held together with religion and societal mores.

Parma spun with safety and repression. I'd ride my bike most evenings escaping my troubled household, roaming the streets, sometimes venturing to the next town, Seven Hills, with its rolling hills that were no challenge for my young, strong muscles. Summer offered me escape, and I escaped as often as I could.

What motivated my mother to choose Parma? She wanted something new, a house no one else had ever lived in, with no one else's memories and scents. She'd grown up in a boarding house run by her great-grandmother, Mary Brown Williams, sharing space with strangers. She'd been an interloper in her own life, dependent on hospitality and charity from this or that relative, succumbing to their tastes, their likes and dislikes. A newly built house was like a blank canvas to her. She could put her own mark on it.

But more than that she wanted a house that matched her newly created life, not like the tornado house with its dark corners and creaky stairs where, no matter how hard she scrubbed the walls and floors, certain odors lingered. In this new house, she and my father could start anew, could be different people.

Our house was one of the first built on our block. The subdivision was so new, the builders had yet to pave the street. There were no lawns, no garages. The house reeked of new wood and fresh paint. Every time a car passed our house, a trail of dust lingered behind it. My mother complained of the dirt and dust.

Once shed of the city and its isolated pockets of diversity, she must have realized the daringness of her choice of a white suburb. Was she laughing up her sleeve like her father likely did during World War I when he passed for white in the North in Indiana? Was she fearful someone would find out her secret? Or had she by this time felt that if her husband hadn't guessed then nobody would?

Though she kept her opinions to herself, she followed the burgeoning civil rights movement that was heating up across America with particular interest.

In 1955, our first year in the Parma house, Rosa Parks was arrested for refusing to give up her seat on a Montgomery, Alabama, city bus, sparking the Montgomery bus boycott and bringing Martin Luther King, Jr. to the forefront of the civil rights movement. A year earlier, the Supreme Court's ruling in *Brown v. Board of Education* overturned the 1896 *Plessy v. Ferguson* decision. State laws on segregation were deemed unconstitutional. Public schools could no longer discriminate on the basis of race, paving the way for integration.

Whatever she felt about these legal changes that had ruled her life and determined it, forcing her to make the difficult decision to leave her home and pass as white, she never said. And whatever progress was being made for racial equality in the United States, it had little to no effect on my mother's personal circumstances and her day-to-day existence in the white suburb. It was almost as if she was in a witness protection program.

Closer to home, tensions were rising in the rigidly segregated East Side of Cleveland where the majority of African Americans lived. In 1966 the predominantly black Hough neighborhood erupted into a race riot purportedly sparked by the owner of the Seventy-Niners' Café who refused to give a black customer a glass of water and subsequently posted a sign outside the café that read: NO WATER FOR NIGGERS. The riots lasted six nights and resulted in the death of four African Americans.[2]

In the working class town of Parma, many white people's attitudes toward racial segregation held firm, regardless of the changing laws. Their attitudes were born of cultural racism, fostered in the tight ethnic Cleveland communities, where many of them grew up. My father was one of those racists.

Though the streets of Parma offered safety, more immediate dangers of another kind resided inside our tiny Cape Cod tract house on Lincoln Avenue so alike in appearance to the other houses it was not uncommon in the dark to pull into the wrong driveway, which my father did on more than one occasion.

It's one of those rare July days when the sky is so untroubled everything appears brighter, crisply defined. In the long concrete driveway that leads from our house to the garage, I practice shooting basketballs as my father taught me, arcing the ball as I aim for the hoop. The repetition of the practice matches the slow lazy day. My mother drags the garden hose across the back lawn and then waters the tomato plants near the garage. Their greenish orbs hang heavy on the vine as if they too have had enough of summer.

It's late afternoon. Soon my father will be home from work. Already I'm planning the long bike ride far from home when the sun shimmers into evening.

From the corner of my eye I spot my brother sneaking into the house through the side door, not bothering to interrupt my game as he usually does by swatting the ball from my hands and taking a wild shot. Something is up.

After my mother finishes the watering, she coils the hose and places it behind the house. She rarely works in the yard, her domain confined to the domestic, cleaning and cooking. Even this briefest of tasks in the glare of the summer sun requires her big floppy hat and long-sleeved cotton blouse and slacks.

Turning to retrieve the ball that has bounced away from me, I see Mrs. Nakao, our neighbor, walking down our driveway. She's never come to our house before. And that alerts me.

My mother looks up and says hi.

Mrs. Nakao is a small woman with a pretty face. "Alvera," she begins. I can tell by the way she stands hunched and furtive as if she can make herself smaller, and the soft tone of her voice that something is wrong and she's come to ask something of my mother who is not her friend, only her neighbor.

I glance toward the house and see my brother's face at the kitchen window and know that whatever reason Mrs. Nakao is here has something to do with my brother and Mrs. Nakao's son, Jimmy, who is my brother's summer friend.

"The boys were playing," she says, not raising her eyes, "and well . . . Did a woman come by here?"

"No. Why?" my mother answers, tilting her head.

"The boys were taunting that new boy who moved in at the end of the block. It might have gotten out of hand. There was some shoving, some name-calling. The mother stormed over to my house very angry. Jimmy said the other boy started it by calling him a dirty Jap. I told her I'd talk to Jimmy and you."

"Alvera, would you handle it," she pleads, briefly touching my mother's arm. "You know I can't say anything." The "you know" hangs in the warm summer air rife with meaning, words she's hesitant to say but that she senses my mother would understand.

An uneasy expression comes over my mother's face as she considers what the woman is asking her to do. Then she agrees to talk to the irate mother. "I'll talk to her," she says.

Later when I learn of my mother's mixed race, I remembered this incident and wondered what thoughts swirled through her mind being asked to be the white emissary with this other white woman. Of course, she was the logical choice to intercede with an incensed white mother who might hurl racial slurs at Mrs. Nakao, so visibly Japanese American. The war was still fresh in everyone's minds.

I can see my mother straightening her shoulders, brightening up her makeup, then walking to the woman's house, facing the angry mother with the confidence that only a white woman could have with another white woman.

I hear her measured words: "I'm sure the boys didn't mean any harm." Leaving the irate mother to figure out which boys she was talking about.

My father's racism was a reflection of his upbringing in the close-knit Cleveland Bohemian neighborhood. Though he never used the N-word, he was vocal about his bigotry using words such as *jig-a-boo*, *spear chucker*, and *coon*, deriding the African American race for lack of ambition and criminality.

My mother reprimanded him with little vigor. "You shouldn't talk like that, Hal." Was she afraid to be too insistent, bringing too much attention to the race issue?

Quixotically, my father's bigotry didn't extend to an African American man who worked for him when he was the maintenance supervisor for a building on Euclid Avenue in the heart of downtown Cleveland, his last position before alcoholism ravaged his body—another medical discharge of sorts.

There's a photo of my father and his men in the makeshift kitchen he installed in the basement of the building where the men could cook their meals. Because my father and his men's workday started around seven in the morning, sometimes they would make breakfast before beginning work. My father spoke highly of this black tradesman with the unusual name of Argosy.

Once when my mother's patience wore thin with my father's racism, the barbs hitting too close to home, though he didn't know that, she protested, "How can you talk about colored people that way and work with Argosy?"

My father huffed. "Well, he's not like the rest of them." In my father's universe of selective racism Argosy, the hard-working black man, got a pass, was exceptional, and most likely proved my father's rule about black people being lazy and shiftless.

Would my mother have received the same pass as Argosy or would her deception been beyond forgiveness?

And how did she endure his racist remarks? Did they beat on her like a hard cold rain? Or had she convinced herself that she deserved it for the lie that sat at the heart of their marriage? Is this why denial was the cloak she wore night and day?

The slow ticking silence is broken only by the sounds of my mother filling our plates as we sit around the cramped kitchen table festooned with a scalloped white bowl of waxed fruit that crowds the table but that my mother refuses to move. The claustrophobia of the space does little to encourage closeness. We are sardines in a can.

Tonight it's pork, sauerkraut, and dumplings. The food holds little interest for me. I'm chronically underweight with jutting bones and safety pins to cinch my skirts' waistbands.

I can tell by the mottled red of my father's face that he is seeped with drink. At thirteen I recognize the signs, watch for them, like storm clouds on a horizon, harbingers of danger, alerting me to take shelter as quickly as I can. His drink this evening is sherry: acrid smelling, sweet, and inviting. His pores seem to ooze with the scent.

Glancing past my brother and father who sit opposite me, I can see the living room, the door with its three oblong windows, my father's recliner, and the stairs leading up to my bedroom, my refuge.

When my mother sits down, my father stops eating and glares at her. "You didn't have shoes until you met me." The disdain in his voice makes me stop eating as well.

I look across the table at my brother. He's shoveling food into his mouth, his head down. I know he's thinking up something funny or outrageous to say, something to deflect what we both know is about to happen.

"I had shoes." My mother's answer is tinged with outrage. The sleeves on her white blouse are rolled up, exposing her shaved arms that seem wounded with perfection.

My father starts eating again, stabbing at his food as if it is the source of his anger; his face now has a purplish hue like the drink in the strange turquoise plastic glass.

"Before you married me you didn't have shoes," he blurts at her with contempt as if he can't figure out why he's sitting eating her food, staying in this marriage.

I shift in my seat wanting the meal to end, for my father to rise from the table, and go into the living room, turn on the television, and fall asleep in his recliner.

"Of course, I had shoes before I married you," she says. "Don't be ridiculous."

I don't know if I want her to continue defending herself or to stop talking. My stomach clutches around my food.

"You were walking around the bayou with no shoes. If it wasn't for me, you'd still be there with the crocodiles."

"I never lived in the bayou." Her voice is smaller now, quieter.

I want to come to her rescue. "She grew up in New Orleans, in a city," I want to say. But I'm afraid. I stare at my plate. I've hardly touched my food and I know I won't escape the table unless I eat most of it because my parents' escalating anger will need a place to land.

"I don't know what you're talking about. I had shoes," she says. "I had really nice shoes."

My brother has powered through his food and asks for seconds. My mother pushes away from the table.

When she sits down my father continues his punitive theme as if his words are lashes, opening flesh, getting under my mother's skin. "You're lucky I married you. Now you have shoes."

She doesn't answer him. She's defeated, crushed by his cruelty. I can see the depression descend as she rises from the table and clears the plates, in the slump of her shoulders, in the way she stares out the tiny window into the suburban back yard as she washes the dishes.

Thinking back on that long ago meal, I wonder if my father had a suspicion about my mother's racial identity, not conscious, just a hunch, some inkling like a tickling at the back of the throat. Had he begun to recognize the clues that she dropped like breadcrumbs—her avoidance of the sun, her wearing makeup to bed, and her reluctance to visit New Orleans—for what they were? Or was he in a drunken mood that evening and my mother was his target of choice in the tiny green house on Lincoln Avenue.

But those days when alcohol didn't rob my father of all reason, didn't cloud his brain, he was a different man—humorous, patient, and instructive. When my brother was an infant, Saturday was my day with my dad. We'd make trips to the hardware store where I'd travel the aisles with him marveling at the different gadgets or watch the men saw wood for my father's carpentry projects. From him, I learned about carpenter pencils, how to plumb a line, hammer a nail straight, and paint a wall. Though he was an alcoholic, he was a functioning alcoholic who never missed work and provided for his family.

Sometimes we'd drive through the Cleveland streets and he'd point out buildings or houses he'd worked on. Once he showed me a church spire rising into the sky piercing the ordinariness of rows of roofs.

"See that. I did that. I made that."

He showed me a world outside the house, a world of action and creation, not the realm of a housewife. I wanted to live in that world, not the self-defeating, confined world that my mother inhabited, full of helplessness and boredom.

But there's no escaping the toll his alcoholism took on us, or the dilemma of his love. My father loved me as only an alcoholic could— sloppily, in fits and starts, wavering and unpredictable. I'd wait for his love full of fear and longing, gauging the distance I'd have to travel to reach it or escape it, the price I'd have to pay in the process, and all the time I'd wonder if it was worth it.

Then when I was seventeen, I no longer wondered. One evening during dinner he told me there was no money for me to attend college, that whatever money there was would go to my brother for his college education. I'd worked extremely hard my last year in high school and had earned all As. My parents had taken me to tour Dayton University, the college I wanted to attend, leading me to believe that they supported my decision and would help me financially.

"Girls don't go to college," he snarled. "Girls get married."

What had I done? I wondered, that he would be so cruel. I said nothing stunned into silence by his punishing tone.

"If you want to go to college so badly, you can pay for it." Then he seemed to soften. "You can live here but summers you'll pay rent."

At that moment I felt his love fall away from me and I let it.

❖

For the rest of my life, I would be a late bloomer, playing catch up while others zoomed ahead in their degrees and careers. It would take me a long time and it would be after I married and had children, but in my late thirties and early forties I earned a MA and a PhD in English, eventually teaching at the University of Illinois at Chicago (UIC) and Roosevelt University in adjunct positions. I was too old, too saddled with family, for any university to seriously consider me for a tenure track position.

By the time I earned my PhD from UIC, my father had to stop drinking because it almost killed him, though he never admitted he had a drinking problem. My father and mother attended my graduation ceremony. When the speaker asked the parents who helped their sons and daughters to earn their degrees to stand, my husband told me, my father stood. My mother had the good grace to remain seated.

22

Keeping Up Appearances

MY MOTHER LEANS toward the bathroom mirror and begins her day by putting on her face. I perch on the edge of the blue bathtub and watch her morning ritual. The floor-to-ceiling cabinet door is open, displaying the three shelves of beauty products: liquid foundations, face powder (both loose and solid), mascara, rouges, face creams (night and day), cleansers, pore tighteners, dark shadow removers, eyebrow pencils and liners, and a pot of makeup brushes as varied as an artist's array of paint brushes. I'm not allowed to touch any of these beauty items without permission. And my mother knows where she's placed each one so I'm wary to disturb her arrangement. Though when I dare I mentally note where the item was placed and return it to that exact spot, right down to how it was positioned.

Her hair is pinned back from her forehead held by three silver clips that resemble metallic insects as long as a grasshopper, revealing a naked face made vulnerable by cold cream, looking nothing like my mother. She retrieves her bottle of foundation, then shakes it before opening. She applies the foundation in upward strokes.

"Always apply your foundation this way, upward, to prevent wrinkles and sagging," she cautions me.

I watch in fascination as her skin is transformed from its dusky olive shade to a lighter shade, not too light to be noticeable, but absorbing the olive tone of her skin as if she's received a shock from which she's yet to recover.

The foundation shade is new and she asks me if I think it fits her. "Is it too light?"

I'm not sure. But I say it looks good, and my answer satisfies her.

Then she takes out an assortment of eyebrow pencils, chooses one and pencils in her eyebrows. The shade is never black as she explains because that would be too black and look penciled in, would look fake, even though that is what she is doing, faking her eyebrows, which she's skillfully plucked to a narrow line.

"Always wear makeup, Gail. Make sure when your husband comes home from work that you have your makeup on and that you're dressed nice. You never know what temptations he'll have out there in the work world."

Her advice bristles. Even then I had no intention of being a housewife.

"Why do you wear makeup to bed?" I ask. It's the 1960s and young people are opting for a more natural look.

"Because you never know if you'll get sick in the middle of the night and have to be taken to the hospital. You want to look your best."

"But mom, if you're sick, what does it matter what you face looks like?" I'm fourteen and starting to question my mother's advice about beauty rituals among other things. It won't be until I'm close to fifty that I'll heed any of my mother's makeup strategies, preferring light powder instead of her machinations.

"You'll get better treatment at the hospital if you look presentable. But that doesn't mean you wear the same makeup to bed you wore all day. No. My sister Shirley would do that. It's not good for your skin. Cleanse your face of all makeup, then reapply a light coat of foundation before bed and pencil in your eyebrows."

Not that I'm agreeing with Aunt Shirley's carelessness, but my mother seems just as wrong in her insistence in wearing makeup to bed.

She applies her rouge subtly, smiling so her cheekbones emerge. As if she's a painter, she selects one of the many makeup brushes from the large jar where they sit brush end up, dabs the brush carefully into the box of loose powder, and with the exactness and skill of an artist she dusts her face with the fine powder. Her face brightens as if her mood has lifted. Lastly she circles her mouth with lipstick and blots her lips on a tissue. The day has begun.

Another clue I missed, chalking her obsession with always having a made-up face to vanity, how beauty becomes even more dangerous as it fades.

But on that fall morning of motherly beauty secrets shared, she was still beautiful, still desirable, and skillfully hiding beneath the lighter shade of a liquid foundation she chose from the shelf of her own making.

Years later when my daughter and I visit her in the assisted-living center she is still applying her face every morning. Still starting her day in a lighter shade though with a less steady hand.

23

The Mystery of the Two Felicites and the Burden of Proof

"When evidence is contradictory the problem of proof becomes more complex."

—Kimberly Powell, Genealogy Expert

A T AN INTIMATE party on a warm summer night in the suburbs, the conversation winds its way to my book project about my mother and her racial secret. When a friend asks me how it's going, I reply without thinking, "You know, cracking the whip." Then I make a whip-like sound.

My friend responds sharply, "You should be used to that."

Her attempt at humor falls flat, at least with me. Our other friend gazes off into the night yard as if the remark came from someone out there. I let it go with a warning about her own suspect ancestor she's been researching. We've all had too much to drink, each nursing our own private sorrows.

What stings is how vulnerable I feel, as if I've done something I should be ashamed of, that this is my fault for having the temerity to reveal my African heritage, which makes me fair game for racist comments. No one would ever know of my African heritage if I didn't reveal it. All three of us are as pale white as the moon. It's as if my mother is there, whispering to me, "See, this is why I didn't tell anyone. This is what happens. Even friends see you differently."

Even though I've yet to find any evidence of a slave in the Frederic line, it's a given that there are slave ancestors, however distant in time. And it's a given I want to find them. How else can I fully and deeply understand my mother's ancestral story?

There are too many ghosts I need to lay to rest. Too many voices wanting to be heard.

The next time my friend and I talk, she apologizes, citing too many glasses of wine as her excuse, repeating how she was appalled by what she said. We've been friends for over ten years. I'm not willing to let our friendship go over a drunken comment meant to be humorous.

"No problem," I say. But I see her differently and maybe myself differently as well. A flaw I hadn't expected in such an educated, savvy woman. None of us are perfect, I think, myself included. I don't have the energy to explore her particular brand of bigotry.

The impetus that generates the discovery of an enslaved ancestor begins in the same way that the journey to find my grandfather Azemar Frederic began, with an omission, a space demanding to be filled—an absence of story, blank pages in a family photograph album, and the need to leave no family member unspoken for, especially those who had no voice.

The long thread back to the enslaved ancestor begins haphazardly with my third great-grandmother, Felicite Mayronne/Merrone/Meyrone and her marriage record.

I realize that in telling Bernard and Felicite's touching romance, I've neglected to investigate her. Even her surname confounds me, Mayronne/Merrone/Meyrone, so many variations resulting in so little information. She is merely a cipher—someone's wife, someone's mother. A free woman of color so beloved by her husband that he married her late in life when the ban on interracial marriage was lifted, proving that their relationship was not only long-term but loving. Bernard felt no need to have a *plaçage* arrangement with another woman. Felicite and their children were enough for him.

Where she met Bernard or the circumstances of their union are unknown. What I do know is that when they met she was a young widow with three sons. Her first husband, Noel Daniel Montesquieu, was a free person of color, making theirs an endogamous marriage.

Within four years of Noel's death, Felicite is living with Bernard and their daughter Philomene. Was she looking for a protector for herself and her sons? Was she thinking that an intimate relationship with a white man, even one who was new to the city, would provide her with the security she needed to raise her young sons? Was she willing to accept a *plaçage* arrangement, hoping it would turn into a life-long relationship? She'd once been someone's legal wife. Did she think she could demand from Bernard Lanabere the same marital fidelity and devotion? Even though, as a free woman of color living with a white man, she had no legal rights?

Bernard and Felicite don't appear in the census records until 1850 and by then her sons from her first marriage are not living with her. When Bernard finally slipped a wedding ring on her finger in 1873, Felicite must have felt some measure of satisfaction that she had chosen wisely.

Based on Felicite and Bernard's marriage record, Felicite's mother is Catherine Dauphin (my fourth great-grandmother) and her father is Manuel Meronne. Here's where the dilemma of the two Felicites lies and where the genealogical burden of proof becomes onerous. Catherine Dauphin, a free woman of color, had twelve children, possibly more. In the exhaustive list of her children, there is no Felicite. The closest in name to Felicite is Aimee Felicitas. And there are no fathers listed in any of the baptismal records for Catherine Dauphin's children. Additionally, there are no other Felicites born around the time of Felicite Meyronne's birth.

The baptismal record for Aimee Felicitas Dauphin is dated May 1810 and names the mother as Catharina Dauphin. The father is unnamed. Aimee Felicitas is a "natural" child, meaning illegitimate.

The question is are Aimee Felicitas and Felicite Meyronne the same person? Why it is crucial that Aimee Felicitas, daughter of Catherine, be Felicite Meyronne Lanabere is because Catherine/Catharina Dauphin is the linchpin in the Frederic family slave story. Catherine Dauphin's mother Marta was an enslaved woman. If the two Felicites are not the same person, then I have no slave story to tell. I have no way of knowing who our African ancestor was. I have no way to finally and irrevocably put a name and story to the DNA I carry and that my mother carried.

If I'm to prove they are the same person, I'll need direct evidence from primary sources. The birth year offers no reassurance only adding to the uncertainty that Aimee Felicitas is Felicite Meyronne.

Aimee Felicitas: birth year 1808, baptismal record
Felicite Meyronne: birth year 1813, marriage record
Felicite Meyronne: birth year 1816, death record
Felicite Meyronne: birth year 1811, 1850 census

With so many different birth years and knowing that ages and birth years were often inaccurate, they just might be the same woman. But I still haven't met the genealogical standard of proof for resolving conflicting and contradictory evidence.

The only unturned genealogical stone in this investigation is Felicite's father, Manuel Meronne, whom she names as her father on her marriage document to Bernard Lanabere.

I ask Judy Riffel to investigate Manuel Meronne, reasoning that in one of his records she might uncover evidence that Felicite Meyronne is the same person as Aimee Felicitas, which would verify that Aimee Felicitas's unnamed father is Manuel Meyronne.

Though Judy pieces together the circumstances of Manuel Meyronne's life (born in New Orleans in 1790, son of Francisco Mayronne and Feliciana Bunel, both white, of French extraction, and slave owners), she's unable to prove that Manuel Meyronne is the father of Aimee Felicitas or that Aimee Felicitas is Felicite Meyronne Lanabere.

Even though Felicite Meyronne Lanabere names Manuel as her father on her marriage record, there is no other document supporting her claim, including Manuel's probate files. If he was Felicite's father, she was just one of many children he had with various women of color. After his wife's (Louise Cantrell) death in 1823, he fathered children by two different women of color, Catherine Moriere Fazende (Rosalie in 1827) and Cidalise Landon (Joseph in 1831). Whether these relationships were *plaçage* arrangements is difficult to know.

With no solid proof that Aimee Felicitas is Felicite Meyronne, I'm left with a dilemma many genealogists face when the records don't support their suppositions and often their desires.

In a last-ditch effort to confirm these two women are the same, Judy suggests I research all of Catherine Dauphin's children and try to connect at least one of them to my Felicite.

She ends her advice with a caveat: "This could be very time-consuming."

Seeing no way to do this time-consuming task without flying to New Orleans, I shelve the genealogical research temporarily and do extensive research into Louisiana's colonial period and slavery, then I write a first draft of that section of the book based on Judy's research and the supposition that Aimee Felicitas and Felicite Meyronne are the same person. It's a risky gamble and one that could cost me countless hours of research and writing. But my gut tells me the two women are the same person.

Then I learn of another way to research Catherine Dauphin's children that doesn't involve flying to New Orleans. Jack Belsom mentions Chicago's Newberry Library's vast genealogical collections, specifically the sacramental records of the Roman Catholic Church of the Archdiocese of New Orleans (Earl C. Woods).

"Do you live near Chicago?" he asks.

"Near enough."

"Why not go there. Sure would save you time and money."

For months I've been requesting baptismal, marriage, and death records from the Archdiocese of New Orleans Archives. As much as I enjoy receiving the official certificates with the embossed seal at the bottom, at twelve dollars per document, it was starting to add up.

In the excitement of researching and writing, I'd forgotten about the Newberry as a possible genealogical research site.

I plan a research trip for the following week. But it doesn't happen. A few days later I wake to excruciating lower back pain and can barely get out of bed. It will be months before I'm well enough to make the two-hour train trip and overnight stay in Chicago. In the interim I keep writing and researching and praying that my hunch about Aimee Felicitas and Felicite is right. It's as if some trace of my grandmother Camille's second sight beats inside of me, urging me on against all logic.

The women wait in the wings, eager to have their stories told. I wait with them, whispering that they will not be forgotten, that it won't be as if they were never here, that someone will know them, will acknowledge their existence—these voiceless women. Isn't that what we do for our family—tell their stories so they're not forgotten? And in telling their stories, I tell my mother's story as well.

The Newberry is my last resort. In advance of my research days, I request the specific volumes of the sacramental records related to the baptism of Catherine's children closest in age to Aimee Felicitas. Because of Judy's warning, I'm expecting to spend at least two days, maybe more, at the library.

The genealogical collections are housed on the second floor. Once I obtain my reader's card on the third floor, I gingerly take the steps down to the second floor, the warmth of the heat pack easing my back pain. After I present my card and copy of my online request to the librarian, she hands me two yellow pencils for note taking, and directs me to table F14.

"Someone will bring the books to you," the dark-haired, petite young woman explains.

It's nearly 2 p.m. I'll have three hours to read through the books. If I can't find anything, I'll return tomorrow at 9 a.m. As I wait patiently for the librarian to bring me Volumes 8, 9, 10, 11, and 12, I read through the list of Catherine's children, reading and rereading baptismal dates, sponsor (godparent) names, and Judy's suggestion about tracking down Catherine's other children.

Children of Catherine Dauphin, native of New Orleans
1. *Maria Luisa Isavel, b.?, godmother to brother Evaristo in 1821*
2. *Guiellmo, bt. 14 July 1799, age 4 months. Sponsors: Juan Joy, Englishman, and Margarita Sinetre*
3. *Constancia Catarina, b. 15 Dec. 1800, bt. 25 Jan. 1801. Sponsors: Felix Tala and Constancia Tala*
4. *Johan Baptista, b. 15 Dec. 1802, bt. 15 Feb. 1805. Sponsors: Baptiste Dauphin and Maria Theresia Dauphin*
5. *Terrence, b. 1 Dec. 1806, bt. 25 Nov. 1807. Sponsors: Pierre St. Dos and Marie Claire Boute*
6. *Aimee Felicitas, b. 15 Nov. 1808, bt. 2 May 1810. Sponsors: Juan Castille and Martina Dauphin, child's aunt*
7. *Joseph, b. 1 Nov. 1810, bt. 5 Jan. 1813. Sponsors: Luis D'Auterive and Maria Rosa D'Auterive, la joven*
8. *Marthe, bt. 27 Oct. 1815. Sponsors: Jean Vernoir and Constance Catherine Rilieux. Bd. 30 Oct. 1815*

9. *Leonard, twin of Louise Elisabeth, b. 30 Sept. 1816, bt. 3 June 1817.
    Sponsors: Leon Dauphin and Eugenie Porera?*
10. *Louise Elisabeth, twin of Leonard, b. 30 Sept. 1816, bt. 3 June 1817.
    Sponsors: Gaspar Borasse and Felicite D'Autrive*
11. *Alphrede, bd. 27 June 1819, age 8 months*
12. *Evaristo, b. 26 Oct. 1821, bt. 24 Aug. 1824. Sponsors: Augusto
    Boundet and Maria Luisa Ysavel Dauphin, child's sister*

Then it hits me. I've made a mistake. A wave of panic rushes through me. Searching through the sacramental records isn't going to tell me anything I don't already know about Catherine's children. Judy's already given me that information. What was I thinking? Why am I here? My lower back begins to ache and throb.

Carefully, I push back the heavy wood chair and stand, feeling sick. I can't leave, I tell myself. I have to at least look through the books. Maybe Judy missed something. Though I doubt that. She's extremely meticulous.

The books are a light gray with black lettering. With resignation, I lift the heavy book, Volume 8, 1804–1806, and turn to page eighty-two: "Johann Baptiste; Sponsors Baptiste Dauphin and Maria Theresia Dauphin." The information matches Judy's information. As expected, there are no informational variations in Volumes 9, 10, and 11.

Reading the 1815 baptismal record for Catherine's eighth child Marthe, my eyes flick back and forth between the book's baptismal record for Marthe and Judy's notes, my heart sinking as I realize the records also are exactly the same. I have only more volume to check, Volume 12. It's nearly two forty-five. It'll be a short research day.

Then my eyes light on an entry above Marthe under a different surname: D'Autarive. Below that name is a marriage record dated November 22, 1815. The record reads: "Isavel Virginia (Luis and Felicite Meyronne) native and resident married Luis Bouligne." Felicite Meyronne's married name is D'Autarive. Of course, the woman isn't my Felicite Meyronne because in 1815, she was still a child. But is she related to Manuel Meyronne, I wonder?

Then I move on to Volume 12, the last volume. "Louise Elisabeth (Catherine), twin of Leonard, b. September 30, 1816, bt. June 3, 1817. Sponsors: Gaspar Borasse and Felicite D'Autrive." I double check the information with Judy's, see that it's the same, and am about to close the book when it hits me. Felicite D'Autrive née Meyronne is Louise Elisabeth's sponsor.

My mind floods with the historical significance of sponsors in nineteenth-century New Orleans. How they were often chosen by parents to help raise the status of their child, to gain social advantages. My heart beats wildly as I go back through the books and look for D'Autrives. The surname has four alternative spellings: Dauterive, D'Auterive, D'Autarive, and D'Autrive. Using the D'Autrive marriage, baptismal, and death records, I piece together Victoria Felicite Mayronne D'Autrive's life. Without question she is Manuel Meyronne's sister. They share the same parents and he is the sponsor for the baptism of her daughter Felicite Fanel.

With only an hour left before the library closes, I quickly order the other volumes of the sacramental records, Volumes 6, 7, 13, 14, 15, and 16. Every entry for the D'Auterives adds more direct primary proof that Felicite Meyronne D'Autrive is the sister of Manuel Meyronne. In sponsoring Catherine Dauphin's tenth child Louise Elisabeth in 1815, Felicite D'Autrive, Manuel Meyronne's sister, confirms the link between the Meyronne family and Catherine Dauphin. The quality and weight of evidence proves that Aimee Felicitas Dauphin is Felicite Meyronne Lanabere. They are the same woman.

I marvel at the serendipity of the discovery, the "what ifs" that had to occur for me to make this discovery: If my eyes hadn't momentarily strayed to the entry above the Dauphin entry; if Catherine Dauphin hadn't asked Felicite D'Autrive to be the godmother of her child Louise. And even stranger, if Felicite Meyronne hadn't married a man whose surname was D'Autrive, alphabetically placing it before Dauphin in the sacramental books.

How am I to explain these bizarre serendipitous happenings? How am I to explain that not only was my hunch right, but that Felicite has been waiting over two hundred years for me to find her so I can tell her mother's story of enslavement and freedom?

24

Modeling Whiteness

"Looking white is, in many ways, contingent on *doing* white."
—Allyson Hobbs, *A Chosen Exile.*

MY MOTHER HAD no manual on how to act white, no guidebook, and no set of instructions. Her light skin said white, but she knew that whiteness was more than a skin color. If she was to pass successfully, she had to not only look white but also act white. Movies were her training ground as well as her escape.

In the era of double features, she went to the movies sometimes twice a week. From the time I was six years old until adolescence, I was her companion and escort to the Friday night double feature at the local movie house. She favored the dark, moody dramas of unrequited love where the heroine retained her honor at all costs or the dark Hitchcock mysteries with their secrets and surprising revelations.

During my childhood I remember vividly *Giant*, *The Night of the Hunter*, *Mogambo*, *The Caine Mutiny*, and *A Place in the Sun*, movies that were too mature for me and sometimes frightened me with their disturbing themes about tough choices, sexuality, and evil. The eerie image of Shelley Winters's drowned body at the bottom of the lake, her hair floating around her, disturbed me for years.

From movies she learned how white women dressed, styled their hair, spoke, gestured, and dealt with troublesome men. Though she seldom smoked, when she did she mirrored Bette Davis, flicking her cigarette ash coyly with that frisky glint in her eye that said, "I'm in charge but you can try." Smart brunettes like Rosaline Russell and Joan Crawford intrigued her with their sassy remarks and independence.

She disliked Marilyn Monroe for her overt and crass sexuality and dumb blond act. Though one year for the neighborhood Halloween party she masqueraded as Monroe, donning a platinum wig, red satin dress with a thigh-high slit, black gloves, fishnet stockings, and a long cigarette holder she pretended to smoke, inhaling and blowing out nothing. I was transfixed by how her personality changed, how seamlessly she became another person. Gushing in a breathless Monroe voice she asked, "How do I look?"

Her obsession with movies ran so deep she named me after a movie starlet, Gail Russell, a 1950s actress who succumbed to alcoholism and died alone in 1961 at the age of thirty-six in her apartment surrounded by empty liquor bottles.

When I asked her why she chose Gail as my name, she answered that when I was born I had blue eyes and dark hair just like Gail Russell, whose beauty she desired for me. She shrugged her shoulders. "But your eyes changed and so did your hair."

The movies were a release for my mother. In the dark theater she could cry without explanation, something I rarely saw her do at home. Her identification with the women on the screen was transformative, as well as instructive, blurring the line between the real and the imaginative. For those two hours she was Susan Hayworth, Hedy Lamar, Lana Turner, women faced with impossible decisions who manage to survive. For the time we sat together in the darkness she could also be herself, appreciating her own performance. How she'd tricked a society intent on putting her in her racial place.

Whether from the movies or from growing up in a boarding house schooled by her great-grandmother, my mother viewed good manners as a sign of good breeding. From the time I could talk, I was instructed to say "thank you" and "please." A swift reprimand would follow my failure to do so.

"Manners will take you anywhere in society, even further than money," was one of her mantras.

I always attributed her strict emphasis on manners solely to her Southern upbringing. But acting white is part of appearing white. Being so polite, so well bred, how could anyone doubt her whiteness.

If manners and good breeding were my mother's interpretation of what it meant to look white, she reasoned that her daughter, who was a reflection of her, should have all the grace and charm that her own childhood had lacked. Though I'd been taking ballet and tap classes since I was four with the intention of imbuing me with grace, my mother felt I needed an extra polish. In the summer before I turned fourteen, she enrolled me in charm school—an eight-week class for young ladies given by Higbee's department store in downtown Cleveland.

According to my mother, charm school would teach me how to be a *lady*. She was convinced that anyone could escape the prison of poverty and class if they were privy to the secrets of good breeding.

But at thirteen I was wise to her true intentions. As much as charm school had to do with good breeding, it had just as much to do with her dream of me being a beauty queen, which now in light of her racial secret seems both subversive and vaguely risky.

Every once in a while my mother would suggest I fill out an application for a beauty pageant. And whenever she did, I knew she wasn't seeing me, what she was seeing was herself or how she wanted to be seen. My mother was beauty queen material, not me.

Tall and thin with heavy glasses and fine, wavy hair that had a mind of its own, I preferred the company of books and close friends. To walk down a runway in a bathing suit being judged seemed to me demeaning and horrifying. Maybe I was her stand-in, her last chance, her doppel-gänger—the white self no one could doubt or question. My whiteness was unbreechable. I was the payoff for her passing—a white daughter who could walk a runway with other white girls—no questions asked.

In 1960 African American women were barred from competing in the quintessential beauty pageant, the Miss America competition. And not until 1984 would Vanessa L. Williams become the first African American to win the title of Miss America, thirteen years after the Miss America contest allowed African American women to enter.

My mother revered beauty contests and felt that for a woman to win a beauty contest was an achievement worth pursuing. So she was not to be deterred. Every Saturday for eight weeks, I went to charm school—a thirty-five-minute bus ride from Parma to downtown Cleveland. In her zeal, my mother convinced my aunt, my father's sister, that her eldest daughter, Yvonne, needed charm as well. Yvonne was three months younger than me and we both had been named for movie stars. I was named after Gail Russell, and Yvonne was named after Yvonne De Carlo. Clearly, our mothers had agendas when it came to their oldest daughters.

Charm school was held on one of the department store's top floors where large windows opened onto the city, flanking the room, casting unflinching light on every flaw that needed to be corrected.

The first class, we were given black spiral-ringed notebooks with "The Higbee Charm School" emblazoned on the cover in gold letters. The teacher, Miss McGuire, was a tall woman with a long, graceful neck who walked as if she barely inhabited her clothes, which were always dark and tailored. She instructed us to record our progress in our notebooks. We were to paste in clothes cut from magazines and write down ways to improve our physical appearance.

That first Saturday Miss McGuire measured and weighed us. One by one in front of the other girls, we had to submit to the tape measure and the scale. With the precision of a surgeon she wrote down the numbers next to the outline of a woman's body—breast, waist, hips, height, and weight.

For some inexplicable reason I still have this charm school notebook, a relic of a bygone era, when beauty was defined by grace, a part of my girlhood that explained my unrelenting self-criticism that still dogs me today. And in light of what I know about my mother's mixed race, the notebook is also a document of 1959's white middle-class America, at least the white America I knew, defining the narrow goals set for white middle-class young women, all centered on physical appearance.

Statistically speaking, in August 1959 I was five feet three and a half inches tall and weighed 105 pounds. My body proportions were symmetrical, both bust and hips thirty-three inches. Next to the outline of my body and my measurements was a quote: "When you praised her as charming, some asked what you meant. But the charm of her presence was felt where she went."

We were cautioned to watch these numbers and that at the end of the eight weeks Miss McGuire would measure and weigh us again to check our progress. It was all about before and after, the notion that a woman was evaluated by her body stats. The reward for all this watching and self-discipline would be a fashion show where we would walk a runway and model a Higbee's outfit.

My notebook had headings like: "Charming of Form," "Grace in Motion," "Charming of Face," and "Charming of Dress." There was a cautionary play on the word charm: "Remember: Charm − C = Harm." There were body and hand exercises, examples of how to stand and sit, how to enter and exit a room, how to glide walk, how to ascend and descend stairs, how to apply makeup, how to use accessories, how to achieve a bandbox look.

The most important lesson I learned in charm school wasn't in my notebook and wasn't intended. The last class before our runway show, Miss McGuire demonstrated on each girl how to pluck our eyebrows. It was going well until she came to the last girl who had thick eyebrows that nearly ran together. This poor girl also had a faint mustache.

As Miss McGuire began to pluck and pluck away, the girl flinched in pain. Finally exhausted, clearly frustrated, Miss McGuire gave up. She put her silver tweezers down in defeat and in front of the class said to the girl that it was impossible, that she couldn't do it, there was just too much hair, and that the girl would have to seek professional help with her eyebrows.

The girl hung her head in embarrassment, her face red, biting her lip, trying not to cry. We all shifted in our seats nervously, careful to keep our legs together, our ankles crossed, not wanting to call attention to ourselves.

The girl never returned for the runway show. I have no memory of that fashion show. But charm school solidified my determination never to enter a beauty contest. I couldn't stand up to the scrutiny. Charm school reinforced my self-consciousness, fostered by my mother, her belief that every hair had to be in place and every movement choreographed, not so much in a pursuit of perfection, but of uniformity. To stand out in an uncharming manner might suggest other unsavory things about you.

On the last page of the notebook is the solitary outline of the same woman's body I'd outlined on the first page. The word *After* is written above her head. In eight weeks I grew half an inch, my weight was still 105, my bust and hips now thirty-four inches. Instead of a startled expression on the woman's face, now she smiles. Miss McGuire gave me a "Very Good" rating. I showed my mother the rating. She nodded her approval but said nothing. I'd passed but I could have done better, "Very Good" isn't "Excellent," obviously there was room for improvement in the never-ending quest for charm and beauty.

To my mother's dismay, a few years after charm school one of my best girl friends from Miss Angela's dance studio, Judy Adams, not only entered a beauty contest but was crowned Miss Teen USA. Judy was a natural beauty with long wavy blonde hair and that beauty queen smile, toothy and sincere.

As my mother and I watched the crown being placed on Judy's head, she turned to me and said, "Yes, but she's not much of a dancer."

By then I was a member of the Cleveland Civic Ballet Company, entrenched in dance, all notions of beauty pageants gone. I was perfecting myself in a different way.

After my mother's death, I joined a grief group facilitated by the local hospice center. One evening I finally found the courage to share with the other group members the devastation I felt at the loss of my mother, this woman who had been such a force in my life, who forged me as if I were raw metal and she was the smithy. Verging on tears, I pieced together what she meant to me, leaving out any mention of her secret. When I was done, after the other members had offered me their support, Liz the facilitator said, "Gail, you have such grace about you."

My mother would have loved that, I thought.

25

Marta

"With much love and affection and services of the mother, no prices at all."

—Louisiana Slave Record 1783, reasons for Marta's manumission.

I'M MOVING BACK in time, each birth year, death date, marriage, census report are like ghost towns seen from the road offering little but a broken sign flapping in the wind, buildings and barns crumbling into the tall grasses, turning back into nothing. Everyone is gone. There's no one to ask about the people who once lived here. This is what it is like to unearth the past through the visage of cold documents. I hold the dry paper, read the facts, and envision my people.

When Judy's email arrives with the news I've been expecting, I realize that she sounds like one of my mystery novel sleuths.

"In studying other church records as well as some of the notarial records, I've developed a theory that Catherine Dauphin was the daughter of Pierre Dauphin and Marta, his former slave."

Then she backs up her theory by directing me to the 1783 manumission by Pedro Dauphin of Marta (twenty-four) and her four children Agustin (seven), Juan Bautista (five), Francisco (three), and Catiche
(1.30). The preciseness of Catiche's age, 1.30, irritates me as needlessly
mathematical, reminding me of her value as property. The manumission names Pedro as the children's white father. The reason Pedro Dauphin gives for freeing Marta and her four children is: "Much love and
affection and services of the mother."

"I believe Catherine may be the same Catiche, as I found nothing further under Catiche," Judy says. "Based on the relationships given in various baptismal records, I am fairly certain that this is Catherine's family."

My enslaved ancestor has been found. She bears but one name—
Marta. She is my portal to slavery's ugly past. She and her mother
are the progenitors of the Frederic African blood. The discovery opens
yet another door into Louisiana and American history of the colonial
period. It shows the muddled history of race relations, illustrating yet
again the mixing of the races and the legacy of slavery writ large in so
many people's DNA, whether they know it or not. She is the Eve in our
family story of mixed race.

All afternoon I return to the manumission documents, each time
experiencing a spark of anger tempered by insight when I read: "Much
love and affection and services of the mother, no prices at all." Pedro
Dauphin's statement goes to the core of slavery and patriarchy. What
choice did Marta have but to submit, body and soul? What choice did
she have but to render services to the man who owned her?

Historian Lawrence Powell's observation that "[s]lightly more than
40 percent of all slaves manumitted from 1771 to 1803 reached freedom
through 'gracious' emancipation" does little to tamp down my disgust.[1]
Nor does the fact that French Louisiana, and especially in urban areas,
"differed from other mainland slave societies in one notable respect: the
number of white men willing to free slave mistresses and their mixed-
race children, or at least acquiesce in other avenues by which they could
reach freedom."[2]

Am I to feel gratitude for Pedro's kindness in freeing my ancestor and their children? Though the circumstances are radically different, I'm confronted with the same question I asked about my mother's passing for white: What was the cost to her? What was the cost to Marta for her freedom?

When I delve into the historical background of Marta's life, I find that her lineage is as deeply rooted in Louisiana's early colonial period as those of the German Coast farmers, who I believe are my ancestors and are credited with feeding New Orleans and saving the struggling Louisiana colony. The irony is that without their slaves working the rich alluvial land along the river, wet nursing and tending their children, and cooking their food with the spices and flavors of Africa the Louisiana colony wouldn't have been saved. Not only did they provide physical labor for farming but also skilled labor from cabinetmakers to metalworkers to surgeons. Slavery was the business that the colony and the country invested in to be profitable, to be viable. And the African slaves were the people who paid the price.

Marta, my fifth great-grandmother, was born into slavery in 1759 during the Louisiana colony's last days under French rule. Pierre/Pedro Dauphin (fifth great-grandfather), the father of her children, was born in Louisiana in 1754. His parents, Joseph Dauphin and his wife Ana/Mariana, both natives of France, owned Marta and her mother, Maria.

Making an educated guess at my sixth great-grandmother Maria's birth year, based on the birth year of her daughter Marta in 1759, it's likely Maria was born no earlier than 1744 or 1745, giving credence to her being born in the colony and that Maria's mother, my seventh great-grandmother, was brought from Africa. If Maria's mother was brought from Africa, then she came on one of the early slave ships.

The first slave ships arrived on the Mississippi Gulf Coast between 1719 and 1721, approximately twenty or so years after Louisiana became a French colony. These nineteen hundred Africans were the first of six thousand slaves that John Law promised to ship to Louisiana as part of his charter with France to turn Louisiana into a tobacco colony.[3]

If Maria's mother was on one of these early slave ships, then she probably was from the Senegambia area of Africa, between the Senegal and Gambia rivers of West Africa. The first slaves brought to Louisiana were from that area and were identified as Wolof, Bambara, and Mandinga.[4] Almost all the slave ships to Louisiana originated from the port of Lorient in Africa.[5] By 1731 when the Company of the Indies left the colony, slave importation had waned.[6] Despite the death rates that had reduced the charter generation of Africans by three-fifths, within a decade of their arrival, Louisiana, had become a black majority colony.[7]

Whether Maria was born in the colony or not, what I am certain of is that Marta's mother was Maria. They are listed in a 1769/1770 partition of the estate of Joseph and Mariana Dauphin, Pedro/Pierre's parents. The heirs are Françoise Dauphin, Juan Dauphin, Josef Dauphin, and Juan Pedro Dauphin (an emancipated minor). The three sons take some land (German Coast) and a group of slaves. The other slaves associated with that estate are: (1) Barataria; (2) Jauno; (3) Juana, wife of Sans Chagrin with four children; (4) LaJoye; (5) Maria with one child; (6) Marta with her mother; (7) Sans Chagrin, husband of Juana; (8) Sans Souci, husband; and (9) unnamed adult. It appears that Maria's one child is Marta and that Marta's mother is Maria.

Slave narratives attest to the dread experienced by slaves when a slave owner died and his or her estate was transferred to their heirs. Depending on the financial situation of the heirs, often slaves were sold and separated from their families.

Delia Garlic, who was born into slavery, describes the separation of families. "Chillens was separated from sisters and brothers and never saw each other gain. 'Course dey cry. You think they not cry when dey was sold like cattle?"[8]

Fannie Moore relates the manner in which women were sold. "It was a terrible sight to see de speculator come to the plantation . . . de 'breed woman' always bring more money den de rest, even de men. When they put her on de block dey put all her chillen around her to show folks how fast she can have chillen. When she sold her family never see her again. She never know how many chillen she had. Colored chillen and sometimes white. 'Taint't no use to say anything, 'cause if she do she just get whipped."[9]

If the heirs of the Dauphin estate had sold the inherited slaves in a public auction, Marta and her mother would have most likely experienced the same fate. Though the inherited slaves weren't publically auctioned, they were separated and dispersed among the heirs along with their parents' other property. Pedro/Pierre inherited Marta and Maria.

According to Ancestry.com, Pedro Dauphin owned property in the German Coast Township, situated along the Mississippi River and above New Orleans, bounded on one side by his brother Joseph Dauphin's land with whom he was in partnership with in a sawmill.

To understand the milieu Maria and her daughter Marta inhabited as enslaved women in eighteenth-century Louisiana, I access the archival civil records for two German Coast parishes: St. Charles Parish, 1770–1803, and St. John the Baptist Parish, 1804–1812. Besides Pedro Dauphin, the Frederic family also owned property along the German Coast. Though I've yet to prove one way or another if Ursin Frederic descended from the German Coast Frederic family.

The archives provide snapshots into the river parishes during the Spanish period and as an American territory, giving a legal accounting of everyday life in the parishes in terms of slave sales, manumissions, and treatment of crimes and misdemeanors of slaves. These records provide a perspective to help me understand the legal positions of enslaved people, as well as slave owners in eighteenth and nineteenth-century Louisiana.

In relationship to slaves and their masters, the civil records indicate how the local authorities enforced the *Code Noir*, or Black Code. As early as 1724, the first slave code, *Code Noir*, was initiated, outlining the treatment of slaves, including under what conditions they could be freed and, once freed, their rights and obligations. The code granted slaves the right to a religious education (Catholic), the ability to be hired out by their masters or work for hire to earn wages, and to bring their masters to court for mistreatment.[10]

In the German Coast Parishes' civil archives, I could find no such redress made by a slave regarding mistreatment. The *Code Noir*'s intention was to limit opportunities for emancipation.[11] The *Code* also prohibited marriage between whites and blacks whether slave or free, as well as prohibiting owners keeping slave concubines.[12] But what appears on paper as a law doesn't necessarily translate to what actually happened.

The German Coast civil archives indicate that the Frederics were active in buying slaves, which comes as no surprise. But when I read the details of one transaction involving two siblings, the callousness of the legal transaction becomes too real. Silvain (eleven) and sister, Marguerite (ten), are separated and moved like pawn pieces or worse, livestock.

Besides slave and land sales, marriage and succession contracts, the St. Charles Parish Original Acts contain accounts of slave runaways and the famous 1811 slave insurrection. Runaways were treated harshly. Not only would they be whipped, sometimes as many as two hundred times, but their lacerated skin was rubbed with sponges soaked in pepper and vinegar, followed by a branding of a fleur-de-lis.[13]

Harriet Jacobs in her slave narrative *Incidents in the Life of a Slave Girl* recounts a particularly horrifying punishment that elaborates on the use of brine. The strong brine was used to prevent the flesh from mortifying and to promote healing.

Her account of the punishment of a slave named James is particularly horrendous. After receiving a hundred lashes, James is put in the cotton gin and given only a piece of bread and a bowl of water daily. The slave who delivered the water and bread was not to speak to James under threat of a similar punishment. After four days and five nights the water was not used and a horrible stench came from the gin house. When the press was unscrewed, James's body was discovered partly eaten by rats and vermin. Jacobs concludes that perhaps the rats that had eaten the bread had gnawed him before he died, thus explaining the water not being used.[14]

The St. Charles Original Acts 1808 Depositions Regarding a Runaway Slave contains an extended account of a runaway slave named Charles involving the exchange of gunfire between the runaway and the plantation's overseer (a white man), which resulted in Charles being wounded and dogs tracking him into the sugarcane fields where he is captured.[15]

The central issue is not whether he fired in self-defense, but whether he could see whom he was firing on. In other words, was the moonlight sufficient to determine a black man from a white man? All the witnesses testify that the moonlight was sufficient to determine the man's race. Though Charles denies knowing he fired on a white man, he is sentenced to death. On the same day that Charles was condemned to death by hanging, an appraisal of his worth was conducted. He was appraised at $300.

In the Spanish's mania for record keeping, manumission acts were also recorded. One particularly stands out and illuminates the complicated layers of slavery (February 21, 1798). "Catherine Silvie, a free Negro, formerly belonging to Pierre Vieux, declared . . . that she granted freedom to the slave named Baptiste (fifty-two) whom she acquired from Jean-Louis Jardin (Girardin), a free mulatto, in recognition of the faithful service rendered to her by Baptiste during a period of illness."[16]

Did a romantic relationship develop between Catherine and Jean-Louis that prompted her freeing him? Or was the reason given the true reason. Regardless, it was not uncommon for emancipated slaves to own slaves and then free them. During the colonial period, the institution of slavery was so pervasive and accepted that the Ursuline nuns and the Jesuits owned slaves. Two-thirds of free households contained slaves.[17]

That my ancestors stood on opposite sides of the slavery fence as the oppressors and the oppressed adds to the complicity of my family's racial history, both clarifying and mudding the question of what it means to be a mixed-race person descended from slaves and slave owners.

After Dauphin emancipated Marta, she continued to live with him and bore him seven more children. As a free woman of color who'd been a slave, what options were open to her? Regardless of whether their initial sexual encounter was forced or not forced, it was a rape. After all Marta was his property. Pedro had all the power. If she gave her consent to his desires, unquestionably her consent was weighted on his side. Some historians suggest that certain enslaved women used their sexual powers to manipulate their white masters. I find that viewpoint difficult to understand. Having been born into slavery as property of the Dauphin family, Marta learned early that she was subject in all things to their will.

Harriet Jacobs's slave narrative gives insight into what a slave woman endured sexually. As Jacobs explains, "The slave girl is reared in an atmosphere of licentiousness and fear. The lash and the foul talk of her master and his sons are her teachers."[18] As property, women are of no value to their owners unless they continually increase their owners' stock.

Jacobs's white master's sexual pursuit of her is unrelenting, though he never rapes her. His particular brand of control is still a violation.

Rather than submit to him, Harriet asserts her own brand of freedom and has a sexual relationship with another white man in the town, closer to her own age, who shows interest in her plight.

"It seems less degrading to give one's self, than to submit to compulsion. There is something akin to freedom in having a lover who has no control over you, except that which he gains by kindness and attachment."[19]

But when she gives birth to a girl fathered by her white consort, she despairs. "Slavery is terrible for men; but it is far more terrible for women."[20]

Marta most likely didn't have the option of finding a white protector. Was her decision to have seven more children with Dauphin after she was freed her way of working within an oppressive society? Was she, like Jacobs, eking out some measure of control? Did she tell herself that at least her owner was near to her own age and she might win his favor, securing freedom for herself and her children? If she did, her and her children's emancipation proved her right, as did Dauphin's will.

In Pedro Dauphin's will dated April 3, 1800, he declares that he is "sick in body, in my full senses, memory and natural understanding." He also states he is unmarried and has eleven mulatto natural children of the Negress Marta. Astonishingly, he divides his property in half, giving one portion to Marta and the other portion to be divided equally among his eleven children. In the event of Marta's death, her half is to be divided equally among their eleven children. In bearing his children, in succumbing in all things to his desires, Marta secured the economic future of her children. Regardless of how I view my ancestors' sexual relationship, there is no question that it was a committed one.

It comes as a surprise to find their relationship cited in historian Kimberly Hanger's book *Bounded Lives, Bounded Places* as an example of how mixed racial relationships contributed to the burgeoning and prosperous free black caste. Hanger discusses the long-term common law relationship between Juan Pedro Dauphin and his slave Marta, stressing the importance of kinship among family members as a means for free people of color to enhance their economic and social status. The free black Dauphin family combined their resources to purchase property. In 1802 Francisco and his older brother Augusto, both born into slavery and later freed by Dauphin, gave to three of their younger brothers a large plot of land in Barataria (the haunting ground of privateer Jean Lafitte).[21]

Sexual relationships with free black consorts were also a pattern with Pedro Dauphin's brothers, Joseph and Santiago, who both lived with free women of color.

However Marta viewed her sexual capitulation to Pedro Dauphin, she remade herself from an enslaved woman to a free woman of color with property and prosperity that was handed down to her children. For a woman who was never even given a surname, she raised her status considerably in a slave owning culture. I'd like to think her canny survival instincts were passed down through the generations.

Not until almost one hundred years later, when Marta's great-granddaughter Philomene Lanabere, daughter of Felicite Meyronne and Bernard Lanabere, marries Leon Frederic, Sr. will Marta's familial line join the Frederic line.

Without doubt the mixing of African and European ancestry is present in other ancestral threads. But none that I could find appeared so early in Louisiana's history, illustrating how some white men took advantage of their positions of power over black women. Considering the Jim Crow laws my mother lived under, how the one-drop rule determined her life choices, I see how the sins of the white fathers were laid upon their children.

But even after I discover Marta, it changes nothing about my sense of racial identity. I have no claim on black identity, no right to declare myself even mixed race. And yet, my African ancestry is there in my DNA: 7–9 percent, more than one-drop, enough that up until 1983 in Louisiana I would have been designated as black.

What does it mean for a blatantly white woman to tell the story of her distant slave ancestor? "What gives me the right?" I ask myself. Is

7–9 percent African DNA enough? Does it matter that it's me telling
her story, as long as her story is told?

My search has never been about claiming a black identity. It springs
from another place—the desire to know what my enslaved ancestors
endured, how they assimilated into their time and place, and how they
survived. I carry their DNA like a badge of honor.

26

Breaking Up Is Hard to Do

My 1958 Diary: Parma, Ohio
August 1: Mom and dad were arguing.
August 4: My parents are at it again.
*August 13: I sure wish Dad was not always feeling sorry for himself. And mom
would be more affectionate.*
*December 31: Two of my hopes for the New Year—a happy family and no
nightmares.*

THE SOUNDS OF screaming wake me, filtering through the house,
up the stairs to my bedroom where sleep has become unpredictable, filled with nightmares and night terrors, whispering voices calling
my name. I lie still afraid to move, listening to my mother shout at my
father, "You're crazy, you're crazy, you're crazy."

I hear a thud. A door slams. Motionless in my bed, I listen hard into
the now quiet house for some signal—more shouting, more doors slam-
ming—telling me what to do next. Nothing, just the wind rattling the
window, wanting in.

My nightlight glows yellow on the other side of the large room cutting the darkness.

It's hours before I fall back into a restless sleep. In the morning I study my parents' faces and see no bruises, no sign that anything has happened.

All that day at school, I wonder why is my father crazy? What has he done to my mother that she screams it through the house in the middle of the night like a warning to us all? "You're crazy, you're crazy, you're crazy."

Soon after that incident my mother joined Al-Anon, a support and discussion group for the family of people suffering from alcoholism. She attended weekly meetings with her friend, a neighbor, whose husband was also an alcoholic. It seemed as if our neighborhood was plagued with alcoholics of every description from the binge drinker who frequented The Lincoln Inn at the corner of our street and often drank himself to unconsciousness to my father who never missed work, never binge drank, but was always buzzed.

Though my father was aware of where she went once a week, he never said anything about the meetings as if that was her problem and it had nothing to do with him.

From Al-Anon she learned how to live with an alcoholic, imparting some of that advice to me.

"Never answer them back," she said. "That's what they want, a fight."

And her behavior did change as a result of Al-Anon. When my father started in on her with his alcoholic rant—the drip, drip, drip of his toxic words, repeated over and over—she'd ignore him, leave the room, put on the television or go to her bedroom, and he'd be left alone with no one to inflict his abuse on.

By then I had my own strategy: disappear. I couldn't be in enough after-school activities from drama to ballet. And when I wasn't doing an activity, I disappeared to my room above the house claiming homework or I rode the streets on my bike, dreaming I lived somewhere else.

But I had to come home eventually.

As committed as my mother was to the Al-Anon tenets, sometimes the pressure of living with an alcoholic and having no family support would erupt into physical violence on my mother's part.

One Sunday after a dance rehearsal in Cleveland for the Cleveland Civic Ballet Company, I return to find the mirror that hangs in the kitchen adjacent to the sink gone. In its place is a darker yellow square where the light never reached.

"What happened to the mirror?" I ask my mother who seems subdued, sitting in the living room reading the newspaper, the house unusually quiet, my father and brother not there.

"Your father couldn't stand that my friend and I went to hear Billy Graham. He just kept at me, picking and picking away." She's crying. "I went to hear Billy Graham speak, a religious person. But your father couldn't stand that. He's so jealous. So I picked up a soup can and threw it at him. It hit the mirror and broke it." She dabs at her face with a tissue. "Well, that shut him up."

I imagine my father's boozy jealousy spiraling, as he sat alone drinking, while his wife and her friend had an enjoyable afternoon that had nothing to do with him. I see my mother snap, grabbing the soup can, and flinging it at the mirror, the need to break something, to silence my father, to stop the pain that was gnawing at her.

Not for the first or last time, I wish they would divorce and end everyone's misery including their own.

The letter is frayed, falling apart, has been in my deceased father's wallet for many years. It's addressed to my father from a Cleveland lawyer who my mother retained.

After his death while cleaning out his bedroom drawer, I'm shocked to find the letter secluded in his wallet like a calling card, a reminder of how close she came to following my advice.

From the age of twelve my mother sought my counsel asking me if I thought she should divorce my father. I was twelve, what did I know of these things? All I knew was she was patently unhappy and that our home life was chaotic and my father's drinking escalating along with his emotional abuse. I had no knowledge of finances, how we would live without my father's income. Where we would live. I felt she wanted me to say "yes," to assure her that this was the right thing to do. And so I said "yes."

Sometimes she'd counter my yes, questioning how we would live without his paycheck. And then I'd know that it was just talk, that she would never divorce him.

Only now do I realize that in that question of divorce was another question. Can I go home to my people if I can't make it on my own? Maybe that's what stopped her—the prospect of crossing back over to the other side.

The letter is dated May 2, 1961.

I have been retained by your wife, Alvera, for the purpose of filing an action against you for separate maintenance and support.

In view of the fact that there are two minor children involved, I feel it is my duty to do all in my power to attempt to affect a reconciliation before filing my petition.

I am confident that a great deal of trouble and expense can be avoided for both you and your wife if you are interested in saving your marriage and preserving your family unity, by you coming in and discussing this matter with me before Friday, May 5.

I am sending this letter in a plain envelope so that your wife needn't know that I have written to you. I strongly suggest that you see me for the mutual welfare of your family.

The letter is a man-to-man correspondence. The little woman is out of control. Your wife wants a divorce. You need to nip this nonsense in the bud. The deception of the plain envelope infuriates me.

The way I see it, the letter is a betrayal of my mother's confidence in the lawyer. It had taken her a long time to seek a divorce. It had taken her knowing that the coffee I poured from his thermos while he drove me to high school was laced with alcohol. At six thirty in the morning his need for drink was all consuming. Morning to night he was always slightly intoxicated. When I'd pour the coffee I'd catch the pungent scent of whiskey.

There was never a divorce or even a separation, just this frail letter, this relic. This fragment of a different mother, who for a brief time stepped out of the shadow she'd lived under for so long, the shadow of an alcoholic husband, decent provider, suburban home—her safe harbor turned treacherous. Perhaps my father promised not to drink anymore while driving his daughter to school, a promise he wasn't physiologically or psychologically able to keep without help.

I like to think, but I'm most likely wrong, that if she'd divorced my father, she might have had the courage to tell me who she really was. Or was that identity so erased that it no longer had anything to do with her? Had she divorced my father, I doubt that she would have returned to New Orleans. She'd left that part of herself forever. There was no going back. Under the crush of her childhood, the isolated years of passing and secrecy, maybe she didn't have the strength for one more journey, one more crossing.

It occurs to me that the shame she felt about her mixed race might have tinged her belief that she deserved a better life. Perhaps she was doing penance for the secret she kept from her husband.

Sometimes I wonder if my parents' troubled marriage was only a troubled marriage, that my mother's secret was beside the point in their mélange of misery and had nothing to do with her unhappiness.

Yet I persist in shifting through the past, looking for clues like an archeologist digging through the layers of time, piecing together the past with nothing but pottery shards, animal bones, and hunches, nothing definitive to go on, just debris laid out on a steel table that could mean anything or nothing, depending on how you looked at it.

27

Who's Your Daddy?

Fall 2015

"**Y**OU'RE GONNA WANT to see this." My husband, Jerry, pokes his head into my office, a converted bedroom cocooned in bookcases, painted a flamboyant turquoise as if the walls were a tropical sea. From the look on his face, I can tell he's found something significant about Ursin Frederic, my other mystery man.

Most days while I write in my upstairs office—where over my desk hangs an Edward Curtis photograph of a Native American in a canoe waiting as I wait every day for the words to come—my husband is in the kitchen tediously combing the notary archives. Sometimes jazz music fills the empty silence of the kitchen, sometimes the low hum of the television.

For weeks, he's been scrolling through the online Historical Notaries' Indexes, by Notary for the Parish of Orleans. The volumes are listed by the notaries' names and are dated 1770–1966, covering the French, Spanish, and American periods. In total, there are eighty-seven notaries with multiple volumes, ranging from 1 to 276. Of course, he's confined his search from the late eighteenth century through the middle of the nineteenth century, the period of Ursin's life. Surprisingly, he's taken to the task, allotting one to two hours most days. He keeps meticulous notes of any reference to a Frederic, an Arnoux, and a Dauphin, though the main focus of his search is Ursin Frederic. What began for him as an onerous task has become an addictive obsession. He's as determined to find Ursin's parents as I am.

This colossal undertaking is a last-ditch effort to locate documentary proof of Ursin's parentage. I'm betting that buried in one of the historical entries is a succession record naming Ursin Frederic as an heir and proving decidedly that Ursin is related to the Frederic family that settled on the German Coast in the 1720s, which would make my mother's paternal line one of the first white settlers in Louisiana. There are bragging rights associated with being descended from the German Coast Frederic family. But it's more than that. The possibility of being a descendent of these first settlers might mitigate some of the shame my mother bequeathed to me about her heritage and any lingering uncertainty I still harbor about revealing my mother's secret. Though my mother is gone, I still feel the sting of her shame.

I've never found any birth, baptismal, or succession records to support my supposition that Ursin is related to the German Coast Frederics except two verifiable but inconclusive facts. The first concerns Ursin's military service. In 1814 he joined a militia unit raised in Plaquemines Parish to fight in the War of 1812. Plaquemines Parish is where Adam Frederic, grandson of first settler Johann Conrad Friedrich, lived until the hurricane of 1793. After which Adam and his family moved to Faubourg Sainte-Marie, New Orleans. Although Ursin lived in New Orleans at the time of his enlistment, his decision to enlist with the men of Plaquemines Parish suggests familial ties to the parish and to Adam Frederic.

The other fact is just as indeterminate. In the 1811 New Orleans City Directory, a J. L. Frederick resided at the corner of St. Philip and Rampart. This is the same address given for Ursin Frederic, cabinetmaker, in the 1822 New Orleans city directory. Also, Jean Adam Frederic and J. L. Frederic lived two households away from each other. But

I was never able to prove that any of Jean Adam's sons was the father of Ursin; the birth dates didn't match. Nor was I able to locate a J. L. Frederic. It's as if the man never existed.

Even with these tenuous facts, I'm confident enough that Ursin is descended from the German Coast Frederics that I've included that information in my genealogy presentations, reasoning that even if I don't have undeniable proof, the journey is as important as the destination. Standing in front of an audience, I feel a sense of satisfaction, if not pride, in being descended from the German Coast Frederics who fed New Orleans, saving the city from starvation and helping to settle the Louisiana colony, adding their unique story to America. I joke that my mother who insisted there was no *K* at the end of her name because that would make us German was wrong. The original Frederics were German. The lighthearted joke strikes at the heart of my story. The state of Louisiana caged my mother into a life of hiding and secrets based on only a part of her heritage. The German Coast ancestors balance that story—a teachable moment, a way of saying nothing is black and white, literally.

Jerry and I puzzle over the notary record dated May 14, 1827. The notary is Louis T. Caire. The transaction is a sale between Ursin Frederick dit Lestinet and John Gabaroche: "Sale Gabaroche (John) de Ursin Frederick dit Lestinet."

My husband shows me another notarial record using the name Ursin Frederick alias Lestinet as one of the involved parties: "Sale Frederick (U. dit Lestinet) des Heritier de M. te Piernas."

My first thought is that this is Ursin Celestin Frederick. It can't be my Ursin Frederick. I've never seen any document using the name Lestinet. I run upstairs, page through my notes to check Ursin Celestin's death date. He's still alive in 1827. Ursin Frederick could be Ursin Celestin. But wouldn't he use his middle name Celestin in any legal transaction?

When I return to the kitchen, Jerry is jotting down the information on the two sales transactions. I tell him that it could be Ursin Celestin and not my Ursin.

As I stare at the heavily inked entry by Caire, I ask him. "Do you think *alias* means what it means in English?"

He says maybe.

"But what does *dit* mean?"

He shrugs his shoulders. "Why don't you look them up online?"

Besides *dit* and *alias*, there are other perplexing French words in the Caire entry: *heritier de*. Does that mean inherited from? Have I found a succession record?

"I'm going to finish up Caire." Jerry's attention has already moved on, back to the notary entries.

Once back in my office, I close the chapter I was working on and Google the French term *alias*, fairly certain it has the same meaning as the English word *alias*. I'm right. *Alias* in French means, "also called," "otherwise known as." Why would Ursin be using an alias?

Next, I Google the French word *dit*. What I find sheds some light on the mystery of Ursin's alias Lestinet. A *dit* name is an alias given to a family name. But unlike alias names, a *dit* name is given to many persons. "*Dit* in French means 'say' and in this context, it means 'called.'"[1]

Applying that definition of *dit* to Ursin means Ursin Frederick dit Lestinet had an ancestor named Fredrick, but he chose to use the name Lestinet instead. So he is Ursin Frederick called Lestinet. The original surname was Frederick, passed down to him from an ancestor, while the *dit* name is the name he and/or the family is actually called or known as. But why use a *dit* name? And who is Lestinet? And is this my Ursin Frederic?

My mystery writer self immediately creates crime scenarios in which Ursin is engaged in criminal activities that necessitate an alias, a *dit* name. It's not that far fetched considering his son Leon Frederic's penchant for gambling and subsequent arrest. As tempting as it is, I hold off on casting Ursin in such a nefarious light and continue researching the significance of *dit* names.

The website *Genealogy Today* calls the use of *dit* names in French, French-Canadian, or Acadian ancestral research the "*dit*" phenomenon:

a unique but straightforward French-naming convention. "Within a French culture, it is possible to know a family by two, interchangeable surnames or by the two surnames linked as one family name." The *dit* name could be acquired in many ways, one of which was from the family's regional place of origin. Was Ursin distinguishing himself from the other family branch of German Coast Frederics? Is he still related to them? The German Coast Frederics originated from Rotenburg, Baden-Wurttenberg, Germany. If Lestinet refers to the place of origin, then it's looking less and less likely that Ursin is descended from them.[2]

As fascinating as the *dit* name is, it's also a nightmare for a genealogist, who's been searching one surname and is unaware of a *dit* name.

The translation of the French words *heritier de* supports my hunch about an inheritance and clarifies the type of sale's transaction. *Heritier de* means "heir to." It's clear that the sale involves property that was inherited. But who is the inheritor: Ursin or Piernas?

What I discover next about Ursin and his parents sends me reeling. My husband's dogged persistence and hard work has unlocked the secret to Ursin's parentage, adding another chapter not only to the Frederic family saga but also casting light on another little known or forgotten piece of American history. All because of the two words: "dit Lestinet."

That afternoon I order copies of the notary documents of the two sales transactions from the Notarial Archives Research Center in New Orleans, requesting digital and paper copies. It takes the archivist several days to email me the digital copies. They're in Spanish. Judy Riffel agrees to translate the documents.

In less than twenty-four hours, I have proof of Ursin's paternity. But it's not the paternity I expected. But nothing has been as I expected since I started investigating the Frederic family, those many shaded characters of history, popping up in the most unlikely of places with the oddest tales to tell. Ursin, especially, seems as if he was challenging my detective skills, saying to me, "Did you think this would be easy?" Going against the genealogist credo: The ancestors want to be found.

On May 14, 1827, Joseph Ursin Frederick dit Lestinet sold to John Gabaroche land and buildings bequeathed to him by Mr. Joseph Lestinet, his father.

The document reads: "The lot and buildings here above described and sold belong to the vendor [Joseph Ursin Frederick dit Lestinet] for having been bequeathed to him by Mr. Joseph Lestinet, his father."

I linger over "his father." Finally, after more than six months of searching, I know who was Ursin Frederic's father.

The details of the sale line up perfectly with the names and addresses found in the 1811 and 1822 New Orleans city directories. The property, which was purchased for $4,150 (about $100,000 today), was left to Ursin in Joseph Lestinet's will dated 1811 and is located on Rampart Street and St. Philip Street. This is the same address cited in the 1811 New Orleans city directory, which listed J. L. Frederick as owner. The property also is the same one in the 1822 directory listing Ursin Frederic as a cabinetmaker and owner. J. L. Frederic is Joseph Lestinet Frederick.

"I feel fairly confident we have the right man. In many ways, it's good we went through this exercise. Your persistence paid off," Judy adds.

She was so excited about the news of Ursin's paternity that before emailing me the notarial translations she embarked on her own hunting expedition, tracking down Joseph Lestinet.

Joseph Lestinet Frederique was a soldier in Hallywl's Swiss Regiment, Fourth Company, formerly known as Karrer's Regiment. Hired by France to guard the garrisons in the French colonies, the Swiss regiments were mercenaries, owing no allegiance to France other than a monetary one. They were supplemental to the French soldiers stationed in the colony and by all accounts superior to them.

Though the Swiss regiments occupy a brief footnote in the French colonial period, these soldiers had a reputation for valor, physical maturity, and a penchant for hard work. The Louisiana contingent of the Swiss regiments fulfilled a contract struck between the French monarchy and a military entrepreneur under the command of Colonel François Karrer, who was required by the monarchy to supply four, later five, companies of troops for colonial service.[3] They were professional soldiers.

In 1719, the first regiments of the Swiss Company were raised for colonial service and based in the French colonies of Saint Dominique, Martinique, and Île-Royale. Joseph Lestinet was not among these regiments. It wasn't until 1731 when the Company of the Indies tenure was ending in Louisiana did political conditions allow the consignment of Swiss soldiers to the Mississippi region.

As professional soldiers, the composition of the Swiss regiments drew from a variety of European regions: Germany, Denmark, Sweden, Poland, Luxembourg, Comte Chiney, Alsace, Lorraine, Savoy, Baillage de Gen, and all of the allies of the Swiss cantons. About 40 percent were non-Gallic.[4]

Joseph Lestinet was one of the non-Gallic soldiers. A native of Lestat in Alsace, he was born around 1743 in Brisach, Germany, just across the Rhine River from Neuf-Brisach in the department of Haut Rhin, France. Lestate in Alsace is likely the place called Selestat in Haut Rhin, France, not far from Brisach. Although not one of the German Coast Frederics, Lestinet was German. His death record also attests to his German heritage, stating that he was from Brisac, Germany.

Joseph was stationed in Louisiana with the Fourth Regiment of Hallwyl's Regiment. Though it's unclear when he arrived in Louisiana, in November 1763 his name appears on a marriage contract. Joseph requests his commandant's permission to marry Margueritte Daumas/Domas. The marriage contract states that he is a widower. His fiancée, who is a native of New Orleans, is also widowed. On the marriage contract his name is Jean Frederic Listine, son of Jean Frederic Listine and Anne Marie Marie.

What strikes me is his age. Give or take a few years, when he marries Margueritte, he's between twenty to twenty-three years old and already a widower and a professional soldier living in a struggling colony.

Though little is known about the social backgrounds of the Swiss regiments, army life in the eighteenth century attracted two types of men: those on the social margins and those who saw army life as a honorable profession.[5] Which type Joseph was it's impossible to know for sure. But for all the hardships he endured as a professional soldier, including having to pay for his own food, clothing, and equipment, he married and stayed in Louisiana after the Swiss regiments were disbanded in 1763.

Possibly he was persuaded to remain, because of the inducements the government was offering the Swiss soldiers. Jean Baptiste LeMoyne Bienville, who was the general director of the colony at the time, viewed the retention of the Swiss mercenaries beneficial to the colony. In times of crises, these trained soldiers would offer professional protection with the least disruption. The government inducements were generous. To those soldiers who became farmers or those who were skilled craftsmen the government gave three-year subsidies for food, clothing, ammunition, and exemption from taxes. Marriage was encouraged as well, since the government viewed marriage as a catalyst for permanent settlement.[6]

Regardless of the government inducements, almost none of the Swiss soldiers remained in Louisiana after the regiment. They were quick to leave the place known as the "wet grave."

But something made Joseph Lestinet remain in Louisiana. Whether he saw the government subsidies as his way of starting a new life in a new land or whether it was his new wife or maybe nothing waited for him back in Germany.

Whatever his reason, he seems perfectly suited to this place of reinvention and flux. Even the various transformations of his name—Johan Lestinet Frederique, Jean Frederic Listine, and Joseph Frederic—attest to the transformative nature of his life from German mercenary to

Louisiana property owner and craftsman. It's as if he was trying out different personas, searching for the right one.

There's no record of what happened to his second wife Margueritte Daumas/Domas, but in 1777, Joseph marries Marie Seizen also known as Marie Gautier. For Joseph, it's his third marriage. For Marie Seizen/Gautier, it's her second. Surprisingly, while she was married to her first husband, Pontardi, and with her husband's permission, she had two children with Joseph in 1772 and 1783. Both children are girls: Genevieve and Margueritte. I can't even imagine how that conversation went. Her first husband's infertility couldn't have been the reason for procreating with Joseph, since Marie also had children with Pontardi, the last one born in 1775. After Marie's husband's death, she marries Joseph, legally cementing their relationship.

In 1778, a year after their marriage, Joseph Frederic and Marie are living together on St. Ann Street, the same street my mother was born on. Fourteen years later Ursin is born, but his mother is not Marie. Ursin's mother's story reveals another ignominious chapter in the history of French colonialism in the Louisiana territory and adds an unexpected bloodline to the Frederic family tree.

28

Luison Santilly: Metisse

"Slavery is not an indefinable mass of flesh. It is a particular, specific enslaved woman, whose mind is active as your own, whose range of feeling is as vast as your own; who prefers the way light falls in one particular spot in the woods, who enjoys fishing where the water eddies in a nearby stream, who loves her mother in her own complicated way, . . . who excels at dress making and knows, inside herself, that she is as intelligent and capable as anyone."

—Ta-Nehisi Coates, *Between the World and Me*

IN JOSEPH FREDERICK Lestinet's will dated 1811, he declares Ursin his natural child and names Ursin's mother, stipulating her race, and thus clarifying Ursin's race as well.

Written in French, the translation reads: "I declare that with the metive Louison Santilly I had a child named Joseph Ursin aged twenty-one who was baptized as my natural child and I recognize him as such." In two years, Joseph will die at the age of seventy.

The word *metive* is perplexing. There is no corresponding French word. The closest French word to *metive* is *metisse*, which refers to a half-breed woman. The word *miscegenation* is derived from the French word *metissage*, which means the mixing of Frenchmen and Indians.[1] *Metisse* derives from *metisser*, to mix. In Spanish *mestizos* refers to the mixed off-spring of unions between Indians and whites.[2]

Considering the misspellings of names and the inaccuracies of dates on legal documents, it's highly likely that the notary misspelled *metisse*, indicating that Ursin's mother, Louison Santilly, was half Native American or "a half-breed." Louison was a Creole in its original meaning, created in America, in the New World, as opposed to being created or born in Europe.

The certificate of baptism from the Archdiocese of New Orleans Archives gives Ursin's name as Joseph Ursino Lestine, a child of Joseph Lestine and Luisa Jantilly. He was born August 1, 1792, and baptized May 20, 1793. His baptism is recorded in the book for slaves and free people of color. Ursin's half sister Genevieve, legitimate daughter of Joseph from his marriage to Marie Seizen/Gautier, is one of the sponsors. The priest who performed the rite is Rev. Luis de Quintanilla. Joseph Ursino was baptized at the St. Louis Parish Church.

The original handwritten Spanish baptismal record for Joseph Ursino tells a more complicated story. The original entry is a study in the uncertainty of racial identity during the Spanish colonial period in a population where miscegenation was widely practiced.[3] In the original entry, after Ursin's birth date, the priest wrote something, marked it out making it illegible, wrote something on top of that, and marked that out as well. The priest indicated that Ursin is the son of Louison, followed by "free quadroon," which he marked out and wrote above it "free mestista," then marked out those two words.

Initially the priest wrote that the father was unknown but crossed that out and wrote "Joseph Lestine" above it and inserted "natural" before son. In the margin he wrote below Joseph Ursino, the name Santilli, then marked that out and wrote "Lestine" above Santilli and "natural" son.

From all the mark outs and added words, it appears that Ursin's father later acknowledged him as his son and the priest made the necessary changes. During the colonial period, such negotiations between a parent and a priest were not uncommon in determining racial identity.[4]

The changes to Luisa/Louison's race are more difficult to explain. Perhaps the priest had no knowledge of her genealogy and he assumed she was a quadroon based on her light skin and facial features. Identifying people of color whose lineage was not known to a white priest was imprecise, erring on the side of African as opposed to Indian. As Stephen Webre points out, whites viewed "a reddish complexion as characteristic of both Indians and mulattoes."[5] Additionally, during the Spanish colonial period, the majority of people of color were of African descent, not Native American descent.

Historian Kimberly Hanger, in her study of the free black society in colonial New Orleans, 1769–1803, concludes that racial identity in New Orleans' hierarchical, patriarchal society was very malleable and subjective. "A person's racial designation depended on who recorded it, what purpose it served, and when it was recorded, and what physical characteristics were considered most relevant."[6]

Regardless, when Joseph Lestine acknowledged Ursin, the priest felt compelled, maybe by Ursin, to specify Luisa/Louison as Indian as opposed to African. But why did he cross out "free" as well as "mestista"?

It's possible that the priest crossed out "free mestista" because he may have been indicating that as an Indian she was already free. When the Spanish took over governing Louisiana in 1769, they outlawed the ownership of Indian slaves. Many were freed officially while others were not because they couldn't prove they were Indian. Even after the Spanish published an edict declaring all native peoples free, in many cases masters didn't obey the edict.

But why cross out "mestista"? Possibly Joseph Lestine wanted to cover up the fact that Ursin was a quarter Native American. He wanted his "natural" son to have all the advantages of white privilege and none of the stigma associated with people of color, even people of Native American descent.

This mixing of Native Americans and Europeans in large part was the result of Indian slavery. By the Spanish period many Indian slaves were mixed race, the offspring of unions between Indians and whites. In Louison/Luisa's case, she was white enough to be viewed by the priest as three-quarters white. There is no indication on any records which tribe she was descended from.

All this finagling over racial ancestry demonstrates the legal and social taint associated with African ancestry, which plays out well into the twentieth century in Southern states and with the legalization of the one-drop rule.

A case in point of how crucial it was not to have any taint of "colored" blood in any ancestral document is the infamous reign of Naomi Drake and her list of "flagged names." Drake headed the Bureau of Vital Statistic in New Orleans from 1949 to 1965. She kept a list of "flagged names" that she deemed were the names of Negro families. If she could prove African ancestry, however distant, however small, she would change that person's race in the official records of the City of New Orleans from white to black. Even a church document dated 1793 that racially identified Ursin's mother as a quadroon, even though marked out, would be suspect and possible proof of African ancestry. And disproving African ancestry was next to impossible.

The 1982 case of Susie Guillory Phipps, who sued the State of Louisiana to have her racial classification changed from "colored" to "white" demonstrates how tenacious the state was in maintaining a person's given racial designation.

When Phipps applied for a passport, she was turned down because her race on her application (White) was different than the race on her birth certificate (Colored).

Phipps's response to the "colored" designation on her birth certificate was, "Take this color off my birth certificate. Let people look at me and tell me what I am."

To substantiate the "colored" designation, the state of Louisiana traced Phipps genealogy back to an eighteenth-century enslaved female

ancestor, Margarite.[7] Although Phipps wasn't able to get her racial classification changed from colored to white, her case shone a national spotlight on Louisiana's history of racial discrimination and racist culture and
was responsible for the overturning of the one-thirty-second rule.

The letter I received from the State of Louisiana in 1995 when I
questioned my mother's "col" racial delineation is reminiscent of the
Phillips case. "If you consider your genealogy different or more specific
to one race, you may submit a request for change of racial designation.
You will be required to submit information, which shows a preponderance of evidence to support this. We will be happy to review it."

Of course, in 1995 I had no idea of the racial fluidity of my mother's paternal heritage. Nor of my own DNA, which would prove a preponderance of European ancestry. But my mother's DNA could have
told a different story of racial preponderance, leaving her race as "col"
on her birth certificate.

Joseph Lestinet couldn't foresee the future ramifications for the Frederic line of his son having a mestista mother as opposed to a quadroon
mother. Whatever his motive was in compelling the priest to clarify his
son's race, he understood the importance of erasing any smirch of African ancestry on a legal record. And if Ursin's service in a white regiment during the War of 1812 is any indication, he succeeded. Nowhere
in any official record, except his baptismal certificate, is Ursin referred
to as a free person of color.

Regardless of Joseph Lestinet's motives, Ursin had other ideas about
maintaining a "white" bloodline and the importance of removing perceived racial taints. All of his sexual liaisons and subsequent offspring
were with free women of color, from the emancipated slave Marie
Polline to Roxelane Arnoux with whom he had four children, one of
whom was Leon Frederic, my third great-grandfather. All of Ursin's
children's baptisms are recorded in the book of slaves and free people
of color. Clearly this is where he drew his racial line.

Thinking about Ursin's various liaisons with women of color, it hits
me that although almost 129 years separate Ursin Frederic's birth from

my mother's birth, he, too, had to decide which side of the color line he was going to live on.

They share other similarities as well. Considering the circumstances of Alvera and Ursin's lives, in some sense their fathers abandoned them. Though Ursin's father acknowledged him as a natural son, bequeathing property to him, even donating a slave named Alix to him in 1803, Ursin was still illegitimate. Taking into account the high preponderance of unsanctified unions in the late eighteenth century of all races, Joseph Lestine/Lestinet did marry Marie Seizen/Gautier, a white woman, and had four legitimate children with her. Ursin was his only bastard son.

My mother was left to be raised by her great-grandmother and then her cousin Tessie, having no idea that her father Azemar wanted custody of her.

Whichever side of the color line they chose to live on, black or white, I suspect color was only part of their decision. Something, I've yet to understand in how they viewed themselves, said this is where you belong or this is where you want to belong.

Could Ursin have married a white woman? I don't know. In terms of legality, during his lifetime interracial marriage was illegal in Louisiana. Would his altered baptismal record pass muster with the Catholic Church considering it was recorded in the register for slaves and free people of color? What I do know is he sought out women of color and sired children with them, contributing to the three-tiered racial system in New Orleans. Ursin knew that his children, as free people of color, would be hemmed in by the legal system and would be held in a lower status than whites.

When America took over governance of Louisiana, as early as 1808, the legislature curtailed the rights and privileges of the free people of color, making it clear that they were legally inferior and subordinate to whites.[8] And yet, this was the world Ursin chose for his children, if he did have a choice. However diluted his "colored" blood was from his "mestista" mother, he felt most comfortable with women of color like his mother.

Or maybe I'm looking at Ursin incorrectly. Maybe he felt wholly white and like so many white men of his time he was enjoying *plaçage* arrangements with none of the burden of matrimony, indulging in the white patriarchal system.

Ursin's mother, Luison/Louison/Luisa Santilly/Jantilly was the daughter of a Captain of the French Marine Troops, Pierre Santilly (sixth great-grandfather), and an unnamed Indian slave. When Pierre Santilly married Marie LaTourneur on March 10, 1760, Santilly's wife brought to their marriage half of her first husband Jean Gueydon's estate, which included seven slaves, three of whom were Native American.

Santilly notes in the inventory that a runaway Indian female slave was believed to have died running away. The three remaining enslaved female Native Americans are:

> Angelique, Indian, twenty-five, and her daughter, Henriette, ten; Catin, Indian, twenty

Based on the ages of the three females, any one of them could have been Louison's mother (my seventh great-grandmother). Within five years of Pierre Santilly's marriage, he fathers Louison with one of these Native American enslaved women. Louison is born into slavery in 1765.

In 1773 Pedro Francisco Santilly, native of Paris, notarizes his will, stating that he is thirty-eight years old and has been in the service of His Majesty for nineteen years. He promises freedom to six slaves, five of whom are mestisas, after his and his wife's death. There's no reason given for the manumission.

The Indian slaves are:
Henrieta

Maria

Suzana

another Henrieta

Maria Luiza.

Of the five mestisas, Suzana, Henrieta, and Maria Luiza are the daughters of the deceased Indian woman Angelica.

He mentions in his will that if his wife should need to sell them, he revokes their freedom, which would have been illegal during the Spanish period.

In June 1783 Santilly records a second will, just prior to his death. He declares in the second will that he has no children with his wife, Maria LaTourneur, and leaves all his property to her. He names for his universal heirs his nephews and nieces who reside in France. He can't sign because of a "shaky pulse."

Shortly after the 1783 will, Pierre Santilly dies in New Orleans. An inventory of Santilly's first estate dated September 30, 1783, lists several Negro slaves and the last slave is a "mestisa" named Luison, aged eighteen, with her son Adelard, aged two, and an unbaptized daughter aged two months. It's unclear if Luison is Maria Luiza from Santilly's first will. In neither the first nor the second will does he acknowledge Luison as his daughter, possibly because Santilly's white wife outlives him.

Marie LaTourneur Santilly dies in 1787, four years after Pierre. In her will she declares that she owns a Negro named Valentin, thirty-eight, a Negress Naneta, twenty-eight, and a Negress Marana, twenty-two or twenty-three. She doesn't mention any Indian slaves, possibly because she freed the enslaved Indian women as per her husband's request.

Like so many enslaved people, there is little else in the records about Luison. The history of Native American slavery in Louisiana is almost as murky and troubling.

The first record of Native Americans being held as slaves in Louisiana is in the 1708 census, which counted eighty Indian men and women among a total population of 278.[9]

From the early 1700s French colonists engaged in Indian slavery either by purchasing or rescuing slaves captured in local Indian wars or by participating in slave raiding expeditions. The French colonists usually killed the men and enslaved the women and children.[10] Although Louisiana Indian slaves belonged to several tribes—Panis, Alibamon, Taensa and Chitimachas—"the Chitimachas of Bayou Lafourche were the most significant ethnic component in the early slave population of lower Louisiana." As the largest tribe in the Mississippi Delta at the time, the Chitimachas were engaged in war with the French who were trying to colonize the area.[11] Possibly Luison's mother was a Chitimacha.

As in many of the New World colonies, efforts to enslave the Indian population were less than successful, leading to the importation of enslaved Africans. The French explorer, Nicholas de la de Salle, wrote in 1709 that Indian slaves "only cause trouble and from whom we receive very little service since they are not appropriate for hard labor like the blacks."[12]

Demographics of Indian slaves in the eighteenth and early nineteenth century support the failure to enslave Native Americans.

1708   Eighty Indian slaves, mostly women
1721   161 Indian slaves, 17 percent of all colony slaves
1771   120 Indian slaves, less than 3 percent of colony slaves
1808   Several hundred Indians held as slaves, descended from Indian families.[13]

In comparison, the rise in African slavery tells a different story. In a 1726 census of the Louisiana territory, enslaved blacks totaled 1,540 compared to 229 enslaved Indians. By the Spanish period the number of enslaved blacks was five thousand while the number of enslaved Indians remained about the same as four decades earlier.

Unlike African slaves, Indian slaves and their descendants seem to have been assimilated into Louisiana's larger white and black populations. The last slave child clearly identified as an Indian in a baptismal record was in 1792 at Natchitoches. The same year Ursin was born.[14]

Other than property in a slave inventory and her name on Ursin's baptismal record, I could find no other record for Luison/Louison/Luisa Santilly. I can only guess at the Native American tribe she descended from and what were the circumstances of her mother's enslavement. How she met Joseph Lestinet remains another mystery.

I'd like to think that her mother was the nameless runaway Indian female slave listed in the inventory for the 1760 marriage contract between Santilly and LaTourneur who was believed to have died running away.

In my version she doesn't die. Though she has to leave her daughter behind, she considers it the price she has to pay for her freedom. Luison will learn by her example.

My genealogical quest is complete. And none of it is what I anticipated and all of it is welcome. I glance again at the artwork that hangs over my writing desk. The Native American man still waits patiently in his canoe among the reeds, gazing off into the distance, his back to me. A slight breeze ripples the water. But he is so still, lost in his thoughts, ready for whatever comes.

I look at the other artwork over my desk—a poster of an ancient Native American woman. "The Navajo are so skilled, they can actually weave themselves into a rug," the poster reads, reminding me that in every rug the Navajo women wove they included a flaw. Art is not about perfection but the creative journey. For over seventeen years her beautifully etched face has stood resolute, her photograph bordered by the rug she wove with its one flaw.

As if I need more proof of my affinity for Native people, on my desk there's the hero woman kachina, the coyote turquoise fetish, the white buffalo fetish; on the bookshelf, the medicine bag and the books about Native American culture; and finally the mystery novel, *The Lost Artist*, that I wrote about the Trail of Tears, the Timucua Indians, and a fifteenth-century lost art treasure.

It's as if I've known, without knowing, that the story of my family would start with a Native American woman.

29

Going Public

January 20, 2015

THE EVENING THE show airs, that night I dream of my parents. Mom and I are in my girlhood bedroom, that aerie above the small Cape Cod house in Parma, Ohio, sorting through papers, drawings, and a box of mementos from my childhood. A warm yellow glow fills the room, which is both different and the same. Gone is the door to the attic behind my bed that frightened me as a child. I imagined demons and ghosts emerging from the attic intent on haunting me in the night.

In the dream, my mom is generous and pleased, wants me to have these things. Then my dad comes into the room with another box, which he abruptly drops on the floor. "Here you can have these," he says brusquely. Before I can open the box, he turns and leaves. True to his nature in life, that tinge of anger just below the surface.

To my surprise, the box is overflowing with our old home movies—those visual links to my childhood.

When I wake in the dark room from the dream, I realize I've never dreamed about my parents together since their deaths. Staring into the dark, I feel that same warm glow from the dream lingering as if their spirits were hovering nearby. The dream seems to be about my coming to terms with revealing my mother's secret on a national TV show. My mother's uncharacteristic generosity, letting me take what I want, and my father's willingness to part with the old movies represent their bequeathing me my past, letting me choose what I want to claim. Finally, I have come into my inheritance.

The next day, in a flurry of emails, strangers across the country reach out to me via my website. Over coffee, I read their emails quickly, holding my breath against any hurt they may contain. But in an overflow of understanding, most of the emails are glowingly positive.

> *I loved your desire to connect with your past, and was touched by your reaction to learning more. Our nation—wonderful as it is—has not made it easy for people to accept an Other who is perceived as different, an outsider. I admire your Mom for her courage and for making the very difficult decision to hide such an integral part of her being, and I admire your courage to seek, to find, and to reconcile with your amazing history. Haydee Rodriguez*

Another person encourages me to write about my mom's story: "I absolutely loved your fascinating family history as seen on *Genealogy Roadshow*. What a quintessential American story! How wonderful if you could write a book about this real-life mystery."

Then there are the emails from people offering me help in my research.

> *I wanted to say, Bless you and your loved ones, deceased and living. It was so brave and humble of you and your family to share your experience on* Genealogy Roadshow. *Keep searching, because as a semi-retired librarian and archivist, you may find wonderful surprises. We have free people of color in antebellum America that moved to Ohio before the Civil*

War, including USCT veterans. I have been a volunteer genealogist and family historian for over thirty years. The ancestors will guide you! P.S. You may email me, because I do not answer phone numbers I do not recognize, or if you ever want to call, send the number for me to note. Mrs. J Thomas

Over the next year, Ms. Jeanne Thomas and her daughter Abby Grace Iona Djama-Adan will be invaluable resources for my research, giving me links to Fold3 for military records, articles on free people of color and passing, and even suggesting the names of two friends in New Orleans who would be willing to offer me lodging. Each of her emails cheers me on with its positivity: "You could find many more wonderful surprises!!!!"

I realize that by sharing my mother's story publically, I've been taken in by another family, the family of genealogists.

When I ask Jeanne her opinion on writing a nonfiction book, her answer is resoundingly positive:

We would both buy and recommend you do a nonfiction book about your family experience, including PBS's Genealogy Roadshow. *This could encourage and give courage to others who seek their true origins. Each book ever read about one's discovery of ancestors has been enlightening and inspirational. There are regrets for some who find out revelations, and the wonderment of why decisions were made, etc. remain with ancestors.*

Kenyatta Berry emails me as well, saying our story was her favorite of the entire series. "I find your ancestry fascinating and hopefully you will continue on the path to discovery." She too encourages me to write a book. "I am thrilled you are writing a book about your family."

My daughter, Lauren Robinson, who teaches English at Andrews High School in Tinley Park, Illinois, receives an email from another teacher who taught *To Kill a Mockingbird* recently to her English literature class and saw our segment of *Genealogy Roadshow.*

We had a really great conversation about race and the motivation behind your grandmother's decision to live as a white person. A very Caucasian-looking student revealed that his father is black and his mother is white. Students were dumbfounded because you'd never guess by looking at him. And then Tracy Sukalo popped in class to explain the genetics behind skin color.

Tracy Sukalo, my daughter explains, is a science teacher at the high school.

The most moving email I receive is from a young mixed-race woman who lives in a Chicago suburb.

I come from a very racially mixed family. Some of us are blonde, some are extremely light, some are brown. As for me, I am pretty fair and have long thin hair. Most of my life people have asked me, "What are you?" especially black people. Uuhh!

People usually think that I'm Hispanic or at least mixed, and some-times they're just unsure. I do come from a very bi-racial or multi-racial family. As a result I definitely have a few of my own racial issues to be honest. Looking the way I do I have personally never been accepted by the black community for the most part, a concept called colorism, you may have heard of. Kids teased me and called me white (though I don't look white to most white people I don't think, but by black standards definitely not black enough).

Most black people would say that I am completely politically incor-rect but I understand your mother better than many black people might. I understand. I believe that she fully believed that she was ultimately giving a better life to you and ultimately she likely did. Unfortunately, I know that she paid a huge price in doing so—having to deny her entire family and not even being able to be fully proud of herself and who she really was. How-ever, I surmise that she thought: "For one generation there will be a price. Nevertheless, for my children and their children and all my generations they will have an opportunity for the best of life." Coming from her time I'm

sure she was right and I totally understand! Even in this time, there are
clearly advantages. It's sooo complicated.
     I wish you luck finding your relatives. Paris L. Smith

Her email stops me in my tracks as I try to absorb the layers of meaning and emotion this young woman has shared about being a mixed-race person. I reread her email and start to cry, seeing my mother in a different light. To have someone else, a stranger, so eloquently understand my mother, the bittersweet price she had to pay to better herself and her children and in the process hide who she really was.

The good wishes and attention are reassuring and welcome, and also uncomfortable. I feel exposed. I'm not a public person. I'm a writer who spends a bulk of her time in a small upstairs bedroom creating fictional characters, solving murders I create, emerging for an afternoon walk. *What did I expect?* I tell myself.

I respond to every email except the two negative emails I receive. One person clearly has an agenda related to a book she's written about race, and the other person seems unbalanced and fearful, harboring the same kind of fear that inspired the one-drop rule and my mother's decision to pass and hide her racial identity.

Besides emails from private individuals, I receive emails from people representing public institutions, librarians and genealogical societies, inviting me to speak about my mother's story and *Genealogy Roadshow*. One email was sent at 11:43 p.m., almost immediately after the show aired.

With a heady glee, I accept all of the invitations, naively oblivious to the consequences of talking about race in a public forum. Like talking about love, none of us really knows how to talk about it or what we're talking about. Though we all have so much to say.

30

What We Talk About
When We Talk About Race
Audience Participation 2015

"The truth is that, for most of our nation's history, many of the people who we consider to be 'white' today, would be 'colored,' 'Negro,' or 'black' in times past."

—Stephanie Jones-Rogers, Professor of History,
University of California, Berkeley.

"WHAT ARE YOU anyway?" The bluntness of the woman's tone puts me on edge.

In the dimly lit library auditorium I can barely make out her features: dark hair, blue top, middle-aged, a face as pointed as her question. I've been talking for an hour, telling my mother's story and how it became a segment of PBS's *Genealogy Roadshow*, sharing that intimate moment when I confronted my mother with the truth of her racial identity, trying to convey (and hoping the audience understands) the poignancy of her reaction.

That morning I'd worked on the book, writing the section defining Creole and racial designation in Louisiana from 1970–1983, when the legal standard for Negro was changed from the one-drop rule to the one-thirty-second standard, and I'm a little touchy about the question of "What am I?" Mainly because I'm firm in my belief that race is a social construct, meant to keep nonwhites economically, politically, and socially suppressed. Do I unleash that information on this woman?

"What do you mean what am I?" I don't like her tone, but I don't want to appear defensive nor miss a teachable moment. The audience is staring up at me, a plethora of expressions on their faces from anticipation to empathy. I tell myself that this is what can happen when you put your mother's story out there. You have to be prepared for these types of questions. But I don't feel prepared. It's only the second presentation I've done since the show was televised.

The woman doesn't get the subtlety of my response. "Well, I'm looking at you and I can see what you look like. But," she struggles, "what are you?"

What she doesn't say, but what is implied, is that I look so white. But I've revealed that I'm not 100 percent white. My appearance isn't to be trusted. That seems to bother her.

The audience shifts in their seats. "Do you mean what my DNA says I am?"

"Yes, that's what I mean."

Why isn't there a HIPAA law for racial identity? What right does she have to ask me this? But by standing here and telling my mother's story, I'm free game. That's what I signed up for.

"I'm 7 to 9 percent black and 86 percent white. The majority of my DNA is Scandinavian and British Isles."

Her hand goes up again. I forge ahead as if I didn't see it. I reiterate the Louisiana one-drop rule and then talk about the one-thirty-second law. I barrage the woman with facts meant to show her the foolishness of her question. Since she's already told everyone she's Jewish, relating a story about Madeline Albright and how she didn't know she was

Jewish, I compare the Nuremberg law with the Louisiana law. "Don't you get it?" I want to scream at her.

For a moment I think I've shut her down, but she raises her hand again. And because no one else is raising their hand, I have to acknowledge her.

"What is your father?" That same blunt tone in her words.

I feel like a pinned insect, not the exotic butterfly with the iridescent green wings but the dung beetle from a third-world country. I refuse to say the word white. "He was Bohemian." I launch into my Great-Aunt Catherine's story of how the Kalina family built a boat and sailed from Bohemia to America, landing in Baltimore and then moving to Cleveland where there was a Bohemian community. I joke about the mythology of that story.

The woman's hand goes up again. "But you don't know that he's only that. For all you know he could also be Jewish."

Now I get it. Now I see she has an agenda. And it has to do with her own Jewishness, with people who don't know they're Jewish and maybe walking around not knowing, maybe disparaging Jews. If I'd had the presence of mind, I should have said being Jewish doesn't show up on a DNA test.

Instead I say, "And wouldn't that be interesting. Like I said before one big gumbo. And I love that."

This time she doesn't give me the courtesy of raising her hand as if she and I are having a private conversation. "When you found out about your grandfather and his race what did you feel?"

I let out a deep breath. "I was stunned but welcomed the richness of my heritage. Like I said one big gumbo."

"That's all you felt?"

What does she want me to say? I was horrified. I was disgusted.

In desperation I reply, "I judge people by their characters, not by their skin color."

Many of the audience nod their heads in agreement.

Before the woman can conjure another question, the librarian's hand bobs up like a lifeline, rescuing me from this strange woman. She asks if I'm writing a book about my mother's story?

"Yes," I smile with relief.

After the presentation, the librarian apologizes for the woman and tells me I handled it very well. I'm not convinced.

On the drive home through the summer night, the softening sunset clouds like mountains on the horizon, with the expressway crazies whizzing around me as if their destinations were dire, I mull over the woman's question. "What are you?"

I sensed even as she was asking her absurd question that it had little to do with me and more to do with her fears about race and racial purity. If I could be other than I appear, then anyone in this country could be other than they appear.

As I exit the expressway and take the sharp curve down the ramp, a shot of anger and dismay courses through me.

How dare that woman ask me what I was? What difference does it make to her? What I am is beside the point. Or maybe what I am is the point. Even I don't know how to talk about race.

At the bottom of the ramp, I turn right and head home to Libertyville feeling disappointed in myself, in people's prejudices and biases.

My only consolation is I'm no longer silent. I'm engaging with audiences about my mother's racial secret. And in turn, I'm attesting to this bizarre dialogue about race.

My mother groomed me too well all those years ago when she told me the story of the old black woman shoved off the banquette by a white man who called her a nigger.

I can almost hear her say, "That's the kind of story that needs an audience."

And then there are the inexplicable occurrences. Before a packed room of fifty genealogical society members, as I take questions, one woman jumps up and says, "I have a gift for you. Can I come up there and give it to you?"

How can I turn down a gift?

This is the third time she's commented on my presentation. Each time the petite Asian American woman has praised my mother's courage and stressed the importance of this story.

Standing beside me, she addresses the audience as if I've handed over my presentation to her. "Actually it's a gift for everyone," she says, swinging her arms wildly. "Please everyone join in."

In a wavery soprano voice she bursts into song. I'm flabbergasted. The song is about love and God. I've never heard it before. Nor has the audience because no one is singing with her. As she sings, I see the president of the genealogical society pop up from her seat and hurry to the front of the room to stand by my other side.

Something is clearly wrong.

My mind is whirling, not sure what to do. Looking askance at the singing woman, I spot a fanny pack around her waist, the zippered pouch in front for easy access. Is she dangerous? Does she have something in her pack, another gift for me?

What if she keeps singing? I call on all my experiences teaching in the city—the unruly students, the substance abusers, and the hostile students. I have to get control back from her.

As soon as she finishes, before she can launch into another song or zip open her bulging fanny pack, I quickly say, "Thank you. And there's one more thing I forgot to say."

There's nothing I forgot to say. But it works. The woman walks back to her seat.

Afterwards the president explains to me that the woman has mental problems, which makes me wonder what in my talk sparked her instability to bloom into the gift of song.

After the event, as I'm exiting the building, heading for the parking lot, I realize, too late, that the singing woman is following me. She's frantically telling me how much she enjoyed my talk. The parking lot is poorly lit, and the woman keeps talking and walking with me. To my dismay no one else is in the parking lot. I quicken my pace though hampered by the rolling suitcase of books I brought to the event.

Before reaching my car, I say, nonchalantly, "What's the best way out of the lot if I want to get back on the highway?"

Somehow the practicality of my question cuts through her chatter. "Just go out over there." She points to an exit.

"Thanks." I scurry into my car, throwing the suitcase in the back seat and locking my car door. I'm so shaken up that I make a wrong turn and drive for ten minutes before I realize I'm heading in the wrong direction.

Winding down the dark country road, I question if it was only her mental instability that inspired the Asian American woman to sing? Or did my mother's story of racial oppression strike a chord with her, igniting passions she could no longer contain that had to find expression in song.

After the first few talks, I decide to end my presentations with my mom's picture, a studio photograph of her in her early twenties, when she was living in New Orleans. Her image remains on the screen as I take audience questions: her serene smile, the white delicate flowers in contrast to her dark tightly curled hair, a slender gold crucifix around her neck, her makeup cleverly applied—as if her image defies my presentation.

Some audience members seem to think she looks Cuban. The power of suggestion, I surmise, because I revealed Roxelane Arnoux, my fourth great-grandmother was born in Cuba. What is this need to label when the visual markers don't support a racial reality?

In two separate presentations, two audience members ask me what my DNA is. The first time I'm asked that question, I'm a little taken aback by the woman's boldness as if she were asking for my medical records. The second time I'm prepared.

"Depending on which test, I'm either 7 or 9 percent African and 86 or 90 percent European." I don't add any explanation.

My answer seems to baffle the two different women as well as the audiences. I see the bewilderment on their faces as they try to come to terms with my white skin and my mixed ancestry. As if everything about a person can be known by looking at them.

One woman says, "I thought it would be more." The other woman says, "I thought it would be less."

There's no escaping my feeling of being dissected, objectified racially. What are they seeing in me that I'm either lacking in blackness or have too much blackness? And again why does it matter? What is this need to take me apart racially? Isn't the point of my mother's story that we have to stop doing this to people?

If I hadn't stood in front of them telling them my mother's story of passing, telling them about the mixing of races that reaches back in our family to the eighteenth century and beyond, they would never know I carried 7–9 percent African ancestry. I would just be another middle-aged white woman they would barely notice.

At a genealogical society meeting, an older white woman who doesn't seem to understand the implications of the one-drop rule asks me why they just couldn't do blood tests back then.

The question throws me. Before I can answer, another white woman calls the woman out. "You're just showing your own views about this, your own ignorance."

It's an uncomfortable moment. I'm relieved the outspoken woman squashed the other's woman question, but I have a spark of sympathy for the older woman that I can't explain. She lowers her head in embarrassment.

It's the twenty-first century and still no one knows how to talk about race in America. The stain of slavery seems to lie under everyone's skin like a latent disease there's no cure for. Even scratching the surface seems to cause the disease to breakout in the most unpredictable way.

31

What We Talk About
When We Talk About Passing

La Porte, Indiana, 2015

T HE BRILLIANT OCTOBER sun glares through the car window as we pull into the Salvation Army parking lot in La Porte, Indiana. My husband, Jerry, has driven the two plus hours from our house to La Porte. The lot is almost full, but Jerry reminds me that it's a community center and there may be other events scheduled for the afternoon. Secretly I hope I'm the only event.

I'm the guest speaker for the La Porte library system's biannual Book Club Luncheon. Butterflies dance in my stomach as I walk inside the building and see the crowded room. A woman named Susan, who introduces herself as the public relations person for the La Porte libraries, escorts me to a far table at the back of the room, takes my memory stick containing the slides for the presentation, and tells me to wait until the announcements are over.

As I wait, I scan the room, counting about fifty people in attendance, mostly women, mostly white, though to my surprise and delight there are two African American women sitting together at one of the tables.

This is the first time I'll be telling my mother's story to a racially mixed audience.

Once I begin, I find myself occasionally glancing at the two African American women, gauging their reactions, wondering if they are taking offense to what I say. Are they judging my mother harshly for passing as white, for turning her back on her family in the process? Are they seeing her as a traitor to her race?

I can't get a read from their expressions. And it makes me nervous. I realize I'm having an inner dialogue with myself as I talk to the audience, making it more difficult to concentrate, sometimes pressing the remote too hard, skipping a slide, having to go back, losing the rhythm of the sequence of the slides and the topics.

When I reach the last part of my talk where I read the email from that young woman who describes what it's like to be a mixed-race person who doesn't seem to fit anywhere because of how she looks, a wave of anxiety shoots through me. She criticizes blacks for not accepting her.

I consider editing her comments about the black community, afraid the African American women might be offended. I realize it's impossible to do that without losing the poignancy of her sentiments. And should I do that? To not read her email and end my talk now would be too abrupt and cowardly.

I take a deep breath and start to read. "Most of my life people have asked me, 'What are you?' especially black people."

I keep going. "Looking the way I do I have personally never been accepted by the black community, for the most part, a concept called colorism."

Quickly I look at the two African American women. Their faces tell me nothing.

"Kids teased me and called me white though I don't look white to most white people I don't think, but by black standards definitely not black enough."

I'm relieved when I reach the final paragraph that talks about her reaction to the price my mother paid to pass. "It's sooo complicated."

The audience applauds, realizing it's the end of my talk though I haven't signaled them as I usually do by saying, "Thank You." The two African American women are still seated, haven't left. I open the presentation to questions.

As usual the questions are a blend of questions and comments about people's experience with race, reflective of the audience's own interests. When will the book be published? Do you have a title? Do you know your DNA? This is my sixth presentation. I've been asked about my DNA so often I now expect the question. Something odd or poignant always happens when I talk about my mother, when I talk about race.

Then the questions get more personal, closer to the bone of racial issues.

"Did any family members who passed have dark children?" Is the woman thinking of the well-known Kate Chopin short story, "Désirée's Baby"? After all this is an audience of readers, of book lovers.

"Not that I'm aware of," I answer, recalling my great-great-grandmother Mary Williams's dark skin and how in her case the opposite happened. Her daughter Ada McNicholls was very fair-skinned. How to explain these genetic skin variations, when I don't understand them.

Then a woman sitting at a back table asks me what passing is. What does it mean to pass? I'm surprised that she doesn't know the concept. I make a mental note that the next time I speak I need to explain racial passing, to use the two words together.

I give some historical background about segregation in the South, separate areas for whites and blacks. I relate Uncle Eddie and Aunt Laura's passing story, how they couldn't go home again after they passed.

One of the African American women shakes her head in understanding. We're reaching the heart of racism.

"But that's no longer happening?" the white woman says, confirming her own belief about race today in America.

"Well, there are no separate areas designated by color any longer," I respond.

One of the black women raises her hand and starts to talk. "Oh, it's still happening," she says in an agitated voice. "My grandmother was trying to pass for white in the South. When they found out, they shot her dead."

We're silenced by her revelation and the strength of her emotion.

"When did this happen?" I ask.

"In the 1930s, sometime."

I'm shocked by her grandmother's story and say so.

After my talk, while I sit at the author table as people shuffle past, some buying books, some expressing how they enjoyed my presentation, I notice the African American women are lagging behind.

I'm hoping they'll stop at my table so I can speak to them and get a sense of their feelings about my presentation and to learn more about the woman's grandmother who was shot for passing for white.

A middle-aged white woman tells me she enjoyed my talk. "But you know if it was a generation ago your children wouldn't want anyone to know. Nor would you."

Am I being subtly chastised? "Yes, I know," I answer, thinking that's the point of my story.

Another woman wants to tell me that slavery has been around for over two thousand years.

How do I respond to that? "Does that make it right?" "Why are you telling me that?" She leaves before I can drudge up a response that isn't defensive or angry. Perhaps she just wanted to share her knowledge of slavery, that it wasn't just an American institution.

Finally, only the staff and the African American women remain. To my delight, they do stop at my table. The taller woman with the short-cropped hair and honey-colored skin holds out her hand to me. I take her hand in my two hands. There's a connection with her I can't explain, as if it wasn't me holding her hand, but my mother holding her hand through me, as if I'm the conduit. Our touch reaches back in time to distant ancestors only she can understand fully. Because of the way I look, because of my experience, I can only witness and record.

Then go out and tell my mother's story, the story of mixed-race people in America. She lives it.

The two women share their own family stories about lighter-skinned relatives and darker-skinned relatives with straight hair, the complexity and fluidity of mixed race manifested in the flesh. The ebony-skinned woman, who related the story of her grandmother being shot for passing, explains that her father had straight hair and light skin. She has a delightful gap between her two front teeth.

I nod and listen. I'm grateful to them for their trust in me.

All the way home as my husband and I drive the swift expressways, I think of those two women and what a gift they and the audience gave me. Never once did anyone ask me what I was. They understood. They got it.

The following day on NPR an African American author discusses segregation in American cities, how blacks are confined geographically, economically, socially, and educationally. As she supports her point, I reflect on the woman who asked what passing is and her comment that it's not happening anymore in America. I can hear that African American woman say, "Oh, it's still happening."

Two nights later I dream I'm at a party attended by mixed-race people. A small black child, a girl, runs toward me, her arms outstretched. I pick her up and hold her, glancing around the room to see if anyone objects, if anyone thinks holding the child is the wrong thing to do. After all I am a white woman and a stranger.

The child puts her small arms around my neck, hugs me tightly, and nestles her head into my shoulder. I hug her back. We stand together holding each other in this lovely embrace.

When I wake, the room is still lost in shadowy light but the dream lingers full of portent.

The day before, I emailed the La Porte librarian and asked her to find out who the lady was that told the story of her grandmother's passing and if she will talk to me about her grandmother. The librarian gets back to me the same day. The woman's name is Versie Jeffries. She would be happy to speak to me.

❖

"My mom talked to us about her history," Versie Jeffries explains. "We'd sit out on the porch. This was when we lived in Arkansas. That's where I grew up, in Arkansas, after the family left Mississippi."

How different from my mother whose family stories were edited and secretive in what they revealed and hid. Of course Versie's mother wasn't passing for white. She was what she appeared to be, a black woman.

"My mom was dark-skinned, but she had people in her family passing."

Versie's mom had eleven children, six of whom lived. After the family left Mississippi, they were sharecroppers in Arkansas.

Before she tells me the story of her grandmother's murder, I sense she wants me to know who she is and who her people are. And I want to know that as well. Her family tree is hued with many shades of color from light-skinned relatives to dark-skinned relatives and in between.

"My dad was light skinned with straight hair. When he worked outside, his face would turn dark. But under his shirt he was light," she laughs. I remember her telling me after my presentation about her dad's skin color.

"I was the first one to graduate from high school." I can hear the pride in her voice. "My brothers had to pick and chop cotton. They supported me. We made three dollars a day."

I ask her when she was born, thinking she was younger than me. "1944," she says. She's two years older than me but her life experience seems caught in another time.

There's an effervescence about Versie, as if she's bubbling over with a need to be heard and understood. She lives in Kingsford Heights,

Indiana, which is nine miles south of La Porte. I find myself writing quickly, using my high school shorthand to capture her words. Sometimes I have to ask her to repeat something she's said because I can't get it all down on paper.

All her energy is poured into her volunteer work, which includes serving as president of the American Legion Auxiliary and being a member of the Democratic Committee. She also is an ardent reader. She has two children, a son and a daughter, both of whom served in the military. She also raised two of her nephews.

"Tell me about what happened to your grandmother who was trying to pass for white," I circle back to what initiated the interview.

"She looked white. She had long black hair and was light skinned. She played both sides," she explains. "You know, she would go out with white men and black men. She was doing that for years."

Her grandmother lived in Walls, Mississippi, in the 1930s when Jim Crow was at its height. Though Versie never knew her grandmother, she'd heard the story and has seen photographs of her grandmother, Daisy Mae Green.

"My dad was a teenager when his mother was shot. After that, he was raised by a cousin."

I guide her back to her grandmother's story. "So what happened? Who shot her?"

"These white guys found out what she was doing, and they shot her."

"Did the police go after them? Find out who killed her?"

"Nah. They didn't even try to catch them."

"How do you feel about that?"

"You know how it was back then. I had an unbelievable mother. She'd tell us, 'People will be people regardless. You should show people respect.' Because we were sharecroppers we worked side by side with whites in the fields. When I moved to Indiana we were the first black family in our neighborhood. There was no problem. Everyone treated us the same."

There's one more question on my list that I want to ask her. "How do you feel about people who pass for white like my mother did?"

"Back in that time I could understand. How they treated blacks. I have no ill feelings. She was doing what she had to do to survive."

Neither of us comments on how her grandmother's decision to pass for white cost her her life. Nor how my mother carried her secret north with her away from the potential danger of being found out in New Orleans. If Versie's grandmother had turned her back on her community and gone north, maybe she would have survived as well. With the hindsight of time, there's no way to know.

Versie continues relating how the current generation in her family has mixed with whites and Hispanics, blending the family tree. She knows all about the possibilities and struggles of multiculturalism and multiracialism.

"I don't see color," she states. And I believe her.

But something still nags at me about her opinion about my mother's decision to pass. I probe deeper. What did she think about my mother turning her back on her family?

"It must have ate her alive."

32

Let Sleeping Dogs Lie
DNA Cousins, 2015

"**H**OW COME WE don't have a big photo album like other families?" Paula Danners wondered growing up in northern Wisconsin.

I shake my head in agreement as I listen to her tell her racial discovery story.

We found each other via Ancestry.com, more specifically she found me. Our DNA is a very high probable cousin match, 96 percent. It's taken me a year to respond to her Ancestry.com emails. In all the upheaval of my mother's death and *Genealogy Roadshow*, I just wasn't ready. Her fourth request piqued my interest: "I would love to figure out our connection. My grandparents were from New Orleans and moved to Wisconsin in the 1920s."

A gemologist for thirty years, Paula's been doing genealogical research for ten years and tells me that nothing in her family has ever been easy. "Many secrets unfortunately."

Her Ancestry.com family tree is lush and luxuriant, spreading outward and upward like an old oak. Most of the branches on the tree bear fruit, photographs of her family members. It's almost frenetic in its expansiveness, illustrating her passionate need for family. She's invited me to view her tree on Ancestry.com, and I sent her the same invitation. We want to see if any of our ancestors' surnames match.

"I always suspected something wasn't right about our family, something was off. But I never knew what it was," Paula explains.

There's lightness to her tone that tells me she has come to terms with her own racial identity and her family's secrecy. Her feeling of betrayal, if not gone, then processed, no longer able to sting. Now it's just an interesting story.

Paula's curiosity about her family sprung from the same absence as my own—no visible proof of our people. No photographs to stare at and compare our face to their faces, looking for similarities that bind and comfort.

"Growing up it was only my grandparents and a handful of their siblings, my mom and sister, and my uncle who lived out in California. I didn't even know my uncle's children, my cousins, until I started researching and found some of them in California."

Her grandmother and grandfather raised her until she was twelve and were strangely silent about their respective families. "My grandfather would eat weird food like gumbo and grits and creole food. I was the only kid in my neighborhood who grew up on grits."

Food sometimes is its own clue, I think. We laugh over our fondness for grits as Northern "white" girls.

When her neighborhood changed and became more racially mixed, one of the African American children commented on her skin color. "You have yellow skin. Are you mixed?"

Confused by what the girl said about her skin, Paula went to her grandmother. "Am I yellow? Is my skin yellow?"

Her grandmother deflected the question, acknowledging her yellow skin tone but giving a misleading answer, an answer a child would accept. "That's because you eat so many carrots."

"I accepted that but still I wondered about my skin. I knew we looked Spanish and Indian. That I did know. I'd ask my grandmother questions about our family and she'd say, 'Let sleeping dogs lie.'"

My mother's strategy of deception was different than Paula's grand-mother's strategy. My mother told me half-truths. But both strategies had the same result for us. They fueled our sense that something was being hidden, some secret we were determined to know. Secrets sparked our curiosity.

The clues to Paula's real racial heritage were like seeds scattered here and there throughout her life. Clues that she had no way of piecing together. And then her first child, a daughter, was born in 1993, and all the pieces of her puzzle finally came together in a disturbing way.

"I was a new mom and I'd just brought my daughter Lauren home and the hospital called me. They told me that my daughter had sickle cell anemia.

"'That's impossible.' I said. 'It must be a mistake. You've made an error. She may have a trait for sickle cell, but she doesn't have the disease.'

"When we went to the hospital to be tested they asked for my hus-band's and my ethnic backgrounds. My husband's family emigrated from Germany around 1910 and were 100 percent German. The test eliminated him as a carrier. So it had to be me. I thought, 'Okay, it's the Mediterranean kind,' and had further tests done."

The gene for beta thalassemia, the Mediterranean form of sickle cell anemia, is relatively common among people of Italian and Greek origin because at one time parts of Italy and Greece were rampant with malaria. The presence of thalassemia minor protected against malaria and thus thrived.[1]

I hear the disbelief in her voice even now after all these years and I relive my own disbelief looking at the 1900 census, nowhere as earth shattering as finding out you and your child have a serious disease but shocking nonetheless, tilting your sense of self, how you see yourself in the world.

"It wasn't the Mediterranean kind. It was the African kind," Paula continues. "I carry about 46 percent of the sickle-cell trait in my blood. My daughter carries about 52 percent. I was taken aback."

According to the National Institute of Health about one in thirteen African American babies are born with the sickle-cell trait. About one in 365 black children are born with the sickle cell disease. Paula and her daughter have the sickle-cell trait.

As soon as Paula found out, she called her mother. When she describes her mother's reaction she uses the words, "flipped out."

"The geneticist is a liar," her mother yelled at her. "They don't know what they're talking about. This same thing happened to a distant cousin and it was a mistake."

"I hung up. I was mad at her for her behavior. I'm a new mom with a sick daughter and all she can do is yell at me. That was my reaction."

She waited a few weeks to call her mother back. She wanted to simmer down. "I had to get the truth. This was for my Lauren and me."

"I told her it had to be her side of the family because my father was Spanish. As I explained why it had to be her side, I realized that she didn't know. She didn't know her own parents were Creole, mixed race. Her parents hadn't told her."

Paula outlines the seriousness of their disease. "We can become more anemic than the average person. We cannot live in high altitude places such as Colorado because our blood doesn't get the proper oxygen and can cause anemia. If we mate with another carrier, the child would have full blown sickle cell anemia."

She says what I'm thinking. "People need to know their heritage for health reasons. The sickle-cell trait can mutate. You think you know your heritage but you don't know, not really. I guess that's why I'm so impassioned about my research." She takes in a deep breath. "This may sound corny. But I really believe that most people don't realize they are a mixture of a lot of wonderful nationalities, maybe races. We really need to embrace all that we are and know as a human race. We are all in it together!"

After she learned of her mixed heritage, she became dogged in her search for family. One family member she found related her grandfather's passing story, one that seems as if it came from a spy novel, with literal, not just metaphoric, crossings.

"Around 1902, the Dugas family left New Orleans, moved to Florida, then to New York, where my grandfather was born, and then to Canada. When the family returned to the United States and settled in Wisconsin, my grandfather gave his race as white, which wasn't true. This family member thought moving to Canada was a way for the family to pass for white."

I think of Uncle Eddie and Aunt Laura leaving their family behind to pass for white in Toledo, Ohio, and never returning home again. I think of my mother marrying my father and moving north to Cleveland, Ohio, also passing for white. I think of the Virginia Race Act predicated on the fear that "white Negroes" would slip over the color line and marry white people. I think of what it means to be a "white Negro," which is another way to say a person carries African blood, even the smallest drop tainting them. I think of the lengths my ancestors and Paula's ancestors have gone, the dissolution of families, the secrecy, the loss, and I feel immense sadness for the shame and oppression my people felt.

As if she can read my thoughts, Paula adds, "I also know that my grandparents and their parents did what they needed to do to survive during trying times in our country, but they always kept in touch with their family members that did not pass over the color line via phone or letters. I really hope that my grandparents would be happy that I am trying to piece the family back together again."

The ardent wish and worry of the person who steps out of the secrecy and reveals the truth. Are we being disloyal?

"I'd like to include your story in my mother's book," I pause, unsure of her reaction. "If you want, I can use another name. You don't have to use your real name."

Her voice becomes steely with determination. "I'm done with the hiding. You can use my real name. If you want photos to use, I'll give you them for the book. All I ask is that when the book comes out, you give me a signed copy."

"I can do that," I tell her, savoring the fierceness of her words. The daughters will no longer hide the truth of their mixed race. The daughters stand together in their own truth. We are no longer willing to let sleeping dogs lie.

As our conversation winds down, we try to find where our families intersect, why our cousin DNA is a 96 percent match. But we share only one ancestral name, Williams, too common, with little other evidence to be our missing link.

What we do find is another kind of connection. Paula's Fauria family owned an awning company in New Orleans in the first part of the twentieth century, Fauria Awnings. My maternal grandmother Camille, the gifted seamstress, worked for an awning company, making cloth awnings. Fauria Awnings was the only awning company in New Orleans at that time, so it's certain my grandmother worked for Paula's family's business.

Before we end our conversation, Paula talks about her grandmother's death. "When my mother, sister, and I went to clean out her house, they asked me what I wanted. 'I'm taking the photo albums.' No one objected." She hesitates. "My family seems like they can just walk away from family."

And isn't that what passing is about, walking away from family, not looking back, walking into the skin of another but underneath still carrying your true skin?

33

Lost Family Found
January 23, 2015

THREE DAYS AFTER the show airs, on a crisp January morning, when I open my email I receive a shock. There's an email from Stephanie Frederic. For a moment, I resist reading her email knowing that once I do my life will be altered, will change in ways I can't predict. Then I plunge forward, ignoring the wild thumping of my heart.

> *I'm Azemar A. Frederic Jr.'s daughter who lives in Los Angeles. A friend saw you on* Genealogy Roadshow *and sent pictures and info about you.*
>
> *We are very excited to meet you. My father lives in Alexandria, Louisiana, now. He's from New Orleans. His father was Azemar Frederic and his mother is Modesta Messmer.*
>
> *Please give us a call. We can't wait to meet you.*
>
> *Love,*
> *Your family,*
> *Stephanie Frederic*

As I finish reading Stephanie Frederic's email, I swipe at the tears running down my face. The house is too quiet, my husband still asleep. There's no one to tell yet.

I reread her email as if I missed something or misunderstood.

No, I didn't miss anything. My grandfather's other family, the one I knew little to nothing about, has found me. All the loss and grief from my mother's death isn't washed away, only intensified, but something else has been added to my life: another family.

"What did I always tell you, Gail?" I can almost hear my mother whisper. "When one door closes, another door opens."

My "new" cousin, Stephanie Frederic, welcomes me to the family, a family my mother left so long ago in New Orleans, a family she never talked about, a family she had nothing to do with, may never have known. The joy of discovery is tinged with sadness for her loss and mine and for all the years we never knew each other.

I keep returning to the words "Your family." In losing my mother and being freed from my vow, I've opened the door to family.

Stephanie's father's name is Azemar, that strange name that intrigued me for so long has been passed down through the Frederic family.

When my husband stumbles into the kitchen, I tell him about Stephanie Frederic.

"I never thought that would happen," he says as he pours himself a cup of coffee, then walks over and reads the email over my shoulder.

"So what do you think?" I ask, turning around to see his reaction.

"What about?"

I'm not sure what he's asking. "About Stephanie Frederic emailing me and her friend seeing the show."

He straightens up and takes a long swig of his coffee before he answers. "What are the odds, huh?"

"You mean of her friend seeing the show?"

"Of her seeing the show, making the connection to Stephanie, telling her about it, and Stephanie emailing you. So many things had to happen. Kinda amazing."

Two hours later I receive another email from another Frederic family member, Aunt Alma.

> *I was excited to learn that you and I both were trying to find info on our family. My journey was about as long as yours; however, in locating my parents' marriage certificate, it was confirmed who we belonged to. Looking forward to meeting you.*
>
> *Love,*
> *Aunt Alma*

"Aunt Alma." I roll her name around on my tongue. All my aunts from my father's family and my mother's family are dead. I have an aunt. I have an uncle. What other family do I have?

Around noon LaChanta, another cousin I never knew I had, emails me.

> *Hi, I saw your story on the* Genealogy Roadshow *and Azemar Frederic was my Granddad on my father's side. I currently live in Philadelphia, Pa., and my dad is Delano Frederic. I hope that one day we can meet because there are a lot of us to know. This is so exciting and I look forward to talking to you soon. LaChanta*

I study the family Facebook photos Stephanie and LaChanta post, searching for my mother's face, similarities that identify us as blood. I can see my mother in an early photo of Delano Frederic and in a later photo of Azemar Frederic, Stephanie's father.

My mother's words come back to me. "People always said I looked like my father." Then they too must look their father, Azemar. It's not the photo I've been searching for, but it's close.

In the afternoon when I phone Stephanie in Los Angeles, Aunt Alma joins the call. We talk for almost two hours. We are learning the outlines of each other's lives.

Aunt Alma is a retired elementary school teacher and lives near Washington, DC. Stephanie runs her own film production company, FGW Productions, in Los Angeles and specializes in documentaries. She and Alma chat about the documentary she made about Katrina. Aunt Alma comments about how brave she was in filming it.

Then they ask when they can meet me.

"I'll be in New Orleans in April. I'm going there to do research for the book I'm writing about my mother and her family."

"Just tell us the dates," they both say. "And we'll be there."

Really? I think. *They'll drop everything and fly to meet me in New Orleans?*

After I hang up, I check out Stephanie's website and am blown away. Her production company is FGW Productions. In another coincidental occurrence, her documentary *White Girls* aired last Monday, one day before our *Roadshow* segment. I watch it, fascinated by a topic I'm now very familiar with—passing for white.

Maybe it's the first flush of friendship in the rush to get to know each other, but over the next few months I begin to see that we share more than a paternal grandfather, that I've found a kindred creative soul.

About a month before Jerry and I are scheduled to leave for New Orleans, I receive an itinerary from Lauren King, my first cousin Azemar's wife. The itinerary is titled "Welcome to the Family." My stomach drops when I read through the elaborately planned schedule from the meet and greet dinner on Friday, April 10, to the Sunday church service at the Greater Mount Calvary Baptist Church. My introverted writer self curls into a shell. A party in my honor is the last thing I want. But then the other part of my writerly self asserts itself. What an adventure and so much to write about.

34

Crossing Back Over
April 7–8, 2015

Prayer to my mother asking her for a sign that I'm doing the
   right thing:
"Be the fingerprint on the window,
the breath behind the curtain,
the shadow that lingers after the light leaves."

THE AIRPORT LIMO is scheduled to arrive in fifteen minutes and I
still can't decide which outfit to wear for the photograph Cousin
Stephanie asked me to take. She needs my photo for the camera crew
who is meeting us at the New Orleans airport.

I've changed my clothes twice already. In the first photograph Jerry
snapped, I look washed out, drained of color. It doesn't help that I'm
still recovering from a two-week bout of bronchitis. I'm not usually this
vain. But so much is riding on this trip to New Orleans.

Originally the trip was to be a pilgrimage to discover the city that
shaped my mother, to soak in the atmosphere, breathe in the air, feel the
light and heat on my skin, eat the Creole food, in the hope of conjuring

her, or at the least the spirit of her. How can I write a book about her if I don't immerse myself in her city?

The week of April 7–14 was chosen to coincide with the possible ceremony on Ship Island, Mississippi, honoring the Second Regiment of the Native Guards who were stationed at the garrison during the Civil War (and for a brief time the Third Regiment, Leon's regiment) guarding the Confederate prisoners of war housed on the island, as well as protecting the Mississippi River from Confederate soldiers. Ike told me that the first weekend in April the National Park Service sponsors a memorial service. I want to attend as much for my mother as the book I'm writing. Another connection to family and the past that she refused to acknowledge.

Besides the welcome home party and the ferry trip to Ship Island, I plan to visit the St. Ann house where my mother was born and St. Louis Cemetery No. One to locate Philomene Lanabere's crypt. The remainder of my free time I'll spend at the New Orleans Public Library doing research.

But all that changed ten days ago when Stephanie phoned me with an idea.

"I'm flying back from New York after meeting with the executives at HBO and it dawns on me," Stephanie said. "I have a story for them right here in my own family. I wished I'd thought of it sooner when they asked, 'What else have you got?'"

I listened to her distinctive speaking voice. She still sounds like the TV journalist she once was, strong, confident, and trustworthy. "What do you think about going into a partnership with me?"

As she explained how our partnership would work, a feeling of disbelief yet rightness came over me. The same feeling I had when the *Roadshow* called and said we'd been chosen for the show.

"So Cousin Gail you want to be partners in a documentary?"

After the initial thrill of her proposal, I brought up my one caveat about the documentary: that it would trump the publication of my book. Why would a publisher want the book if the documentary had already told the story? I reasoned.

"I'll put in the contract that the book and the doc have to come out at the same time," she answered without hesitation. "I want you to be comfortable with this."

I'm comfortable—a bundle of nerves but comfortable.

Quickly, Jerry takes the second photograph and emails it to Stephanie. The limo driver pulls into the driveway. One of the biggest adventures of my life is about to begin.

As the limo heads for the expressway, I think that it's no coincidence that two days ago was the first anniversary of my mother's death. Something serendipitous is happening, yet again. When I booked this trip on January 13, I never expected that my mother's lost family, my lost family, would find me or that they'd be hosting a "Welcome Home" party. And without question I never expected to be making a documentary with my Cousin Stephanie, who four months ago I didn't know existed.

"We can't re-create these moments," Stephanie explained to me when we discussed the filming of my New Orleans trip. "We need to capture them spontaneously as they're happening."

It's the second day in New Orleans, and I'm standing on St. Ann Street in front of the house where my mother was born, waiting for the camera crew to set up. We spent the morning at the New Orleans Public Library, where Lisa Martin, the doc's producer, conducted an impromptu interview that felt awkward and strange to me. I had to repeat several times the story of my mother's secret. It's starting to feel like a script that I can't quite get right.

I just can't seem to relax—too aware of the camera. It didn't help my nerves when my cousin Azemar King and his son A. J. showed up in the middle of the interview. I kept trying to catch a glimpse of him and his son and kept losing my train of thought. He's the first Frederic family member I meet. And we both seem to be at a loss for words.

On our drive from the New Orleans Public Library to St. Ann Street, Azemar told me that all the Frederic men are short as if I'd been questioning his height. He's a handsome guy with warm caramel-colored skin and European features. His deceased mother Modesta Frederic King was my grandfather's oldest child from his second marriage, my mother's half sister.

"They say the oldest girl looks like me," my mother once told me. "That's all I know about her." She never said there were more children. She never told me Modesta's name. She never told me much of anything.

When I asked Azemar what his mother died of, he said, "She was just worn down." I don't pursue it.

Azemar has an electric personality. Though his arm is in a sling, it doesn't seem to tame his energy or his fast driving. He's a marine and has seen several tours of duty in Iraq.

As we wait for an airplane to pass overhead before filming, Azemar says, "The house is razed."

I'm not sure what he means. "Is it going to be torn down?" A warning sign festoons the chain link fence surrounding the house: Private Property No Trespassing.

He points to the cinder blocks supporting the house. "No, rehabbed."

I'm relieved as if the house should never be torn down, should never be lost, should remain a monument to my mother's family. Trickles of sweat run down my back, and I curse myself for wearing black jeans, for being nervous, for stealing glances at Azemar trying to find some semblance of my mother but I can see no resemblance.

"This is a shotgun house," Cousin Azemar explains. "That means if the front door and back door were both open and you stood at the front and fired straight into the house, the bullet would pass straight through."

I shield my eyes from the late morning sun beating through the large oak trees and study the cream-colored house—the neatly trimmed windows edged in red, the plywood where the front steps should be, the gravel drive. The unreality of the situation blunts my reaction to seeing my mother's birth house.

If my mother were here with me, would she even recognize this house after all this time, after so many other families have lived here, after so many reinventions? This was the house she never returned to. Though I try to summon her, I feel nothing but the incredible heat and humidity.

"Would you like me to take a picture of you in front of the house?" Azemar asks.

"Sure." I hand him my camera.

Months later when I look at the photo closely, I'll notice how overgrown the trees are in the backyard where my mother and her two siblings posed for that other photograph so long ago. That cherished photograph that she brought with her from New Orleans north to Ohio that I'll pass down to my children. Finally, sewing the tattered ends of her story back together with the silkiest of threads, the thinnest of needles, the finest of stitches.

"We're ready," Lisa says. "Gail, why don't you stand in front of the house, and I'll interview you with the house as backdrop." She wears a black jacket and black studded boots that seem at odds with the hot day and the spring season.

George, the cameraman, hoists the large, bulky camera on his shoulder while Blake, the boom guy, holds the large muffled boom steady.

While we shoot, a rooster walks across the street. Then a black man at the end of the block shouts at us. "Don't put me on TV! If the police see me on TV, I might have to go to jail. There are warrants out for me."

The crew stops shooting and we wait patiently for the man to go back into his house. Then Lisa says, "How do you feel seeing your mother's house?"

I bumble through an answer, not able to access my feelings that seem to have gone underground. I'm not an actress, I want to tell her. I'm a person. I don't know what I'm feeling. I'm overwhelmed.

Toward the end of the interview, I strike one of my mother's theatrical poses and say, "I'm channeling my mother." Everyone smiles. But I can find my mother nowhere. She seems beyond this house, this place that she never wanted to see again.

Did she know that this house is only a mile from the Iberville house where her father lived with his second family? I wonder. Azemar drove by the Iberville house before coming here, telling me about the house fire that destroyed all the family photographs.

"So there's no photograph of our grandfather?" I say as if I have to confirm what he just said.

"We're still looking. Maybe at the welcome party one of the family members from out of town will bring a photograph."

"Have you ever seen a photograph of him?"

"No. But there has to be one somewhere."

In the evening, sitting in our hotel room on Magazine Street, my underground emotions surface. In my journal I write about the melancholy and tremendous sadness I felt seeing the house on St. Ann Street. Because I know my mother will never grow up in this house and that her parents will separate when she's six. That her mother will lose custody and she and her sister Shirley will be shuffled around from one relative to another. Then in 1940 they'll be living with Cousin Theresa Spikes, the schoolteacher. That this house will be the first and last place they will live together as a family.

If only I had been able to tell Lisa that while the camera rolled and the heat poured down and the crazy man shouted at us.

Getting permission to enter St. Louis Cemetery turns out to be an ordeal, an almost insurmountable hurdle. The cemetery has been in lock down since 2013, because of the defacement that year of Marie Laveau's tomb—the Voodoo Queen of New Orleans. Someone snuck into the cemetery at night and coated her tomb with thick pink latex paint. The three-month restoration of her tomb cost the Archdiocese of New Orleans $10,000. Because of the defacement, only family members who have ancestors buried in the cemetery or those taking guided tours are allowed entry. Family members must obtain passes from the archdiocese and prove that they have a relative buried in the cemetery.

The defacement of Marie Laveau's tomb, though extreme, has been building for years. Decades ago someone started the rumor that if people wanted a wish granted by Laveau, they should draw an *X* on the tomb, turn around three times, knock on the tomb, and shout out their wish. Such is the power of New Orleans and voodoo and the careless stupidity of tourists.

Lisa Martin, who has no luck getting the camera crew and us into the cemetery, tells me of other acts of vandalism that seem beyond belief—people reaching into the vaults and pulling out bones, removing rocks from the gravesites. I take it personally since I know that my third great-grandmother is buried here.

Prior to the trip to New Orleans, the only family grave I've located via the Internet is Philomene Lanabere Frederic. Even the Civil War veteran Leon Frederic eludes me. Finding her grave takes on an unexpected importance to me. I want some physical marker that my ancestors existed other than census reports and vital records. I want to touch something that links me to them. If I can't have a photograph of them in life, then at least I can have an image of where they lie in eternity.

I call the Archdiocese of New Orleans and explain that I'd like permission to visit the grave of my ancestor Philomene Frederic who's buried in St. Louis No. One. From Find a Grave, I located her tomb and have a photograph of it in case I need to show proof. Though I suppose anyone could print out a photograph and claim an ancestor.

It takes over a day to reach someone by phone, and I'm losing hope. When I reach someone at the diocese, the woman tells me I have to come to the archdiocese to pick up family passes.

For spring, the weather has been unusually hot and humid, most days reaching ninety degrees. But I will not be deterred. From our hotel on Magazine Street, Jerry and I meander the streets for close to an hour before we find the building on Walmsley. The passes are waiting for us inside the wonderfully chill office. We're told that we could use the passes, made of durable plastic, again and again.

The next morning we set off early. It takes us most of the morning, wandering the twisting and turning paths in the sweltering sun before Jerry finds Philomene's crypt. In desperation he'd shown the photograph of her crypt to a guard.

"Not many that look like that," the guard said. "Try over in that section."

Already two tour guides have stopped me and questioned what I was doing in the cemetery.

Patiently I explained that I'm searching for a family member. That explanation seemed to satisfy them.

When I see the Lanabere tomb I'm overwhelmed by its grandness, how well it's maintained. The face of the tomb is black marble and the family names are etched into the stone. I write down the family names. Two Azemar Lanaberes are buried in the tomb: Azemar Lanabere 1848–1896, Philomene's brother; and Azemar J. Lanabere 1893, who was the son of Azemar Lanabere and Marie Augustine Celles Reinecke Lanabere. Their son lived only four months.

After I record their names, I shove the notebook in my purse. Then I put my hand to the stone as if I could invoke Philomene's spirit. But I only feel the warmth of the marble. As I stand there, with my head bowed, I say a prayer for her and the other Lanaberes.

Even as I pray, I know it's my mother I'm praying for.

35

Welcome to the Family

April 10, 2015

AZEMAR KING SKILLFULLY maneuvers his large black SUV around the parking lot for the second time as the camera crew takes their positions at the entrance to the Event Room where the welcome home party will take place. He seems to be accustomed to camera crews and Stephanie's direction, not at all annoyed, taking it in his stride.

"Everyone's already inside," he tells Jerry and me. "Waiting for you."

I try not to think about the camera crew or the "new" relatives awaiting us. I try not to think about my mother or what she would think of this journey I've made to discover the truth of her family. I try not to think.

We pull up to the door and Azemar jumps out of the car and opens the passenger door for me. I've finally convinced him not to call me ma'am, but I appreciate his chivalrousness.

With the camera crew trailing us, we approach the entrance, and then stop. I take in a deep breath. Jerry opens the glass door and I walk inside. The family is lined up in a semicircle to greet us. I see Stephanie at the end of the line on my left. She's crying. Uncle Fred walks toward me and hands me a gift. Then he hugs me.

"Thank you," I tell him.

"No," he says. "Thank you. We are so grateful to you. You have no idea what you've done for our family."

I accept his gratitude and wonder at it. Then the rest of the family comes forward and introduces themselves, hugging me, welcoming me. Jerry and I are guided to a table and are quickly joined by Uncle Fred, Aunt Alma and her husband John, Aunt Brenda and her husband Maurice.

I can't help myself. I can't stop staring in wonderment at them, especially Uncle Fred. I can see my mother in his face, the same dark eyes, the same facial shape.

"Uncle Fred," I say. "You look like my mother."

He smiles as if proving the similarity.

I open his present. It's a silver embossed heart with a key that inserts into the back and acts as a support. A golden plaque adorns the front of the heart, which bears the words "Grateful Heart."

The two aunts hand me framed photographs of each of their families and Aunt Modesta and Uncle Delano's families.

I've brought gifts for them as well. I give each of them copies of the ten-page research packet about the Frederic family that Rich, the genealogist from *Genealogy Roadshow*, prepared for the show.

As Uncle Fred pages through the packet, he says, "You know I always hated my name Azemar. Kids used to tease me at school. But now that I know how far back in the family that names goes, I'm liking it more and more."

Stephanie comes over and tells me that some of the family members haven't seen each other in thirty years, like Cousin Dell from Philly, Delano's son.

"You've done a good thing," she says, "bringing this family together."

Without knowing, I was the catalyst that reunited this family, as was *Genealogy Roadshow*. If I hadn't filled out that online application none of this would have been possible.

They tell me how they never knew their father had a second family. They tell me how young they were when their father died and their mother left them.

Aunt Alma says, "We were raised by Alma Reilly. It was much later we found out she was our grandmother. All those years we never knew."

"Tell me about your father. What did he look like?" I want to know details about my grandfather, the man my mother told me so little about.

Uncle Fred jumps in first. "My father was real careful about his dress. He wore white starched shirts, shoes shined. That was my job. To shine his shoes. His hair was always combed. He worked at a furniture store. On Saturdays he and his friend would sit on the porch drinking beer. I didn't like that." I can see the distress in his face.

I tilt my head in surprise. This description of Azemar is radically different from my mother's description. "My mother always told me her father never smoked or drank. That he was a hard worker."

"Just on weekends," Uncle Fred answers.

But something about his father's drinking bothers him even though he concedes it was only on weekends. Perhaps as my friend Linda always says, the truth is somewhere in the middle.

"Did anyone find a photo of him?" I'm almost afraid to ask, for surely they would have given it to me along with the other framed family photographs.

They shake their heads. "All the pictures were destroyed in the fire," Uncle Fred explains.

I'm disappointed that I still don't have a photograph of my grandfather. The missing photograph that started this quest so many years ago is still not found. But then I look at my two aunts and one uncle and realize that this was what I was meant to find. I glance around at the other tables, at the cousins. We are every shade of skin from darkest ebony to whitest white and all the shades in between. This is what my quest was leading me to, not a photograph of my grandfather Azemar Frederic, but his other family.

After we eat Azemar King comes over to our table holding an eight-by-ten black-and-white photograph. "Cousin Gail," he says. "Maybe you can help us. We were looking at this photograph last night of my mother and my brothers. But there's this other woman with kids in the photograph, and no one knew who she was."

He places the photograph on the table in front of me. I can hardly believe what I'm looking at. The sight of the woman and her children hits me hard. I blink away the tears that threaten to fall. I'm suspended in time, thrown back to my childhood.

"That's my Aunt Shirley," I say. "My mother's sister. And those are her children, Margaret, Tripper, and Tony." I don't tell them what else I know about Aunt Shirley and her children, that they're now deceased. And that Aunt Shirley died in a mental hospital bruised and beaten. It is too joyous an evening for sadness.

We all stare at the photograph in silence, in awe of what the photograph reveals to us. Many years ago long after my grandfather died and my mother moved north and left her family behind, Aunt Shirley and her half sister Modesta knew each other. There was once a bond between them. At one time Azemar's two families knew each other. But something happened and the families drifted apart, taking their stories with them.

"Hey, Cousin Gail," Azemar says, "you up for another reunion next year?"

"Sure, where?"

"Cousin Dell wants to host us in Philly."

I catch my husband's eye. I can see he's on board, as I am. "Just let me know when and I'll be there."

36

Two Versions of One Family Story
December 2015 / January 2016

A S THE PRESENTATIONS wind down, as the book takes shape, I'm plagued with searing spinal pain, as if the burden of telling my mother's story, the story of racism in this country, has become too much to bear, has lodged in my spine, has taken root. Some days I can barely get out of bed.

But there's one family story that's missing, another absence, another empty space that needs to be filled. That last day in New Orleans at the Café Adelaide, Aunt Alma talked about how her mother disappeared after her father died, her emotions raw as if it had happened yesterday. How can I be a part of this family without hearing that story? Without understanding how it shaped their lives.

With some trepidation, I contact Aunt Alma and set up a day and time to chat. I also contact Uncle Fred because I suspect he'll tell me a different story than his sister. Stories and memories are like that. Although they've embraced me as family, I feel shy about having them relive these painful memories of childhood abandonment.

When I tell Stephanie what I intend to do, she says, "Good luck with that. They don't share much."

Alma Frederic Montgomery is a retired elementary school teacher who lives in the DC area. Both in appearance and actions, she's precise and clear, probably occupational traits developed from her years of teaching young children. Though she's kind, there's a no nonsense attitude about her. On the ferry over to Ship Island, Mississippi, she related how she and John, her husband, volunteered to help after Katrina, traveling south and sleeping in a church.

When I ask about her father, she says wistfully, "My memories are so scattered. I think I knew more than I remembered. I don't have a good memory of him."

What she does remember of him is his being waked in the front room of the house on Iberville and being scared of his dead body in the house. She was seven years old when he died.

"I felt double abandonment. All within one year I lost my father and my mother." She pauses. "We lived with Alma Riley, and I thought she'd adopted us after my father died and my mother left us. Not until fifteen years ago when I went to Vital Records in New Orleans and looked her up did I discover that she was my grandmother. My mother's mother."

"Why did your mother leave you? Was that after your father died?"

"Before he died. She'd come around for maybe a day. I didn't know where she was living. I didn't know at that time if my parents were separated or divorced. I do remember when my father was sick, he told Alma Riley, 'If anything happens to me, will you keep the kids?' He'd had two heart attacks already. The third one killed him. I think he was an alcoholic."

"What about your mother, Modesta?"

"I think she left us to start a new life, maybe to marry a white man. In this school photo of her and me, she looks very white with brown hair, thick hair. All the girls have thick hair from my mom. When I looked her up in the census, every time—1920, 1930, 1940—she was listed as a boarder. She was never related to anyone. Her race was mulatto and her father was Caesar Messmer." She takes in a deep breath and I wait.

"Music was a stabilizer for me." There's a lightness and pride in her voice when she talks about music. She had a full scholarship to Xavier University of Louisiana in New Orleans, where she studied elementary education. Her musical outlet was her church. She worked part-time as an organist.

When I ask her about my mother's decision to pass and what she thought of that, she tells her own story of passing.

"The only time I thought about passing was on a bus trip from Beeville, Texas, to Blytheville, Arkansas, where I was living at the time. I'd gone to Beeville to visit my first husband Kurt who was stationed at an army base in Texas. This was in 1960. It was a long bus ride and the bus went through Mississippi and Louisiana. I was tired. So when I got on in Texas, I decided I wasn't going to the back of the bus where the black people were to sit. So I sat down in the front in the white section. I was doing my Rosa Parks.

"The bus driver looked at me but doesn't say anything, but he kept looking at me. Not until the third stop did he say anything.

"'What are you?' he said.

"'What do you mean?' I answered.

"'You know what I mean. Are you colored or white?'

"'I'm an American.'

"'Go to the back of the bus or I'll call the police.'

"I believe if I hadn't, I wouldn't be here today. I do believe that."

I believe it too, having heard a similar story of a WWII black GI who was taken off a bus in the South and beaten to death because he refused to sit in the "colored" section. But Aunt Alma's story takes place in 1960 not 1945.

I remember Aunt Alma crying at Café Adelaide that last day we were in New Orleans when we had lunch with her, John, Cousin Azemar, and his wife Lauren. She was talking about her mother's abandonment, how her older sister Modesta went to the church where their mother worshiped to see her. Modesta did see her, but her mother didn't see her or pretended not to.

"For all I know, my mother could still be alive, living in some nursing home. I've tried over the years to find her. But she just disappeared."

How can a woman abandon her five children and never look back? How could she never visit them, leaving them to be raised by her mother? As a mother it seems incomprehensible to me. Maybe what Aunt Alma said about her always being a lodger, never belonging to anyone, explains what seems to me heartless.

"The main thing about all of this happening with you and the *Roadshow* is I finally found someone who was looking for us as I was looking for them."

When I talk to Uncle Fred I get another piece of this family's broken puzzle, another insight into their mother and father.

"I was there when my father passed away," Uncle Fred says for the second time, leading me back to the story he wants to tell. I let him. Something about his witnessing his father's death at the age of ten needs to be heard.

"That must have been hard for you," I encourage him. "He died at Charity Hospital, right?" I don't mention what else I know about my grandfather's death, that before his death he'd stayed at Charity for 105 days and that he died of coronary occlusion, heart disease, and gangrene. This is Uncle Fred's story. I'm only here to listen.

"My father had heart trouble, which could have been caused by his drinking. My mother left him nine months to a year before he passed. She might have left because when he drank he got abusive, not physically."

"Emotionally?"

"Yes, emotionally abusive."

Could his emotional abuse have been ignited by his jealousy, the reason my grandmother gave for leaving him?

"It was a July day, and I was the only family member visiting my father. My grandmother gave me fourteen cents to take the trolley to the hospital. I didn't understand at the time that Alma Riley was my grandmother. But I didn't take the trolley. I saved the fourteen cents and walked from Iberville to the hospital."

He's gradually easing himself into the story of his father's death. "When I got to the hospital my father was having trouble breathing. I could tell. Then the nurse ran over, looked at him, and then called for the doctor. My father took in a long breath and then let it out. It was his last breath. I saw it. Real quick they put me in a wheelchair that was always by his bed and wheeled me out of there." He gathers his thoughts. "I was the first one to know he died. I didn't know how I was going to tell the family. When I got home they already knew. Someone from the hospital must have called."

I ask him about his mother. I expect him to say that after she left that was the last he heard from her. But he surprises me.

"After she left, she called and told me where she was."

This is a different story than the one Alma told me, that her mother cut off all contact with the family. I wonder if the siblings ever shared their different stories.

"She never said why she left my father. We'd ride the trolley car and talk. We'd ride to the end of the line and back. I asked her if she was okay. She said yes. I asked her if she was happy. I'll never forget what she said. 'I'm content, not happy.' I always remember that word, content."

There's no rancor or resentment or even sadness that Alma expressed. Fred seems more resigned to his mother's abandonment. He keeps repeating that he always wanted to be a person who was independent, a person who called his own shots. To prove that, he relates a series of jobs he had as a child: from whitewashing graves at St. Louis No. Three cemetery to working in the meat department at the corner market to helping his grandmother set up for the school in her backyard where she taught people to read in the evenings and on Saturdays. Even his joining the air force after high school is another sign of his fierce need to be independent, to travel the world, to get an education on the government's dime, not to burden his grandmother with his education.

"My mother was very pretty, very attractive, very fair. When my mother and I would ride the trolley, we'd sit behind the screen, in the section for the colored people. Sometimes older people would get on and move the screen so we would be sitting in the white section. One time I sat in the white section. No one said anything."

I also ask him his thoughts about my mother's passing. "Your mother saw an opportunity to better herself and she seized the opportunity. That was an individual opinion and desire. If it helped you for your goals, why should a person be held back."

He chuckles. "I passed. I'll give you an example. There's this hotel in New Orleans, the Roosevelt, very elegant hotel. When I was a child, blacks had to go in the back way. When I'd pay the water bill downtown for my grandmother, I'd go into the front entrance of the Roosevelt Hotel and sit on this circular bench and look at the beautiful tapestries. I thought to myself that was their law not mine. One time a clerk said to me, 'Son, you need anything?' I said, 'No, I'm just waiting.'"

Then he tells me another story of accidental passing. "When I was processed into the air force, I had to submit my high school records and on the record for race was *C* for colored. The person who processed me changed my race to white. He must have thought there'd been a mistake but he never said anything. I didn't know it at the time. But I found out later. So I used it to my advantage in the service because I thought it would help with my promotions."

When I ask him about his father's other family, he says, "I never knew my father had another family. He used to take me to visit this lady on Galvez Street. I didn't know who she was. Her name was Shirley that was all I knew."

This was my mother's sister, Shirley. He was visiting his half sister and was never told that they were family.

It seems incredible that my grandfather never told Fred that this lady on Galvez was his half sister. And just as incredible that Shirley never said a word either.

How easily family falls away from each other, I think.

"Is there anything else you'd like to say?"

"I think your book is going to open up a lot of people's eyes."

37

Union Station, Los Angeles, California

Genealogy Roadshow Redux: January 15, 2016

THE MIKE GUY hands me a wire and asks me to thread it inside my blouse while a commotion of tech people ready the set for the taping. As I thread the wire, I listen to La Monte Westmoreland give Kenyatta and me instructions for the taping. He's his usual unflappable self, warm, friendly, and professional.

"Kenyatta, start by asking Gail what's happened since she's been on the show. We'll use footage from her segment as a lead-in."

I sigh, relieved I don't have to recite the story of my mother's racial secret and my seventeen-year vow to keep that secret. Though I'm prepared to do so.

Kenyatta says, "Got it."

About a month ago, La Monte contacted me and asked if I'd like to fly to Los Angeles to do an update for the show. Of course I said yes. He explained that the three *Genealogy Roadshow* genealogists—Kenyatta Berry, Joshua Taylor, and Mary Tedesco—were asked which story had the most impact on them personally, and Kenyatta chose our story. But I don't know why. Maybe during the interview she'll reveal her reason.

"Just pretend we're having a conversation, just you and me," Keny-atta advises me.

"Pretty hard to do with the cameras."

"Okay, we're ready to go," shouts the bearded guy with the baseball cap whose name I can't remember.

Kenyatta and I exchange a knowing smile, and she says, "Gail, we're happy to have you back."

"Thank you. I'm happy to be back."

"So what's happened since the show aired?"

"Three days after the show aired," I begin, "I received an email from Stephanie Frederic welcoming me to the family. She tells me her father is Azemar Frederic, Jr. He's my mother's half brother."

The words tumble out as images flash through my mind—images of family my mother left behind, turned her back on, let go of. I see them lined up to greet me as I walked through the doors of the Event Room. I see us on the ferry to Ship Island as the boat rocked and someone steadied the camera to capture this blended family, who visually tell the story of racial identity in America. I see my mother's shotgun house on St. Ann Street where she was born and the black marble of Philomene Lanabere Frederic's crypt in St. Louis No. One Cemetery. I see Steph-anie Frederic sitting across the table from me at a restaurant last night after having flown from Atlanta, Georgia, to take her new cousin to dinner. Then flying back to Atlanta at midnight.

Someone says, "Stop."

I'm frustrated that I may lose the thread of my story, the momentum that was building. He apologizes and explains that we have to wait until the next train is announced over the loudspeaker.

While waiting, I glance to my right and watch a young woman walk slowly through the station and think of my mother walking through this very station in 1943, eager to test the waters of passing in California. Is she with me here now? Is she thinking, finally my story will be heard?

Finally I will be given a voice and people will know who I was, who I really was and what I had to do to escape racism.

La Monte walks over. "Kenyatta, why don't you tell Gail why you chose her story?" She nods, straightens her back, and rests her hands on the table taking in a long breath, as she gathers her thoughts.

We start filming again. "Gail, I was very moved by your story. I think you were incredibly brave to tell it on national television. You've lived your life as a white woman. That's how your friends and your community viewed you. You had no idea how people would react. It was also brave to keep the secret for so long to honor your mother's wishes. I thought it was very touching that you weren't angry with your mother."

I squirm under her praise. "Thank you," I respond, not sure if she'll like what I want to say about bravery. "But I think my mother was the brave one." It's not false modesty. It's really how I feel. "She made the audacious move to come north and pass as white. She did that for her children so we could have a better life."

"I think you mentioned how she hid from the sun, wore hats whenever she went outside," Kenyatta coaxes.

"She did. She never went outside without a hat." And she did so much more to protect herself from being found out.

"There was always the fear for her of being *outed*, of having someone from her hometown recognize her. And then having to leave her family in New Orleans behind to cross over," Kenyatta adds.

She gets it. She understands what it means to leave family, to reinvent yourself.

"With all that's happened this past year how has it changed you?"

The question throws me. In preparing for this interview, that question never occurred to me. I stumble for an answer and even as I say it, it comes up short.

"I have a deeper understanding for what my mother went through. I see myself differently."

"How do you see yourself differently?" Kenyatta asks.

How can I explain the way I view race and myself now? Not that I was ever a racist, but that I can see deeper into our racial history, how it's a social construct with consequences. From Luison Santilly, the enslaved Native American, to my mother Alvera Frederic Kalina who was enslaved by Jim Crow laws and all the Frederics in between, moving back and forth across the color line, making decisions that impacted their children's lives. Except for Asian, the Frederic ancestors have checked every racial box.

I'm not sure how I answer her. There's too much to say. It would take a much longer time to explain the journey that has brought me here.

The interview ends. Kenyatta and I hug. I walk back to the holding area where the other two *Genealogy Roadshow* alums and my husband are waiting. It's been a good day. I watch the light from the palladium windows dance across the art deco marble floor. I hear the announcement of the arrival of another train.

I think of my mother carefully relating her New Orleans stories to me in the small bedroom in Parma, how she gave me the gift of her life story, to sift through, to bear witness to, to interpret, and then to tell what she could not tell, dare not tell, the true story of her life in all its shadings and shadows and half-truths and deceptions. Preparing me to be the daughter she wanted me to be: secret keeper and storyteller.

Acknowledgments

Iwant to offer my heartfelt thanks to those who gave so generously of their time and expertise during the writing of *White Like Her*. Their contributions were invaluable.

I'm indebted to my savvy and intelligent readers, who I'm fortunate to call my friends: Professor Nancy Cirillo, University of Illinois, Chicago; Professor Hanley Kanar, Illinois Institute of Art; and Professor Linda Landis Andrews, University of Illinois, Chicago. Thanks to journalist and friend, Mary Aiello Gauntner, who kept my spirits from flagging and contributed to the Civil War research.

I am grateful to these generous researchers and genealogists: Genealogy Librarian Sonia Schoenfield, Cook Memorial Library; Genealogy Librarian Ellen Jenkins Jennings, Cook Memorial Library; Genealogist Rich Venezia, Genealogist Judy Riffel; Librarian and Archivist Jeanne Thomas; Researcher Abby Grace Iona Djama-Adan; Archivist Jack Belsom, Archdiocese of New Orleans Office of Archives and Records; Head Librarian Becky Hill, Rutherford B. Hayes Library; Jessica Strawn, Parish of Orleans Civil District Court; Military Historian Isiah Edwards; Librarian and Archivist Gregory Osborn, New Orleans Public Library; and Head Librarian Christina Bryant, New Orleans Public Library.

Without *Genealogy Roadshow* this book probably would have never been written. I owe special thanks to the *Genealogy Roadshow* family, especially Senior Producer LaMonte Westmoreland, Field Producer Sarah Hochhauser, Executive Producer Carlos Ortiz, Executive Producer Stuart Krasnow, and host Kenyatta Berry who understood the importance of my mother's story and offered me support and guidance.

White Like Her is a story of family, both lost and found. I would like to thank the entire Frederic family for their unflinching and warm welcome and for entrusting me with the Frederic family story. I'd especially like to thank Ula Moret, Alma Montgomery, Azemar Frederic, Paula Danners, Versie Jeffries, and Paris L. Gill Smith for sharing their personal stories. I'm particularly grateful to Stephanie Frederic for her encouragement, enthusiasm, and generous spirit. She has been a guiding light throughout the writing of the book.

Finally, I would like to express my deep gratitude to my son, Professor Christopher Lukasik, Purdue University, who deserves special recognition for his genealogical research into the family tree, and to my husband, Jerry Lukasik, whose diligence and patience solved the mystery of Ursin's paternity and whose belief in me has kept me steadfast in this journey of amazing discoveries.

Notes

Foreword

1. Michelle Gordon Jackson, *Light, Bright and Damn Near White: Black Leaders Created by the One-Drop Rule,* (JacksonScribe Publishing Company, 2013), 18.

5: The Vow

1. James Weldon Johnson, *The Autobiography of an Ex-Colored Man* (New York: Dover Publications Inc., 1995), 90.

6: Creole, Anyone?

1. Mary Gehman, *The Free People of Color: An Introduction* (Louisiana: Margaret Mead, Inc., 2014), 77.
2. *The Harvard Encyclopedia of Ethnic Groups*, (Cambridge, MA: Belknap Press of Harvard University, 1980).
3. Louisiana Revised Statues, title 42, sec. 267.
4. Gehman, *The Free People of Color*, 100.

10: Difficult Beginnings

1. Edna B. Freiberg, *Bayou St. John in Colonial Louisiana 1699–1803* (New Orleans: Harvey Press, 1980), 277–279.
2. Cornell University Law School: Legal Information Institute.
3. Merriam-Webster Dictionary.
4. Allyson Hobbs, *A Chosen Exile: A History of Racial Passing in American Life* (Cambridge, MA, and London: Harvard University Press, 2014), 129.
5. Hobbs, *A Chosen Exile*, 128.
6. 1924 Act to Preserve Racial Integrity.

7. *Mixed Race Studies: Scholarly Perspectives on the Mixed Race Experience.*

11: Nothing Left to Lose
1. Hobbs, *A Chosen Exile*, 15, 18.

13: The Case of the Disappearance of Aunt Laura
1. Arthé A. Anthony, "Lost Boundaries," *Creole: The History and Legacy of Louisiana's Free People of Color*, ed. Sybil Kein (Baton Rouge: Louisiana State University Press, 2000), 301–302.
2. Anthony, "Lost Boundaries," 303.

14: Gens de Couleur Libre
1. "Free People of Color in Louisiana," LSU Libraries, October 2015, www.lib.lsu.edu/special/fpoc/history.html.
2. Joan Martin, "*Plaçage* and the Louisiana *Gens de Couleur Libre.*" *Creole: The History and Legacy of Louisiana's Free People of Color*, ed. Sybil Kein (Baton Rouge: Louisiana State University Press, 2000), 57.
3. Gehman, *The Free People of Color*, 11.
4. Kimberly S. Hanger, "Coping in a Complex World: Free Black Women in Colonial New Orleans," in *The Devil's Lane*, ed. Clinton and Gillespie (New York: Oxford University Press, 1997), 220.
5. Martin, "*Plaçage*," 68.
6. Hellen Lee-Keller, "Placage," in *knowlouisiana.org Encyclopedia of Louisiana*, ed. David Johnson, Louisiana Endowment for the Humanities, article published 2 Feb 2011, http://www.knowla.org/entry/764/.
7. Martin, "*Plaçage*," 62.
8. Martin, "*Plaçage*," 62.
9. Martin, "*Plaçage*," 64–65.
10. Gehman, *The Free People of Color*, 2.

15: Leon Frederic, Light Enough to Fight
1. Mary F. Berry, "Negro Troops in Blue and Gray: The Louisiana Native Guards, 1861–1863," *Louisiana History: The Journal of the Louisiana Historical Association* Spring 1967, 165–90.

2. James G. Hollandsworth, Jr., *The Louisiana Native Guards: The Black Military Experience during the Civil War* (Baton Rouge: Louisiana University Press, 1998), 16.

3. Butler to Stanton, August 14, 1862, OR, Vol. XV, 548–49.

4. Hollandsworth, *Louisiana Native Guards*, 13.

5. Hollandsworth, *Louisiana Native Guards*, 16.

6. Berry, "Negro Troops in Blue and Gray," 165–90.

7. Berry, "Negro Troops in Blue and Gray."

8. Butler to Stanton, May 25, 1862, *OR*, Vol. XV, 442.

9. Hobbs, *A Chosen Exile.*

10. *New Orleans Daily Picayune*, May 27, 1863.

11. Joseph T. Wilson, *Black Phalanx*, 195.

12. Hollandsworth, *Louisiana Native Guards*, 21.

13. Hollandsworth, *Louisiana Native Guards*, 40–42.

14. Berry, "Negro Troops in Blue and Gray," 178.

15. Berry, "Negro Troops in Blue and Gray," 181.

16. Hollandsworth, *Louisiana Native Guards*, 46.

17. Hollandsworth, *Louisiana Native Guards*, 48, 51.

18. Hollandsworth, *Louisiana Native Guards*, 53.

19. Hollandsworth, *Louisiana Native Guards*, 54.

20. The Walter Stephens Turner Diary: 39th Mississippi Infantry, May–July 1863.

21. Hollandsworth, *Louisiana Native Guards*, 56.

22. Hollandsworth, *Louisiana Native Guards*, 58.

23. Hollandsworth, *Louisiana Native Guards*, 57.

24. Hollandsworth, *Louisiana Native Guards*, 59–60.

25. Hollandsworth, *Louisiana Native Guards*, 100–101.

26. Hollandsworth, *Louisiana Native Guards*, 101, 102.

27. Hollandsworth, *Louisiana Native Guards*, 106.

28. Hollandsworth, *Louisiana Native Guards*, 106, 107.

29. Gehman, *The Free People of Color*, 91.

30. Hollandsworth, *Louisiana Native Guards*, 107.

31. Gehman, *The Free People of Color*, 92.

32. R. C. Hitchcock to George Washington Cable, September 1, 1888, quoted in Somers, "Black and White in New Orleans," 42.

33. Anthony, "Lost Boundaries," 301.

34. Anthony, "Lost Boundaries," 303.

16: The Vagaries of War

1. Ned Hemard, "New Orleans Nostalgia: Minit Made," *New Orleans Bar Association: New Orleans Nostalgia, Remembering New Orleans History, Culture and Traditions*, 2013, accessed September 2015, http://www .neworleansbar.org/uploads/files/Minit%20Made%202-27.pdf

2. Stephen Ambrose, "Advance to Buna-The 32D 'Red Arrow' Infantry Division in World War II The 'Red Arrow,'" 2014, accessed August 2015, http://www.32nd-division.org/history/ww2/32ww2-2.html

3. Eric Larrabee, *Commander in Chief: Franklin Delano Roosevelt, His Lieutenants, and Their War* (Annapolis: Naval Institute Press, 2004).

17: California Dreaming

1. Shmoop Editorial Team, *Economy in World War II: Home Front*, 11 November 2008, accessed 22 April 2016, http://www.shmoop. com/wwii-home-front/economy.html.

2. Gehman, *The Free People of Color*, 311.

3. Hobbs, *A Chosen Exile*, 113.

18: Antebellum Love and Sex: The Cabinetmaker and the French Grocer

1. John Hanno Deiler, *The Settlement of the German Coast of Louisiana and the Creoles of German Descent* (Philadelphia: Americana Press, 1909, 2004).

2. Richard Stringfield, *Le Pays de Fleurs Oranges* (Plaquemines Parish, Louisiana: Gateway Press, 1989).

3. Jerah Johnson, "Colonial New Orleans," *Creole New Orleans Race and Americanization*, ed. Arnold R. Hirsh and Joseph Logsdon (Baton Rouge: Louisiana State University Press), 42.

4. Kimberly S. Hanger, *Bounded Lives, Bounded Places: Free Black Society in Colonial New Orleans, 1769–1803* (Durham & London: Duke University Press, 1997), 104–105.

5. Martin, *"Plaçage,"* 68.

6. "Faubourg Marigny," *Wikipedia*, accessed August 2015, https://en.wikipedia.org/wiki/Faubourg_Marigny#cite_note-7

7. Dean Reynolds, "History of Faubourg Marigny," *Improvement Faubourg Marigny Association*, 2015, accessed August 2015, http://www.faubourgmarigny.org/ZZ_history_fm.htm

8. Reynolds, "History of Faubourg Marigny."

9. Paul F. Lachance, "The Foreign French," in *Creole of New Orleans: Race and Americanization*, ed. Arnold R. Hirsch and Joseph Logsdon (Baton Rouge: Louisiana State University Press), 105.

10. LaChance, "The Foreign French," 112.

11. William J. Bromwell, *History of Immigration in the United States, Exhibiting the Number, Sex, Age, Occupation, and Country of Birth, Passengers Arriving in the United States by Sea from Foreign Countries, from September 30, 1819 to December 31, 1855* (Redfield: N.Y., 1856), 1–101.

12. Carl A. Brasseaux, *The Foreign French: Nineteenth Century French Immigration into Louisiana, Volume 1 1820–1839* (Center for Louisiana Studies: University of Southwestern Louisiana, 1990), xxii.

13. Brasseaux, *The Foreign French*, xxii.

14. Brasseaux, *The Foreign French*, xxiii.

15. "Enterprise on the Water," Smithsonian National Museum of American History, accessed August 2015, http://americanhistory.si.edu/onthewater/exhibition/2_3.html

16. David Herr, "Intermarriage," in *Compiled Edition of the Civil Code of Louisiana* XVI, ed. Joseph Dainow, 55.

19: Interracial Marriage Hidden

1. Hobbs, *A Chosen Exile*, 129.

2. *"Loving v. Virginia,"* *Black Culture Connection*, PBS/WYCC.

3. Nella Larsen, *Passing*, (New York: Alfred A. Knopf, 1929).

4. Toni Morrison, *God Help the Child*, (New York: Alfred A. Knopf, 2015).

21: Hiding in Plain Sight

1. Al Andrews, "Parma is Unchallenged as Fastest Growing in U.S.," *Cleveland Plain Dealer*, April 1, 1956.
2. The Cleveland Historical Team, "Hough," *Cleveland Historical*, accessed December 2015, http://clevelandhistorical.org/items/show/7.

25: Marta

1. Lawrence Powell, *The Accidental City: Improvising New Orleans* (Cambridge, Massachusetts: Harvard University Press, 2012), 285.
2. Powell, *The Accidental City*, 119.
3. Powell, *The Accidental City*, 53.
4. Powell, *The Accidental City*, 262.
5. Gwendolyn Midlo Hall, *Africans in Colonial Louisiana: The Development of Afro-Creole Culture in the Eighteenth Century* (Baton Rouge: Louisiana State University Press, 1992), 31.
6. Powell, *The Accidental City*, 228.
7. Powell, *The Accidental City*, 75–76.
8. Delia Garlic, *Voices From Slavery 100 Authentic Slave Narratives*, ed. Norman R. Yetman (NY: Dover Publication, 2000), 133.
9. Fannie Moore, *Voices From Slavery 100 Authentic Slave Narratives*, ed. Norman R. Yetman (NY: Dover Publication, 2000), 228.
10. Gehman, *The Free People of Color*, 12.
11. Michael T. Pasquier, "*Code Noir* of Louisiana," *KnowLA Encyclopedia of Louisiana*. ed. David Johnson, Louisiana Endowment for the Humanities, 6 January 2011, accessed November 2015, http://knowla.org/entry/742/.
12. Powell, *The Accidental City*,117.
13. Powell, *The Accidental City*, 85.
14. Harriet Jacobs, "Incidents in the Life of a Slave Girl," Written by Herself, *Slave Narratives*, ed. William L. Andrews and Henry Louis

Gates, Jr.; ed. L. Maria Child (1861) (NY: The Library of America, 2000), 794.

15. Glenn Conrad, *The German Coast: Abstracts of the Civil Records of St. Charles and St. John the Baptist Parishes 1804–1812* (Louisiana: University of Southwestern Louisiana, 1981), No. 52, 10-6-08, 68–71.

16. Conrad, *The German Coast*, No. 1479, 2-21-98, 294.

17. Gehman, *The Free People of Color*, 12.

18. Jacobs, "Incidents in the Life of a Slave Girl," 797.

19. Jacobs, "Incidents in the Life of a Slave Girl," 801.

20. Jacobs, "Incidents in the Life of a Slave Girl," 823.

21. Hanger, *Bounded Lives, Bounded Places*, 100.

27: Who's Your Daddy?

1. Lawrence J. Lachance, "French 'dit' Names," 1996–2016, accessed November 2015, http://www.lachance.org/dit.html.

2. AnnMarie Gilin-Dodson, *GenWeekly*, "What is a Dit Name and Why Is It Important to Family History?" 2009, accessed November 2015, http://www.genealogytoday.com/articles/reader.mv?ID=2913.

3. David Hardcastle, "Swiss Mercenary Soldiers in the Service of France in Louisiana," in *The Louisiana Purchase Bicentennial Series in Louisiana History: The French Experience in Louisiana, Vol. 1*, ed. Glenn R. Conrad (Louisiana: University of Southwestern Louisiana, 1995), 369.

4. Hardcastle, "Swiss Mercenary Soldiers," 370.

5. Hardcastle, "Swiss Mercenary Soldiers," 370.

6. Hardcastle, "Swiss Mercenary Soldiers," 374.

28: Luison Santilly: Metisse

1. Powell, *The Accidental City*, 116.

2. Stephen Webre, "The Problem of Indian Slavery in Spanish Louisiana, 1769–1803," in *The Louisiana Purchase Bicentennial Series in Louisiana History: The Spanish Experience in Louisiana, Vol. 1*, ed. Glenn R. Conrad (Louisiana: University of Southwestern 1995), 353.

3. Webre, "The Problem of Indian Slavery," 356.

4. Powell, *The Accidental City*, 338.

5. Webre, "The Problem of Indian Slavery," 362.

6. Hanger, *Bounded Lives, Bounded Places*, 15.

7. Anthony G. Barthelemy, "Light, Bright, Damn Near White: Race, and the Politics of Genealogy, and the Strange Case of Susie Guillory" in *Creole: The History and Legacy of Louisiana's Free People of Color*, ed. Sybil Kein (Baton Rouge: Louisiana State University Press, 2000), 259.

8. Powell, *The Accidental City*, 333.

9. John C. Rodrigue, "Slavery in French Colonial Louisiana," *KnowLA Encyclopedia of Louisiana*, ed. David Johnson, Louisiana Endowment for the Humanities, 11 March 2014, accessed November 2015, http://www.knowla.org/entry/1424/.

10. Jennifer Spear, "Indian Women, French Women, and the Regulation of Sex" *Race, Sex, and Social Order in Early New Orleans* (Baltimore: The Johns Hopkins Press, 2009), 24.

11. Donald H. Unser, Jr., "American Indians in Colonial New Orleans," *The Louisiana Purchase Bicentennial Series in Louisiana History: Volume II The Spanish Experience in Louisiana 1763–1803*, ed. Glenn R. Conrad (Louisiana: University of Southwestern Louisiana, 1995), 298.

12. Gwendolyn Midlo Hall, *Africans in Colonial Louisiana: The Development of Afro-Creole Culture in the Eighteenth Century* (Baton Rouge: Louisiana State University Press, 1992), 57.

13. Spear, "Indian Women," 163.

14. Stephen Webre, "Indian Slavery," *KnowLA Encyclopedia of Louisiana*, ed. David Johnson, Louisiana Endowment for the Humanities, 23 November 2010, accessed December 2015, http://www.knowla.org/entry/801/

32: Let Sleeping Dogs Lie

1. "Beta Thalassemia," *MedicineNet.com*, 19 May 2015, accessed September 2015, http://www.medicinenet.com/beta_thalassemia/page2.htm.